NO NEW YORK

ADELE BERTEI

NO NEW YORK

A MEMOIR OF NO WAVE
AND THE WOMEN
WHO SHAPED THE SCENE

faber

First published in 2026
by Faber & Faber Limited
The Bindery, 51 Hatton Garden
London EC1N 8HN

Typeset by Faber & Faber Limited
Printed and bound by CPI Group (UK) Ltd, Croydon, CR0 4YY

All rights reserved
© Adele Bertei, 2026

The right of Adele Bertei to be identified as author of this work
has been asserted in accordance with Section 77 of the Copyright,
Designs and Patents Act 1988

A CIP record for this book
is available from the British Library

ISBN 978–0–571–38615–4

Printed and bound in the UK on FSC® certified paper in line with our continuing
commitment to ethical business practices, sustainability and the environment.
For further information see faber.co.uk/environmental-policy

Our authorised representative in the EU for product safety is
Easy Access System Europe, Mustamäe tee 50, 10621 Tallinn, Estonia
gpsr.requests@easproject.com

2 4 6 8 10 9 7 5 3 1

dedicated
to the formidable ghosts
of No New York

may they instruct
and
be
loved

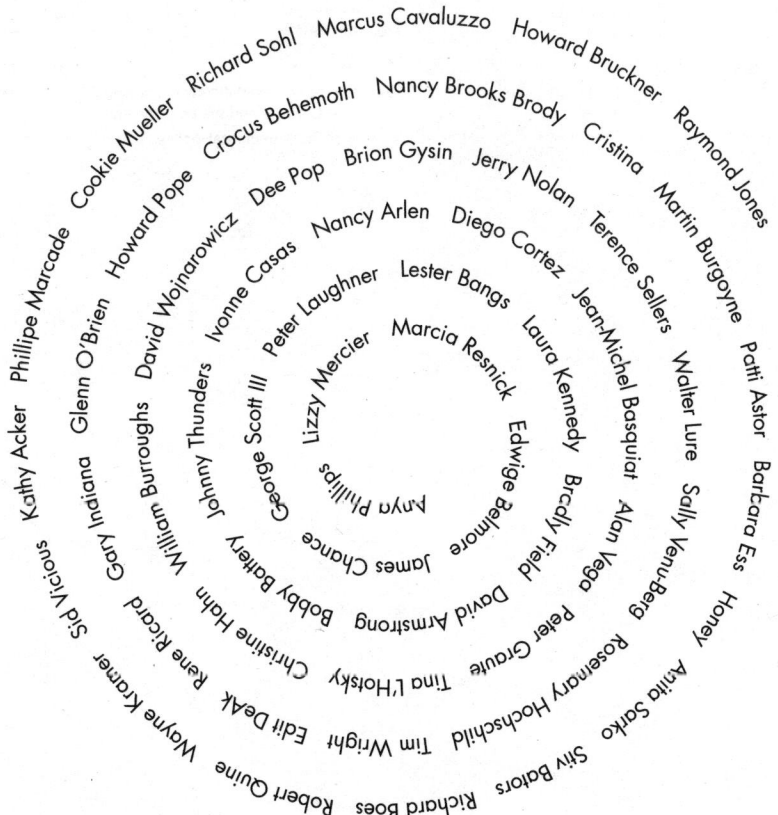

CONTENTS

Preface	1
Heaven and Hell	7
Nan, 1975	13
Peter and Lester, 1977	23
The East Village	35
Surreal Vertebrates	47
Contort Yourself!	53
Grandma's Hands	71
Love in a Blackout	77
Poète Maudit Mischief	83
Kiki	91
Contortions Part II	99
Paradise Lost	117
Idlewildly 3rd Street	133
The Nova Convention	147
Le Faux Garçon	163
Anti-Fashion	175
Where Have the Gazelles Gone?	183
NO-llywood	189
Dancing the Wild Step	223
Berlin to Rotterdam	229
Poppies and Poets	237
Girl Gang Dreaming	245
Bloods Light	251
Bloods 2.0	265
Lock Up Your Daughters	273

CONTENTS

Liquid Sky & the Crack-Up	289
Cabaret to Compromise	297
He(art) Lost and Found	309
Epilogue	319
Acknowledgements	325
Photo credits	327

Preface

New York City was once a haven for reinvention. No Wave was born there, a counterculture that brought punk, rock, jazz, funk, hip-hop, film, art, and outlaw sensibilities into a vibrant and volatile mix. If the Lost Generation strayed because of the wasteland of World War I, we eclipsed their ghosts by howling 'NO' to the dead-eyed cultural and political landscape of the 1970s. Art guerrillas, esoterrorists, and wild Mary Shelleys, we stitched together our own Frankenstein monster. A moveable feast of No. The Parisian painters and poètes maudits of the late 1800s, the Lost Generation, the Beats, the Harlem Renaissance, the Black Arts Movement; these were all scenes rooted in geography, particular times and politics, shifting cultures toward new insights and expressions. No Wave was downtown NYC. Our No New York.

Thurston Moore, Byron Coley, and Marc Masters have all chronicled No Wave with style, plenty of history, killer photos, and even a few scandalous anecdotes about me. And yes, they gave the women well-earned attention. But I wrote this book to dig deeper. What truly set No Wave apart from past artistic movements? The women. They didn't just participate. They set the tone and they lit the fuse.

Women – resisting tired stereotypes and reinventing according to our individual artistic visions. Artists like Patti Smith, Debbie Harry, and Tina Weymouth of Talking Heads were establishing women as equal progenitors in New York's music scene in the mid-1970s. In England, Chrissie Hynde, Poly Styrene, and the Slits were changing the game; the Slits especially were the epitome of the No Wave sensibility. We followed them, seized the right to create new music and sound. Dismantling art's male-dominated paradigms, we ignored the boundaries of gender and genre. In downtown New York in the late 1970s and '80s, the first significant international movement of women artists was born, creating sound, word, and vision as explosively as the men. This was possible, in part, because the imperative to make art was not driven by money or fame, at least not in a commercial or corporate sense. We enjoyed a camaraderie that can only be achieved when women disentangle themselves from competition and jealousy. Collaborative and supportive, we envisioned a new reality of art and friendship, living our freedom through example and through art in all its forms. The female musicians in the scene didn't have a brand like the later Riot Grrrls. To us, brands were a joke. Commercial success was anathema to our goals, as telegraphed in the irony of Barbara Kruger's iconic slogan 'I shop therefore I am' and in the anti-commodification of the Au Pairs song 'Steppin' Out of Line'.

The Irish filmmaker Vivienne Dick filmed a group of us on rooftops in the late 1970s; we called ourselves les guérillères.[1]

For the first time in history, wild visionary women gathered in one place. We rocked, ripped, destroyed, exposed, and made our work alongside men. We shape-shifted, using our instruments, typewriters, paintbrushes, and cameras as extensions of our nervous systems, pushed to the edge of overload. Radical libertines and codebreakers shot Super-8 films and photography. One writer transformed the canon's sacred texts into sexed-up sacrilege, others penned poetry and manifestos while working in dungeons as dominatrices. Most of us avoided labels, yet feminism was inherent in our choices in love and sex, in work and action. Our self-confidence and unfettered imagination emboldened the men around us. There was a spirit of fluidity within a deeply sexual scene. Our lack of

---

1 After *Les Guérillères*, a 1969 novel by Monique Wittig. It was translated into English in 1971.

PREFACE

defining ourselves felt liberating, enabling change in a spirit of flow when change beckoned. The way we moved, dancing through the downtown streets, and the convulsive physicality of making work. All of it, an exercise in sensual freedom.

The lens may be occasionally clouded with nostalgia. And there was darkness. Danger and risk didn't always lead to inspired revelations and good outcomes, especially for women considered feral, or those tempted by heroin's allure. Drugs, gentrification, and the commercial success of many, including myself, eroded the creative energy of the downtown world we had built, and as we moved onto our separate artistic paths, the scene began to fade. AIDS arrived, bringing fear, premature death, shock, and grief. The rise of dance music became a fleeting joy, a temporary, ecstatic flight away from the grip of the disease on the community. More than 100,000 people died of AIDS before the 1980s had concluded, and its toll on the hearts of the queer community and the cultural landscape of New York City was beyond devastating.

Not everyone I mention in this book will agree, not by a long shot, with being identified as a part of No Wave, or a guérillère, or with the way I remember things. I've overlooked many women art- and sound-makers during the period, and a more thorough, scholarly account of the women working during the No Wave movement would fill a critical gap and be an essential addition to our understanding of this era.

Mine is a different kind of contribution – a diaristic rendering of the scene, a memoir rather than an academic history. I'm writing in the tradition of personal chroniclers who documented their cultural moments from the inside, where the intimate becomes a way of understanding larger movements. Sometimes the personal *is* political, and the lived experience offers what scholarship alone cannot. What I can offer is how it lived in me, stitched together through memory and feeling. I've tried to stay awake to the ways certain people, stories, and addictions shaped my life then and now, while still holding these memories inside a wider view; of how much it all felt like something cracking open, both personally and in the sweep of history.

To quote Virginia Woolf, 'Killing the Angel in the house' is a necessary part of becoming a woman writer.[1] There will be dirt. Musicking girls were not supposed to be outspoken or wild like our rock 'n' roll brothers. I was carrying centuries of bottled-up female rage, and dangerous episodes fuelled by alcohol and drugs appear throughout these stories like a game of whack-a-mole. When does bravery become recklessness? And when does addiction turn deadly?

I lived valiantly, sometimes violently and recklessly free, often feeling singular to the point of being in the world, but not of it. That freedom often came at a price. I was out as a lesbian in 1977, two decades before Ellen DeGeneres came out on national TV. My post-No Wave journey through the corporate music world was fraught with obstacles. Toward the end of this book, I will touch on the transition from the personal and creative freedom of No Wave to the conformity and control of the corporate music business.

Ghosts will rise up from these pages: painters, musicians, noisemakers, actors, junkies, activists, filmmakers, poets, queens, criminals, dancers, thieves, writers, drunks, and visionaries. I'm unafraid to dance with ghosts. For the living, our numbers are dwindling. It's time to tell the stories.

---

1 Virginia Woolf, 'Professions for Women', 1931.

Heaven and Hell

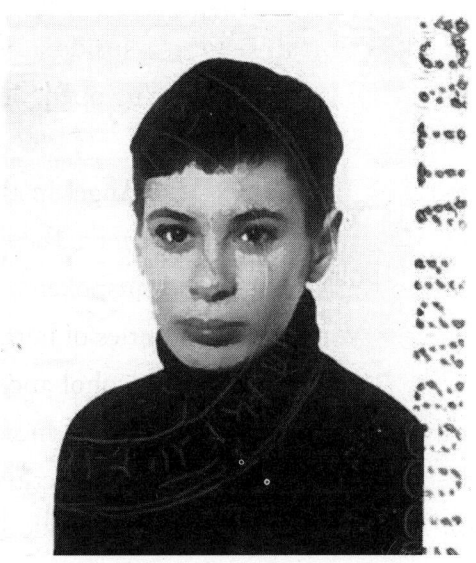

July 1977.

According to plan, I'd set out from Cleveland on a Greyhound bus – to move to New York City and join a band. There wasn't much to carry; the Fender Duo-Sonic guitar Peter had given me, tied in a burlap sack, plus two thrift-store suits, $100 in cash, and a shorn head.

Morning rush hour at Port Authority felt as if I'd been transported to an over-populated planet of amphetamine junkies. Downtown on Avenue A, the destination of my first lodgings, could wait. My first stop was a place I'd visit often and was the antithesis of punk, and all future visits would remain secret. Shoving my way through the crowds to the E train, I got off at 53rd and Fifth Avenue. I had an appointment with an archangel and a demon. Rain hammered down on hordes of well-dressed people trying to dodge the downpour. So many people. The humid smell of rain beating the hot cement excited me, as water rushed to the sewers carrying busted, spiny umbrellas along its course like broken blackbirds swept off by the gutter's current. The sight recalled a painting my mother loved, Van Gogh's *Wheatfield with Crows*. She hung the print flipped upside down, as was her way.

Churches are egoless architecture. St Patrick's Cathedral graced me with a feeling of reverence, provoked by its structural majesty and the incensed air of a space charged with trillions of prayers. Its lacy Gothic Revival style, spires, marble statuary, and the light leaking through its stained-glass windows called to me as a young girl when I leafed through the pages of *LIFE* magazine. Drawn to Catholicism through both the Italian and Irish sides of my family, I'd taught myself to sidestep the dogma and head for the theatrical and bewitching. Frankincense and myrrh in thuribles suspended from chains. The Latin mass, acoustic dreaminess. The costumed priests and nuns and the polychromatic wounds of pain transformed into expressions of ecstasy. The dark sexuality of the art and its Freudian slips eluded me as a child yet always fascinated, promising that no matter the suffering, elevation into the mystic waited.

Depictions of ecstatic gratification gained through pain and suffering can feel intriguing to a traumatized kid, providing some type of perverse hope. Sacred hearts encased in crowns of thorns dripping with blood – these sigils of suffering were common fascinations I would share with Nan Goldin. Nan was one of two people I'd say prayers for on my first day in New York. How shameful – a 'punk' who prayed? (So did Pussy Riot, decades later, to St Maria the Mother in a Russian Orthodox Cathedral.)

Walking the church's periphery, I stopped to read the plaques for each statue and prayer station, pausing at St Therese of the Little Flower and moving on to the altar of St Michael. Lighting candles to say prayers for the people who opened me to new ways of seeing, Peter and Nan, I asked for Michael's ongoing protection. Lucifer peeked his head out from below St Michael's foot. Seeming to wink at me. As if to say, Remember your fallen angel. Defeated, yet still very much alive.

Twelve years later, I returned to St Patrick's in 1989 for the ACT UP (AIDS Coalition to Unleash Power) and WHAM! (Women's Health Action and Mobilization) Stop the Church demonstration in protest with more than 4,000 activists. Nearly 90,000 people had died of AIDS in the USA, with almost 400,000 deaths globally by the end of 1989. Cardinal O'Connor and the Catholic Church continued to oppose condom use, safe sex education in schools, and abortion – a pro-death dogma posing as pro-life. While activist

Tom Keane enacted a symbolic crucifixion in the aisle of the church along with hundreds of other protestors, I lay down on the street for a die-in outside with my queer brothers and sisters, watching police carry protestors out on stretchers, their hands zip-tied. The demonstration demanded attention and was one of ACT UP's most powerful actions toward demanding effective treatment options, which would become available in the early 1990s.

By the time I joined ACT UP, I was newly sober and learning about pathways to redemption. Where the Catholic Church of my childhood taught a theology of wounds, a scripture of necessary violence and suffering, ACT UP taught me that protest is salvation. That silence equals death. And action is life.

St Michael's battle with Lucifer would come to symbolize the dyad of experiences I'd choose in New York City and various cities of empty. To witness darkness is to understand its simplest truth; it is merely an absence. A void I'd dance into and out of until I learned that evil and its cohort pain are far less interesting than their romantic costuming. We are, each one of us, alone. Yet when all seems absent of light, we reach our hands out to one another in the dark. Connection is the holy antidote to a starless sky.

Nan, 1975

I was twenty years old and had already spent two years of my life in Cleveland's gay bars, cutting my queer teeth in the Change, the city's most notorious gay watering hole. The art of serious drinking was a prerequisite for entry into the queer culture of the early 1970s. Genetically prone to alcohol, I was an embryonic inebriate. One photo of my mother pregnant with me shows her happily sauced whilst holding a beer bottle. And when I cried as a toddler, they rubbed Seagram's 7 on my teething gums. Thanks to my drag queen friends and neighbours, the dipsomaniacal genes were cheered into orbit as I learned to drink with gusto, like a drag king Joel Grey on a bender.

The Shaker Club in upmarket Shaker Heights catered to a suburban, well-heeled gay crowd. Flock wallpaper in dark reds and blacks, a mahogany bar, and sconces with candelabra lightbulbs set the scene for cocktails and dreaming. Sit at the bar and you might observe the eyes of a closeted young businessman going sparkly to Roxy Music's 'Mother of Pearl' while exchanging coy glances with a chic transvestite in droop earrings. The Shaker Club catered to a higher class of drag queens; Lady Stardusts invested in passing, preferring designer-clad mystery over the cheap and cheerful camouflage of their poor stepsisters at downtown gay bars like Twiggy's and the Change. Women aching for lesbian experiences appeared occasionally, secretarial types with their big hair brushed back into Farrah Fawcett wings. Fag hags were not ashamed to call themselves as such. And, occasionally, a genuine lesbian hiding in femme drag waited for a kiss from an imperial dagger to smash open her closet door. This action played out against a score of rock and disco platters: Bowie, Mott the Hoople and the Three Degrees. Cleveland's premier DJ Eric Baroush made sure the suburban queers got their love-sexy on with Manhattan Transfer's 'Blue Champagne' (a romantic slow-dip), Bette Midler's 'In the Mood' (for dancers who knew how to swing), and a switch-over to a funky disco confection like 'Rock Your Baby' by George McCrae (for the daggers who knew how to tease-pimp on the dancefloor).

One night out at the Shaker Club, I saw her – a high femme posing like a 1940s movie star. Nan stood chatting with a queen at the bar, casually hot in spike heels and a million-dollar smile. Her head was tilted just so. She sparkled. Nan's look was noir gun-moll glamour with a Parisian flair. She knocked out the entire room.

I took in every inch of her. Seamed stockings on taut calves, black impossibly high heels. White pencil skirt cinched just below the knee, the white V-neck sleeveless blouse with its centrepiece of cleavage. Dark red hair pinned up in a chignon, crowning the top of her forehead in a pompadour of perfectly messy curls. Her skin was nearly translucent, as milky white as her string of pearls. And the way she tilted her head when she laughed – the pearls cradling just so in the embrace of her collarbone. I watched how she dazzled with her smile. Pulled her camera up while chatting with her subject, an older local queen. Nan brought her photo-taking into her conversation effortlessly, the camera an extension of her quick and beautiful eyes. When she turned those eyes on me, she smiled, pulled the lens up, and began shooting. The Nikon might as well have been a gun. She had me at first click.

I was initially intimidated; she had a sophistication I'd never encountered in language and gesture, smiling as foreplay to her eye-to-lens and then – snap! – she caught me before I could strike a pose. She asked intimate questions while dipping the camera up and down between her gaze and her chest. Looking. Considering.

NAN, 1975

Making me feel unguarded, sexy, sad. Excited and confessional all at once.

I had made love to girls before Nan, but Nan's body was not girlish. She was a woman, her full breasts weighted with life. Tiny waist and beneath it a soft stomach and full hips. The neck of Audrey Hepburn flashed through my head when she unwound her hair, red curls embracing the collarbone and tangling there in the little pearls she declined to remove when naked. Her skin was pale, nearly translucent, and the veins in her neck pulsed soft blue.

I told her about my childhood, learning to be a butch daddy in a Cleveland reformatory called Blossom Hill. My natal family blew up when I was eleven due to my mother's schizophrenia and my stepfather's gambling, lack of support, and physical abuse. He was an Italian immigrant. Treated horribly as a boy for his lack of English, he grew up with fantasies of revenge; of being a gangster, a made man with jackpot eyes who never made it past being a numbers runner, only to have two fingers severed at the knuckles for sticking his mitt in the mob's cookie jar.

In keeping with generational trauma, my mother had grown up without knowing the identity of a father. Several generations of Irish women on her side had no husbands and unknown fathers. My grandmother had carried her through poverty and extremely dangerous circumstances as a young girl during the Great Depression. I'd inherited my mother's confusion between sex and love. She was hypersexual; she loved her body and wanted to live and experience it fully and control her own carnality, which is common with women who've experienced sexual assault as children. The cost of her ache for love and freedom in the 1950s was brutal. At a very young age I understood how different she felt trying to live amidst the Donna

Reed aspirants of our working-class suburb. The cruelty of the reality she faced cracked open a portal. My mother stepped through into another reality where her imagination made her a queen who reigned over a world of music and art, dance and beauty. A life free of children to care for. She left us. I wanted to follow where she led.

She could be almost sadistic in this state, a reflection of the oppression she felt tortured by. I never knew which personality I'd be facing each morning: Cleopatra or Medea. Yet, the best of her wild imagination would eventually prove to be my magical badge of courage; through watching her escape from this plane of existence, I learned to take risks, to break away from whatever I perceived as cruelty and ignorance. By the time I was thirteen, I had run away from two foster homes and ended up incarcerated as an incorrigible runaway.

In the Blossom Hill reformatory, we girl-hooligans created families from the same need as the darlings of *Paris Is Burning* and *Pose*. We played at being little gangsters, openly courted each other, danced and performed, and life in jail was like a fantastic movie no one could ever dream into existence. On the flip side of my gangster pose at Blossom Hill was the pitiful waif at Marycrest, the Catholic School for Wayward Girls. Marycrest was akin to Ireland's Magdalene laundries, run by one of the same orders of nuns in Ireland – the Sisters of the Good Shepherd. My favourite nun, Sister Veronica, loved hearing me sing the embarrassing 'Where Is Love?' and 'Who Will Buy?' from *Oliver!*. Although I fancied myself more of an Artful Dodger, as pathetic as it sounds, the *Oliver!* songs trembled in my lonely bones.

Nan had her own family traumas; her sister had committed suicide at the age of eighteen and the loss had left its shadow. She told

NAN, 1975

me she'd travelled to Chicago, Detroit, and now Cleveland to take photos of drag queens and transvestites. She pulled an envelope from her bag and laid out a series of eight-by-ten black and white photographs. Her subjects took on the witness of her camera with an air of naked confidence, yet there was no sense of posing or arrogance in the photos. I'd never seen anything like these images, all arresting in their revelation of character. Some looked vulnerable, others seductive or self-reflective. David Armstrong and his boyfriend Bruce at the beach; these she pointed out were her best friends. Each subject, so natural in their bodies and expressions – as if they felt completely safe to let down their guard. As I searched their faces, I felt like they were saying, Look at my battle, what it's given me. The depth of the wounds, a gateway into the soul of gnosis. Nan's camera gave her friends permission to expose just how beautiful they really were; revealing that struggle and sadness can create a certain grace, a vessel to shield one from the vicious world that labelled gays as freaks and outcasts, which is exactly how it was in 1975 when I met Nan.

Being gay was no picnic in the 1970s. You could be harassed, beaten, or even killed if exposed, and this continues today. There was such shame back then. But in the world of Nan's photos I did not see the shame the outside world foisted on us. I saw a certain tenderness. Hurt, yes, but a dignity inside the pain. Self-acceptance and, sometimes, pride. I understood why she was interested in someone like me; I was androgynous, often passing for a boy. I resisted the line separating gender; I did not want to be man or woman. The vulnerability of my mother, who'd given up her life as a dancer to live inside a suburban box with a man who abused her; the despair of my grandmother, a brilliant piano player whose husband took away her music. Their pain demonstrated clearly that being a woman meant suffering. My refusal of womanhood manifested in dressing like a boy, feeling there was a boy trapped inside my skin, a boy entitled to all the opportunities unavailable to girls. In a world that mistreated women, I took cover behind boyish pose and swagger.

My mask became porous in Nan's presence; she saw right through. She allowed me to see her own fragility; I sensed the pain was deep. Nan didn't define herself as gay or straight, and she talked to me about feeling as if she were a third sex, like the queens she photographed. A gender I could relate to. Nameless and fluid.

In Nan's philosophy, when someone allows their hurt to peek through the masks we all wear, it's more beauty than an eye can behold sometimes. And in giving of herself in word and image, Nan lifted a bit of shame from my heart, teaching me a truth that would become central to my understanding of humanity. Her photographs taught me how to look. To see. It was Nan who said I should move to New York, a world where outsiders celebrated one another.

★ ★ ★

Nan returned to Boston, and we began writing letters to each other. I'd listen to Laura Nyro on *Gonna Take a Miracle*; the combined voices of Labelle and Laura so raw and beautiful on that album – a shiver-inducing roar of women. Each song felt immediate, like they were in the room singing directly to me, to the girls who knew the streets. Girls who wanted to fly. I envisioned Nan as my 'Désiree', the first song I'd ever heard with a woman serenading another woman. Nan was renting an attic flat in a house in Provincetown,

NAN, 1975

Cape Cod, which was small and had sloping ceilings. Lovers David and Bruce were there; these two roommates contributing to the sweet, near-claustrophobic space. The entire bathroom was covered in strips of black and white photo-booth pictures of Nan and her friends. Larger prints mixed it up with images of actors, singers, and saints torn from magazines, tacked up all over the walls, interspersed with Nan's sacred heart and crucifix collection.

★ ★ ★

They played the best music at Nan's place. I heard John Cale there for the first time, his *Paris 1919* album. You never knew what to expect on the hi-fi; it could be Roxy Music followed by Johnny Ace, Eno and Fripp's *No Pussyfooting*, the soundtrack to *Gold Diggers of 1933*, Chuck Mangione's 'Land of Make Believe' sung by Esther Satterfield. A close friend of Nan's visited – the gorgeous Cookie Mueller, a sexy femme with attitude and star of John Waters' comedy *Pink Flamingos*. Hanging with Nan, Cookie, David, Bruce, and all the fascinating people I met that summer felt like stepping through the looking glass into a formidable world of new possibilities; a world where imagination and magic were encouraged. David told me about Jean Genet and how he had written an entire book on a roll of toilet paper in his prison cell. A guard had seized and destroyed it, but Genet began again. Nan must have mentioned my reform school history to David, prompting him to lend me his copy of *Our Lady of the Flowers*. That a writer with no education could create such beautiful prose gave me hope. I read *Our Lady* greedily, sighing over the prose and the Catholic rituals of Divine and the queens, sometimes frustrated with the translation and feeling vexed that I'd never had the chance to study French – how poetic the text must be in its native tongue. For the next decade in New York City I went from job to job, using each as an excuse not to write while fantasizing about committing the perfect crime. Something related to theft: a banking con or a robbery of priceless objects from some hapless art aesthete's precious collection. A crime with a tailor-made prison term that would grant me enough time and solitude necessary to write my own queer-girl version of *Notre Dame des Fleurs*.

Peter and Lester, 1977

In early February 1977, Peter Laughner had presented me with a round-trip ticket for my first visit to New York City. He'd arranged for us to stay at his buddy Lester Bangs' place in the West Village. I was thrilled but nervous and kept nagging Peter about whether it was cool with Lester that I stay there. Would Lester discover me as a girl-hooligan fraud with nothing to offer? I could sing, but a soulful voice and punk did not make great bedmates. As if I'd be breaking into song to impress him anyway.

The Jackson Pollock of phraseology, Lester riffed words like spatters of paint flying from the horn of the Birdman himself. Sometimes his descriptions leaped as high as Parker's, so high up and off the page, I'd yelp in astonishment. His intoxicating sprawls of sentences about music made me giddy. Peter's own journalism was decidedly gonzo and Bangsian, yet he had his own unique spin, enough to gain his mentor Lester's respect and loyal friendship. I considered myself a member of Lester and Peter's church (in which Music is God), but I hardly rated choirboy in their hierarchy of action and expression. I prepared for baptism.

It was springtime when we arrived, the city rainy and everything shiny with buds bursting and people rushing. Myopia smoothed all I saw into soft focus. My New York at dusk was a painting by Monet, the rain smearing misty circles of colour around the glow of the streetlamps on Sixth Avenue. Our taxi pulled up in front of Lester's place – an apartment above the unglamorous Gum Joy restaurant near the corner of 14th Street. Imagining the worshipper of Stooge-ian thrash as a feral-eyed punk, he of the torn black clothing and bughouse hair, the door opened to a boyish man in dirty corduroy pants smelling like stale potato chips. Lester was a doppelgänger for Rob Reiner's character from *All in the Family*. I was surprised, exhaled relief. A Quicksilver T-shirt strained across his paunch as he grinned, took my hand, beckoned me inside, and tackled Peter in a bear hug.

Lester's apartment was a mess of typed pages, assorted rock ephemera, empty food containers and beer cans. A narrow path snaked through stepped-on pizza boxes, leading to the couch where, in the seams and cracks, a confetti of pharmaceuticals mixed it up with crumbs of unknown origin. Messy rooms never failed to pitch a shudder into me, but Lester's chaos felt like heaven. Peter launched right into what drugs they'd be taking. Lester warned him to slow down as if he were trying to protect me from seeing just exactly what these two could get up to. Maybe he wanted to stay at least a little sober himself, but unlikely, from what I'd heard. Peter pulled out a flask and took a few demure sips. A goof. Lester laughed and out came a prescription bottle. They were off to the races without me.

The little pills must have been speed, resulting in a codeine-laced cocktail that had them acting like dopey teenagers in the cab ride down to CBGB. Peter squirmed, all jazzed and jumpy about seeing the Ramones live. He sang 'Now I Wanna Sniff Some Glue' at the top of his lungs, with Lester and me chiming in. As we entered CBs (gratis, courtesy of owner Hilly Kristal's reverence for Lester), the volume nearly lacerated my eardrums. We pushed our way through a packed room of headbangers losing it to the speeding power chords of 'Blitzkrieg Bop'. Joey Ramone was riveting. His girlishness helped neuter the juvenile obsession with Nazis and punk fascism that certain white-boy punks thought cool. Essentially a charade intended for shock value, it was nevertheless disturbing.

PETER AND LESTER, 1977

The band was as tight as a baby's fist and they knew exactly how to work the crowd. Six-foot six-inches topped by a luxurious mane of black hair and hubba-hubba lips, Joey resembled an anorexic hermaphrodite, replete with alien sex appeal. When he sang 'I Wanna Be Your Boyfriend', close your eyes and you'd swear it was Ronnie Spector with a head cold. The Ramones were the epitome of the punk aesthetic; the attitude, the uniform, the choreographed three-chord thrash-and-burn. But, for all that bad-boy attitude, Joey could certainly croon a plaintive melody. I inched my way through the crowd, dreaming of being on that very same stage.

Contrary to rumours of the duo's behaviour, neither Lester nor Peter got rowdy. After the Ramones finished their set, the two spent most of the evening tossing back whiskeys at the bar in a series of heated discussions about music. My desire to explore the New York streets was distracted by wanting to hang on to every word of their crazy brilliant conversation. The more they imbibed, wilder came the words.

We woke up around noon the next day with hangovers. Lester, in his usual chivalrous manner, asked if there was anything I particularly wanted to do. I wanted to see where the great poets and writers hung out. First stop was 10th Street and Greenwich Avenue, a red-brick library and, next to it, a lush garden – once a women's jail that held Angela Davis and Valerie Solanas. We marched along 8th Street past Hendrix's legendary Electric Lady Studios, where Patti Smith recorded *Horses*, and on to the White Horse Tavern, where Dylan Thomas, Kerouac, and Anaïs Nin imbibed and dreamed. Lester was happy to report on Anaïs. Considering himself a feminist, he proceeded to tell me (as bizarre illustration) how Anaïs wouldn't kiss Antonin Artaud because his teeth were black and disgusting from smoking opium. As he spun the tale, I watched his moustache form the words, bristles coated with tomato sauce from the pizza we'd just eaten, and I couldn't help myself, blurting how he'd be shit out of luck pulling any girls himself if he kept wearing his lunch on his lip. He and Pete stared at me, speechless. I thought I'd blown it and I was mortified, but they were just psyching me out. Their faces cracked into laughter, with Lester blushing as he picked up a napkin and groomed. The God of rock journalism wasn't only human; he was a sweet, good-natured slob.

I continued to go easy on the drink, determined that my first trip to New York wouldn't dissolve into a black-out or end with me slugging some creep in a bar that dared glance at me the wrong way. It was the first time I didn't try to match Peter drink for drink. I downed one shot for each outing. Just enough courage to keep things smooth. We spent the remainder of the day in a booth at the White Horse Tavern, me as sober captive audience to the two dipsomaniacs hammering themselves into yet another entertaining and often asinine discussion about Lou Reed.

More booze, a few mysterious pills between them, and a retracing of Dylan's steps on 4th Street followed, with the two of them tearing into Bobby Z for having ripped off Woody Guthrie and Phil Ochs. Aside from a Talking Heads sighting and some trash-rock with Wayne/Jayne County at CBGB, the good stuff that Saturday night happened at Lester's. We listened to fantastic bootlegs I'd never heard, like Patti Smith's *Teenage Perversity & Ships in the Night*, followed by a rare Yardbirds bootleg. Off they'd go again – who was the better player, Jeff Beck or Eric Clapton? – while swigging Romilar, Lester's favourite high. When Lester asked if I liked jazz, I admitted to not knowing much about it aside from Lady Day (beloved) and

PETER AND LESTER, 1977

the Mahavishnu Orchestra (loathed). Lester stood up, a bit wobbly, and swept his arms out in a grand dramatic arc announcing, 'Your jazz education begins here and now.'

Even though he nearly fell over – it was 4:00 a.m., and the two boys were dulling down to a boozy sputter – he pulled out *The Black Saint and the Sinner Lady* by Charles Mingus.

'Mingus spent some time in the nuthouse previous to writing this suite of songs, written as a ballet,' Lester emphasized. 'And if you listen carefully, everything you'll ever need to understand about jazz is right there, within those grooves.'

As the guys nodded off, I stood at the window looking out over Sixth Avenue and the New York night. Not wanting to miss one movement, one note of Mingus from solo dancer to duet to group. Thinking of the possibilities these boy-men were unselfishly revealing for me, I felt a strange rush of fear at being in love with it all: the colours, their words, this music. The horns sounding like so many yellow taxis, cymbals and the night, shimmering out there as I imagined lovers, mothers, drug fiends, workers, runaway kids. Ghosts from every corner of the world walking this avenue below me, stepping in time to a ballet, a vision in Mingus's head and in that moment, my soundtrack to the city. A conviction of notes informed the dreams of the boys who dozed near me, each interior network of blood and bone humming with music. Always with music.

★ ★ ★

Within five years, these two young men would both be dead. I can still see them lying there so peacefully in the New York night, filled with inexplicable hurts known only to themselves . . . acutely sensitive to the beauty and the terror of life and time. Constantly reaching for a blanket of numb to dull the sting of that light. The aching need to express it all . . . fear of failure, of falling, of the absence of gravity. The everything that matters in word and note. I stood there at a new attention, wanting so much. To translate the secret braille of their longing. Wishing for their futures . . . free from the pressure of cool. Without the insult of oblivion.

★ ★ ★

On Sunday, we took a trip to 42nd Street for some visual sleaze and a stop-in at Colony Records on 49th Street, where Peter dropped a bundle on rare discs. It seemed as if every 45-rpm disc ever pressed could be found in the endless stacks. I scored and brought home Patti LaBelle and the Blue Belles' single 'I Sold My Heart to the Junkman'. Inspiration for the last song Peter and I wrote together.

Back at Lester's, the conversation turned to Fela Kuti and Nigerian music. He put on the record *Expensive Shit*, which set me to dancing, and when they got up and attempted to cut a rug – disastrously, as white boys are prone to when it comes to the funk. We played Fela and Lenny Kaye's *Nuggets* until Lester clumsily embraced us both. It was time to say goodbye and split back to Terminal City. The next time I'd see Lester, we'd hardly meet one another's gaze. It would be a very different type of encounter.

Once we returned to Cleveland, Peter began to dissolve. His drinking and drugging increased as his health weakened. Eager to escape the sadness of Peter's failing health, I decided to make another trip to New York for a few days to look around and see if it might be possible to make a life there. I hoped that on my return

PETER AND LESTER, 1977

from New York I'd get a call from him saying he felt great, having re-emerged from someplace that helps broken people restore themselves to bright-eyed packages of wonder.

I took a Greyhound bus to New York in the early morning of 22 June ready for a few days of hanging out, seeing bands, and possibly connecting with a few other ex-Clevelanders. Bradly Field had also moved to New York and was playing drums in a band with a name to vanquish all others: Teenage Jesus and the Jerks. It was a mild day in New York, the cabbie yammering on about the Son of Sam still being at large and the incompetence of the NYPD while I squirmed with excitement about being back in the city: I was about to check in to the legendary Chelsea Hotel. I strolled into the lobby wearing black – everything tight – carrying a GI duffle bag and the Fender Duo-Sonic. They gave me one of their cheaper rooms: a white chenille bedspread on a sagging double bed, a wooden table, a chair. One forlorn dresser and a window facing a brick wall framing another shaded window across an air shaft. This was the famed inspirational home of so many great artists? The room reeked of unhappiness. I dropped off my stuff and headed out to CBGB to see a band called Suicide.

Mars was the opening band that night. The tightly compressed song they played featured Velvets-inspired noise guitars, but a cacophony more insane than anything velveteen, and the guy on the microphone sounded like he was having a psychotic breakdown. His singing reminded me of the times my mother would lose it, her wailing gibberish like a tape being played backward. This new sonic territory felt unhinged and exciting.

Even more astounding was that Mars had a female drummer and guitarist – both were striking in look and sound. The girl playing slide guitar made crazy squeals and noises. Her name was Constance (China) Burg and her wild slide guitar dissonance would directly influence the guitar-playing of Lydia Lunch and Pat Place (the latter would soon be my bandmate). Connie played like a drunken reptile dancing on olive oil. The drummer, Nancy Arlen, held Mars together in an odd, disjointed, whiter-than-white hatch of tightly wound nerves and angst. Mars was the first of the No Wave bands to record. '3E' was their single for Patti Smith's label Mer, produced by Patti's drummer Jay Dee Daugherty.

CBGB was packed with punk rockers, but it was another breed catching my attention. Creatures less cartoonish than the punks, black and grey clothing covered their gaunt frames creating the aura of a sexy, fashionable despair. As if taking cues from Italian neorealism and French new wave on how poverty can be haute. Guys in baggy 1950s pants, T-shirts, and Borsalino hats and scuffed black brogues with bare ankles. The girls in black slips, rumpled vintage dresses, flea-bitten men's suits with fucked-up hair and sexy makeup. I marvelled at what would soon be my chosen tribe.

Mars left the stage and a roadie brought up a single keyboard attached to a few other strange-looking machines on a stand. He placed one lonely microphone on its stand dead centre. I wound through the tight mesh of bodies, closer to the action as a cool character in aviator shades strolled on stage and flipped a switch – a synthesizer pulsed. Not even close to Eno's synth work from Roxy and beyond, this was a vibrational rumble like something from a steel mill, assembly line, dentist's drill. The volume was so loud I thought I'd go deaf. My internal organs shook. Pushing backward, I snaked in between bodies toward the club's entrance as the stage

PETER AND LESTER, 1977

lights began pulsing in rhythm to the drone. I climbed on top of a bar stool, turning around to look at the stage at the very moment the crowd exploded into war whoops; a slight guy sauntered jaguar-like onto the stage. He was wearing shades and a leather jacket, heavy black eyeliner, and a black bouffant dissected by a headband. He stopped. Posed. Louche and regal, draping himself over the microphone stand. The effect: Al Pacino dolled up as a gay hustler on 53rd and Third.

The band called Suicide droned and pummelled, decibels punishing over a cheap, Tinkertoy drum track. The singer, until now as static as a streetlamp, suddenly banged the mic stand onto the stage floor with a loud BOOM and rushed his body toward the audience, as if he were going to bite off the heads of the entire first row. The crowd screamed with delight. He began to croon, all heavy-lidded eyes and vibrato: 'Oh, what have I done? Let's hear it for Frankie . . . Frankie Teardrop!'

Alan Vega worked that microphone like a razor-wielding lover looking to shave your neck a little too close, while Marty Rev continued to punch us with synth waves turned up and off the Richter scale. Vega stabbed at the audience with his entire body, his voice. More than a performance, it was theatre. Antonin Artaud's *Theatre of Cruelty*. The power of it compelling me closer to the stage. That's when I saw him – the imp of the perverse. It was Bradly Field, looking deranged and screaming something inaudible. Trying to be heard above the sound of Suicide. He came in way too close.

'Peter's dead!' He was laughing, his face screwed up in torment.

'Come on, Bradly. That's not funny.'

'He's dead! I talked to Stella! He's dead, and good for him, that stupid fucker!'

His wails moved from annoying to repugnant. I pushed him away but he wouldn't stop. Foam at the corners of his mouth, manic and now gleeful over the death of a friend he once worshipped, he just kept repeating himself. I headed for the door but out on the street, the little demon was following still, yelling his crazy mantra.

'Peter was an asshole and who fucking cares? You don't believe me? He's dead! Ask Lester!'

His words hit me full force as I spotted Lester. Face ashen, Lester saw us and came over, placing a firm palm on the imp's forehead to hold him to the spot, but nothing was going to stop Bradly. He continued to scream and writhe beneath Lester's grip. Lester shoved him against the wall and warned him to shut up. Bradly started to cry. I looked up at Lester and knew before the words hit air.

'It's true. They found him this morning.'

I think Lester wanted to hug me but I felt all my senses on alarm, as if Peter's ghost had just rushed through me. The moment cracked my insides open with a feeling I knew too well. So I did what I'd always done when life punched me in the chest and shook the bees loose. I ran.

The East Village

I boarded the F train, a rickety tin box washed in wild graffiti, changed onto the L, and got out at First Avenue and 14th Street. It was early morning and the rain felt good on my cropped head, a warm baptism for la vita nuova. This arrival scene couldn't have been more different to St Patrick's. The rain smeared patches of the hot concrete sidewalks with filth. Walking along, heavily gated shops selling cheap clothes, suitcases, and children's toys felt like strolling through a decrepit jail. There was not a soul on the street as I turned the corner toward the address of where I'd be staying on Avenue A.

Gazing around, it felt as if I'd landed in an outdoor prison camp, and I thought back to Cleveland State Mental Hospital, the infamous bughouse that once incarcerated my mother in an overcrowded ward for women deemed crazy. Some stores were abandoned, while others had their entrances accordion-gated and chained with windows barred and padlocked. Refuse swirled in little whirlpools as rain pelted the metal trashcans drumming a symphony of the desolate and broken. In too many doorways, vagrants huddled and squirmed, trying to avoid the wet. This was not the city of artists and poets presented by Lester Bangs when Peter and I visited less than a year before. Compared to the West Village, Avenue A was a maximum-security gulag gone to hell. All manner of detritus bobbed on puddles stinking of sewage; dirty rubbers, glassine bags, and cigarette butts, the dismembered arm of a pink doll pointing east. I could see a line of skinny people in black clothes huddled near a hole in a wall and couldn't fathom why none of them bothered to cover their heads in the rain.

★ ★ ★

NO NEW YORK

In 1977, the financial resources of both New York City and New York state were exhausted. Mayor Abraham Beame made flaccid attempts to ward off bankruptcy, and Governor Hugh Carey was desperate to save the city, asking President Gerald Ford for a loan and financial support. Ford vetoed possible bailouts, prompting a newspaper headline in 1975: 'FORD TO CITY: DROP DEAD'. He eventually caved and approved federal support – but the damage was everywhere. Especially downtown.

It was the summer of the blackout, the 'Summer of Sam' when David Berkowitz's dog whispered murder down forbidding streets. Fires ripped through the Bronx and the Lower East Side nightly, and the view from an East Village rooftop provided a dystopian skyline filled with smoking orange light that haloed buildings demolished to rubble. As if the city had been attacked, at war. A wasteland for its surviving immigrants, the East Village would prove to be our very own junkyard of surrealistic mayhem. Crumbling tenements lined the dangerous, poorly lit streets, and the rats far outnumbered us as we danced between them through the ghostly fairytale landscape.

Due to its financial collapse, Manhattan had lost more than a million people since its glory days of Beat poetry and Black renaissance. Walking the ruinous streets late at night, one could feel the ghosts of immigrants now gone whispering secrets into the soles of the feet. Aching for life, for the new.

I arrived at the address I'd been given where an old, bearded vendor gave me the once-over. He yanked at the accordion shutters barricading his shop. The metal screeched up to reveal a shoe repair store and a large tangle of garbage. The vendor kept kicking at it until a filthy man emerged from a chrysalis of rags, rising to begin

THE EAST VILLAGE

an amble down the street. As if this were a daily ritual, the vendor smiled to himself and went into his shop. I took a deep breath and rang the buzzer to the first of many way stations where I'd be laying my head.

Initially, I stayed with a couple who I'd met at Cleveland's Plaza. Linda was nine months pregnant when I arrived, and Rob had already succumbed to the East Village local pastime – smack. Linda was oblivious to his habit, but I clocked it right away, having learned about the junkie nod from Peter. Linda was an innocent. In defiance of any modicum of sanity, she asked if I'd help her deliver her baby in the bathtub. I scanned the ground-floor flat with a shudder: the mattress on the floor, the sad quart of orange juice sweating on the windowsill, the unwrapped packages of diapers and baby onesies. And Linda, so young and so very pregnant. One look at me in 1977 and midwife isn't a title that would ever have sprung to mind.

The impending birth wasn't enough to kick me into taking Rob up on his offer of a 'taste' whenever poor Linda lumbered out of the room. The man was clearly overwhelmed and checking out. And I hadn't even cooled my heels from the trip in and now – boom – I'd scored the role of doula in *The Panic in Needle Park*. As grateful as I was for their warmth, I needed an exit strategy, but didn't know anyone in New York except for Lester. Petrified by the sadness he was sure to unveil in me since Peter died, I didn't dare reach out.

★ ★ ★

Peter had also given me the number of his friend Miriam Linna. Miriam played drums in the Cramps and was the punk Harriet Tubman, funnelling out-of-state kids seeking the artist's life into jobs at the Strand Bookstore. Patti Smith and Tom Verlaine had both worked there. I had one other phone number – digits for Bradly Field, the imp of the perverse himself. The same Bradly who had screamed in a hysterical rant of rage and loss at CBGB, because he loved Peter. And love can be a hurting thing.

He answered the phone as if he had no recollection of our last encounter, inviting me over and gloating proudly about being in Teenage Jesus and the Jerks, as if the incident at CBs around Peter's death had never happened. I had to admit, it was a stellar name. I headed for Delancey Street.

Bradly lived in a derelict building on Delancey above an abandoned Chinese movie theatre. Its white marquee was busted out in chunks, and the dirty windows in the storeys above were half-concealed with newspaper, some panes of glass covered in Hànzì – red characters rimmed in fading gold. I leaped off my feet when one of several half-opened plastic bags of garbage moved, like a magic trick, and a family of rats scrambled out of the bag and into a wooden crate stuffed with rotting vegetable matter. There wasn't a buzzer to be found and judging from the ramshackle condition of the building, I figured he must have given me the wrong address. I screamed his name a few times. Just as I was about to leave, up slides a window on the second floor and I saw his mini-Frankenstein noggin.

'L'il Bit! Here's the key!'

He threw a sock out the window, heavy with keys and a rock, and like a heat-seeking missile it nearly capped me. I cursed my pal Jack for telling Bradly my reform school nickname was L'il Bit. I picked up the sock.

'What's this?' I yelled up at him.

THE EAST VILLAGE

'The key's in the sock, dummy!'

I unlocked an old metal door and climbed two steep, dirty flights of stairs where the imp waited at the top, beckoning me into a 'loft' – something I'd never heard of. The place was a dump. Paint peeled away from the walls, and I saw yet another rodent scurry into a hole in a baseboard. There were patches of nasty carpeting, a kick and snare drum in a corner with two cymbals, some beat-to-hell amps, and a beat-up keyboard. A few guitars were lying around, one on a chair with its stuffing guts ripped out. A swastika flag hung over a flea-bitten couch. Bradly loved outrage. I'd seen punks using this symbol but never thought it was okay or cool.

'So, you're a drummer now. Are you a Nazi too, Bradly?'

'Oh, shut up. You like this couch? It's from the synagogue behind us!'

I didn't get the logic of how a Jewish couch deactivated the poison of a Nazi swastika but decided to swallow my tongue. After all, I didn't have any friends in New York. There you have it, the banality of evil.

Peeking out at us from a crawlspace above was a cherubic face framed by pitch-black bangs.

'Bradly, who's the new tuna?'

'This is L'il Bit. She thinks she's a pimp!'

'Well come on up here, L'il Pimpin'!'

Under her full head of witchy tresses, the girl gave me a cute, scarlet-lipped smile. I followed orders, climbing the ladder to her tree house. The girl had created this tented space with scarves and fabrics in a loft bed area no bigger than a closet. She sat there grinning at me beneath a string of Christmas lights, surrounded by little dolls. Once I reached the top of the ladder and crawled in, I may as well have been a trick. We were practically on top of each other. She was wearing a flimsy dress that showed off her cleavage, and fishnets with gaping holes. Full red pouty lips, a plump baby face. She squirrelled her mouth at me like a little brat, then smiled big and shoved a Ken doll into my hand.

'Here, you are definitely the boy.' She picked up her own doll and commenced dancing it around the blankets like a five-year-old innocent on a living room floor. I was stunned by this strange scene but went with it, picking up Ken and dancing him into a macho mating call. She laughed and propelled her doll toward me.

Then without warning, she took her Barbie, swung it, and socked Ken so hard she decapitated him. Ken's head flew through the curtains of her cubby hole and landed on the floor below, near Bradly's foot. He yelled up at us.

'Hey! What are you two dykes doing up there?'

This was how I met Lydia Lunch.

★   ★   ★

Lydia Lunch was seventeen when we met, a teenage Anna Magnani in torn black slips and fishnets with a baby face and a take-no-shit attitude. She had run away from home in Rochester, New York and found ways to survive through her street skills and the kindness of strangers the likes of Wayne/Jayne County and Willy DeVille. I loved the music of Mink DeVille. Until I arrived in the East Village, I thought of his *Cabretta* album and Laura Nyro's *Christmas and the Beads of Sweat* LP as the ultimate romantic soundtracks of New York City. It was rock gypsy balladeer, smooth Willy, who dubbed Lydia with the Lunch moniker because she'd show up at his band rehearsals with victuals for all. This baby-faced killer was nobody's fool. She knew the right push-up bra, the perfect sneer and a tasty sandwich from Katz's would take her anywhere she needed to go in life. The über-confident snotty punk boys in the downtown scene went nuts for her bratty, sexy package, while the squeamish ran for their lives.

Lydia was a fighter. Like me, she'd clock any guy in the face who looked at her sideways, an instinct honed from childhood sexual traumas we never discussed. Years later, we'd both unravel the horrors we'd buried, but back then we chased down those very monsters the best way we knew how; in noisy, occasionally bloody public exorcisms. She would grow into an artist I've always admired, a provocatrix and a Sicilian sister I'd keep close – sometimes contentiously, but always beloved throughout the decades.

★ ★ ★

Lydia and Bradly put me on the guest list to see her band the next night at Max's Kansas City. The room and stage were a lot smaller than I'd expected but I was thrilled to be at the famous Max's, home of Warhol and the Velvet Underground.

I didn't have a clue about her band, what they might sound like. As far as I knew, Bradly was not a musician nor was he the type to apply himself to months of diligent practice. I imagined their songs to be in line with Lydia's cubby hole playpen, some type of dolly holocaust music, however that might manifest. Maybe Lydia was a baby Patti Smith, but with more of a snarl.

Before the show began, Lydia introduced me to two of her friends; a beautiful Asian girl in liquified Lycra and a cute guy I thought was her boyfriend. The girl was sassy and sharp. A stone-cold fox.

NO NEW YORK

The band came on and Lydia, dressed in a skin-tight vinyl skirt and vest, looked at the crowd as if she'd rather shoot us than give us an inch of entertainment. She had her guitar slung low, with a glass slide on her finger. Bradly was wearing his usual fiendish glare, T-shirt stretched over muscled torso as he sat down in front of a solo snare drum next to a cute Japanese bass player wearing shades and a trench coat. A skinny little guy with an alto sax was with them, all Mick Jagger petulance, shifty little eyes, and a greased pompadour. He sulked and posed, a petite prince of damage in a sharkskin suit. This was James Chance.

Suddenly Lydia screamed at the audience, 'No one here gets out alive!'

In an ear-splitting volume, the bass player started pumping on one note. Bradly began smacking out a single marching beat on that snare like he was beating death into a bunny rabbit. Everyone fell in together; Lydia's warped guitar slice, sax squawk, bass thump and snare smack on the one. Military blasts at an enemy line up – BAM BAM BAM B-B-BAM BAM BAM! – and Lydia started to wail: 'Little orphans running through the bloody snow! Little orphans running through the bloody snow! Little orphans running through the blood through the blood through the–' and she took that glass tube and ran it across the fretboard of her guitar, making it squeal in staccato bursts of pain while the band kept the military beat behind her, emphasizing every word with a sonic blast. This was no baby Patti Smith – more like Medusa resurrected to riot and rip your face off. The music was painful, disturbing, bombastic. And liberating.

I looked around the mesmerized crowd staring at the teenage girl on stage screaming with her guitar and the awkward kid poncing around with his bleating sax. The beautiful Asian girl kept edging her chair closer to mine and I thought, here are the offspring of the broken American dream, picking through the ruins to offer up a new vicious poetry. Shards of sonic glass. Pieces of ache and rage. Belle laide, the French would say. Beautiful ugly. Belle laide.

Any artist Patti Smith mentioned, from Arthur Rimbaud to Vladimir Mayakovsky to Buster Keaton, sent me racing for the library and bookstore. The same had happened when Lester Bangs related his Antonin Artaud story. I hightailed it to the shelves looking for every utterance from Artaud and here on stage was a spectacle he'd predicted in his essays, a phenomenon defined as a 'violent, austere, physical determination to shatter the false reality that lies like a shroud over our perceptions'. Mix with a kind of Dada brutalism, exposing nerves and fascia and you get NO WAVE, a negation of every wave that had come before. And Lydia was its oracle.

The beauty in Lycra tugged lightly on her leather choker, drumming her fingers on my thigh. Beats of empty space were inhaled between the chest-battering hits and then the guitar would suddenly veer off like a car crash with screechy sliding noises, the sound hitting you full throttle. James squawking on his sax, Lydia wringing screams from her guitar . . . The song wasn't even two minutes long and left me gasping for breath. The girl I'd met playing with dollies in her loft bed was this girl on stage screaming an anthem for a scene that would create thunderstorms of artistic rage around the world.

While revelling in the sonic contempt of Teenage Jesus, I whispered in the foxy girl's ear: 'This is the theatre of cruelty.'

She gave me the look. Turned and whispered something to her handsome friend, who asked where I was from. I told him, 'Cleveland, home of the burning river.'

The girl in the Pebbles Flintstone outfit of tied-up Lycra was Anya Phillips. Her escort Diego Cortez grinned, then flashed his camera at the stage.

Lydia screamed in time to her second march: 'Die a thousand times, a crown of thorns, thrown off the shelf, my eyes are burnt . . .'

I had found my way home.

Surreal Vertebrates

The second night I crashed at Bradly and Lydia's, I joined Lydia in her cubby hole while below, a band, if you can call it that, were making strange noises. It was James Chance. He was making skronky, manic runs on an alto sax, clearly now the head of his own band. Lydia had kicked him out of Teenage Jesus because he liked too much contact with the audience, contact that was hostile. Lydia wanted no contact or connection at all. Her attitude was to face-off with the audience as willing victims, there to suffer and be tortured in the name of nihilistic rage.

James Chance was the leader of this new noisy crew. Reck, the bass player in Teenage Jesus, had also left to play with Chance in the new band he was starting. A cute Japanese guy in Wayfarer sunglasses, Reck was dressed in a Japanese noir aesthetic: in black pants, a white dress shirt, and black trench coat. A pair of black dress shoes, worn-out but clean. Everyone was clean. Maybe scruffy, but not vagrant dirty. Reck seemed to keep the most consistent beat of the foursome.

James (now Jamie) Nares was an exceedingly tall Brit. Aristocratically handsome with an alluring mental institution haircut, he was carving away at the strings of a plastic red guitar festooned with electrical tape and big X's, playing dashes of well-placed skronk in the bald spots of the others' attempted rhythms. He also had red X's taped onto his raggedy white dress shirt. Black 1950s pants and bare ankles in black dress shoes that had seen a generation or two on the Bowery. He was playing a rough rhythm and following Chance's cues of where to step in with a stab of sound. Although I didn't know exactly what I was hearing or seeing back then, I understand it now as polyrhythm. Rhythm and silences punctuated with unworldly dissonant squeals. It worked on some crazy level that made you want to hear more.

A creature that resembled a blonde raccoon from outer space was most intriguing of all. The creature was playing guitar with a broken beer-bottle neck, sliding over the fretboard like Lydia, but in a wilder rhythm, bursting then creeping; the sound of an animal during a painful moulting. As the creature turned and danced in its peculiar rhythm, the bubble butt gave her away.

I was used to rock 'n' roll and punk boys being skinny and kind of feminine so Pat could have been a boy, but I was hoping she was a girl. I was in desperate need of female friends who walked the same non-binary line as me. Thin and flat-chested beneath a Warholian striped T-shirt, she wore extremely tight pants low on her hips. Her hair was a sight. She beat James Nares in the psycho haircut contest, white-blonde hair hacked into crispy thistle. Crazy haircuts were often on display in No Wave, as if we were fresh escapees from the film *Titicut Follies*.

★ ★ ★

Pat was doing things to her electric guitar that no one had ever done before, not even Lydia or China Burg. She had what looked like the broken neck of a beer bottle and was running it over the fretboard hardly the way a Muddy Waters bluesman would play. You could tell she knew none of that. Her sound was pure zombie apocalypse. James Chance drew rhythmic cues in the air with a wild floppy hand, and Pat fell in with a weird pattern of unworldly squeals timed between bass notes, moving like a dyslexic snake. All three – Pat, James Nares, and Reck – watched Chance with sharp, attentive eyes.

I was stunned by the sounds, the noise they were making. These were astonishingly new sounds, and I wanted in. Some freaky hybrid

SURREAL VERTEBRATES

of jazz, noise, and punk, it repelled me as much as it intrigued. I climbed down from the cubby, sat at the drums and started pounding out a very simple but kind of funky beat. They all looked a bit surprised but didn't chase me off. The row grew louder into a riot of crazy wild rhythms and noises that felt like a chemical detonation of unknown origin. We finally ended the jam and Pat looked over at me with approval. Avoiding my eyes, James Chance stuttered out the words, 'You, you've got natural rhythm. Do you play keyboards?' I said no and thought that was that. Chance packed up his sax and took off with James Nares.

Pat and I hung out and talked a bit while she twisted a short thistle of bleached hair in her fingers. Pat was a visual artist who had recently moved to New York from Chicago and was discovered by James at CBs one night. He wanted to know if she'd play guitar in his band. She'd never even picked up an instrument until James asked her to, due to the striking way she looked.

★ ★ ★

A few nights later, I went to CBGB to see a triple bill of Blondie, Suicide, and the adorable and wild electric violinist Walter Steding. Lester Bangs was there, as well as Diego Cortez, Anya Phillips, and the artist Kiki Smith. Cheetah Chrome and Stiv Bators, guys I knew from Cleveland, were in a popular punk band, the Dead Boys. It was a very strange contrast of styles that night. Blondie was pop '60s fun with a punk veneer and the sharp-edged sexiness of Debbie Harry, whereas Suicide was pure menace, enough to make your ears bleed. And Walter was charmingly eccentric on his electric violin.

That night James Chance approached me with Pat by his side.

'Hey, you look like a little pimp. Do you wanna join my band?'

I wondered how he assessed me this way, since I never saw him look directly at me.

'To play drums?' I asked.

'I want you to play my Ace Tone organ. I'll show you how.'

I looked around the club, at kids like me. We all seemed so young and vital and curious and cocky. Kids who'd arrived from the same places I'd run from; broken cities, broken families, failed educations – most of us knowing academia had nothing to do with art or freedom, only indoctrination. The hypocrisy of culture breaking us into sharp glittering pieces able to cut through the charade and defy all restraints. We came together from across America, from Europe, from Japan to find one another downtown. We were on fire in a town ripe for the taking, not giving a damn about being accepted on any ideological terms. Life had already beaten the hell out of us and now, we were beating back.

I had never played organ or touched a keyboard, aside from playing bass notes on my grandmother's piano as a girl. Many of us in the scene didn't do what we'd really come to New York City to do. Pat Place and James Nares were visual artists. I was a singer. We picked up instruments we'd never played, knew nothing about. The instruments became extensions of our nervous systems, a way of expression that, unbeknownst to us, would evolve into a movement.

Contort Yourself!

James Siegfried (soon to be Chance) grew up in Milwaukee, the oldest of four children and the son of middle-class educators who loved music. Ironically, this venom-spitting malcontent of a musical prodigy had his first instruction in music by a nun who taught him piano in Catholic school. (It is uncanny how nuns pop up as musical instigators in so many biographical stories.) As he grew, young Chance was a fan of Charlie Parker and John Coltrane, but it was the more abstract free jazz players he gravitated toward: Archie Shepp, Cecil Taylor, and Albert Ayler.

Sun Ra was the Afro-futurist leading James to guide my hands in atonal organ dissonance and rhythm. I wouldn't come upon the musical phrase 'clusters' until it was pointed out to me by a stranger on the Bowery. This encounter occurred after George Scott, Jody Harris, and Donny Christenson had joined James Chance, Pat Place, and me, resulting in what is regarded as the quintessential, most dynamic of Contortions line-ups. I was just leaving Phebe's on the corner of East 4th St, heading down Bowery, when a sizeable fellow ambled toward me. As he came closer, he narrowed his eyes as if to inspect me, then stopped and flashed a smile.

'Hey! You're that girl from the Contortions!'

Because he was Black and knew of the band, I figured he must be part of the free jazz players curious about the unhinged white skronk of the Contortions. Serious players in the jazz loft scene had bounced James Chance from their jams for being too weird and attention-hoarding. Not a man to cede the spotlight to another, James never followed anyone musically, and the loft scene jams were no exception. He'd launch into his white-boy wiggle while trying to provoke an audience sitting on the floor to get up and dance.

'You're the girl on the keyboards!'

'Yep, that's me.'

'Where'd you learn how to play like that?'

'Um . . . my grandmother played piano.'

'Uh-huh. You been listening to Sun Ra playing those clusters.'

He tilted his head in amusement as I stumbled for words, not knowing a cluster from a major C.

'Uh . . . Sun Ra?'

'Like you don't know.'

He smirked, pulled out a pen, and scribbled an address on a matchbook. He complimented me about my timing, saying I should sit in with him and some of the jazz players – I was that good. When I told him I just might do that, he laughed.

'Yeah, but you'll need to put a bag over your head!'

Was he calling me ugly? My face immediately betrayed the insult received, and he laughed, pointing to his forearm skin, then to me. As if to say, you know.

'Serious, now, you should come by and play.' Then he headed toward East 2nd Street.

That night, after a Contortions rehearsal, Jody, Donny, and I went to Fanelli's. Once a speakeasy in the 1920s and '30s, Fanelli's is a classic. It has the kind of atmosphere a film producer would spend serious money recreating for its bohemia-meets-mob-joint feel. A mahogany bar faces small tables with red and white checkered tablecloths, and the walls are plastered with framed black and white photos of boxers, mobsters, and benefactors.

I pulled out the matchbook received from the stranger, realizing I'd never asked the guy for his name. While telling Jody and Donny about the encounter, Jody inspected the address on the matchbook, asking me to describe the guy. I did, and Jody flipped out.

CONTORT YOURSELF!

'Are you kidding? That was Stanley Crouch! He writes for the *Village Voice* and plays the drums. He's a motherfucker! I hear he'll slug you if you rub him the wrong way. You should play with him. They're all free jazz dudes. Do it, if you know what's good for you!'

I eventually saw Sun Ra's Arkestra at the Squat Theater, next door to the Chelsea Hotel. By the end of 1979, they were practically the Squat house band and were defiantly futuristic. And I started reading Crouch's reviews in the *Village Voice*. You could always count on some iconoclastic pepper sauce from Stanley's pen, and apparently, also his mitts. Jody and Donny started teasing me about mine and Stanley's pugilism being a good match, but imposter syndrome prevented me from showing up to play with Stanley's crew. The honorary punk in Crouch would surface in the late 1980s when he slapped a fellow critic who dared to criticize his work. With his love for fisticuffs, he would have fit right in with the Contortions.

Totally enthralled by Cecil Taylor's keyboard playing, I wanted to play like him but didn't have an inch of the discipline required to learn theory, to back up my percussive style on the keys with notes capable of such extreme musical transport. James dropped out of the Milwaukee Conservatory of Music one year shy of a degree and started a local band called the James Siegfried Quartet. Not your usual free jazz line-up, one band member played electrified oven racks. Extremely intelligent and just as shy, his brother David told me that when James was a teenager, he had a transistor radio glued to his ear. This was back in the golden age of AM radio in the 1960s, when midwestern stations were playing music like the Stones and the Animals, the Merseybeat bands, plus garage bands like Question Mark and the Mysterians, the Shadows of Knight, and Sam the Sham and the Pharoahs.

James loved Motown as well, and when he discovered James Brown, he'd found his hero. Mick Jagger would make off with the Brown booty of moves and make them his own, as would Iggy Pop, but James Chance took the lacerating funkster's moves further than any feral animal could dream. Brown was the master of funk, was rhythm personified. Chance wanted to be like him, not only in the burning funk style but in command on stage and behind the curtain, treating his band like serfs and bitching you out if you hit a wrong slice of noise on the offbeat. At first, we all found this amusing. James was no diplomat when it came to rehearsals. He'd show you what to play and if you didn't play it his way, he'd stop the song and call you out, resembling James Brown as bandleader despot. Soon we'd start playing his parts in our own styles, and as a unit the Contortions would evolve a solid style through the experience of gigging. Or, shall I say, assaulting.

James invited me over to try my hand at his Ace Tone organ. He was living in a storefront hole on East 2nd Street between Avenues A and B. I was getting used to a scene where everyone lived in near squalor. Beds were usually mattresses on floors and most sheets looked an uninviting dishwater grey. Hardly anyone cooked at home, but the girls were better at this. Good bread, butter, cheese, and decent coffee and tea could be purchased cheaply. You grabbed a slice of pizza now and then or ate starchy, filling foods at one of the dirt-cheap Ukrainian restaurants like Leshko's or Veselka. (These were the days when art without comfort was comfort enough.)

James prided himself on dressing well, and the only hint of domesticity to be found in his railroad storefront dump was an ironing board and iron. His shirts and sharkskin suits were all perfectly pressed and hanging on a clothesline he'd strung across the room. He motioned me over to his keyboard.

The Ace Tone is a very cool organ from the 1960s with a nasty garage-band bite, much harsher than the Italian Farfisa, a common organ used in 1960s garage-rock like Sam the Sham and the Pharaohs and by Rose Stone from Sly and the Family Stone. Kate Pierson of the B-52s would bring the Farfisa back into the spotlight on songs like 'Planet Claire'. The Ace Tone Top-5 was a Japanese model, with a more aggressive sound than the Farfisa and a wicked, crazy vibrato. James suggested playing it like I would drums, percussively, and showed me the clusters of notes he wanted on some of his songs. Since I couldn't read music, the approach suited me just fine. Initially James wanted me to play exactly what he dictated, and if I strayed a bit, he'd literally pick my hand up and off the keys, toss my hand off the way a mother would a child's hand on a matchbook, play the cluster himself, then pick my hand up and guide it on to the notes, all the while never ever looking me in the eyes. (I wondered whether he had some type of autistic spectrum disorder, like Asperger's. He could never look anyone in the eye for more than a brief second.)

He had a fold-out hi-fi and played a few Fela Kuti tracks. We were all listening avidly to Fela. His music was all about the one, an emphasis on the very first beat of every measure, also employed in funk by James Brown and George Clinton. It would take a few personnel changes for the Contortions to get there, but James wanted that on-the-one funk as foundation to the noise. He also played Albert Ayler and Cecil Taylor tracks, enough for me to realize he'd bit their more extreme cacophonous styles, bending them to his own unique style.

So, James 'played' my hands on the keys until I learned how to manhandle an organ, taking his style and subverting it a bit in the Contortions. As we continued to play together, none of us would follow such a strict 'Chance-ian' paradigm as we did in the beginning. But his signature way of creating polyrhythms and bringing the disparate parts together would remain as foundation. There was a method to the wee dictator's madness.

Lydia's bass player Reck brought in his friend from Japan, Chiko Hige, on drums. With a Japanese rhythm section, James Nares, Pat Place, myself, and the inimitable James Chance in the lead, the Contortions were thus born in Bradly's loft on Delancey Street. James had gotten the band's name from music critic Robert Palmer, who called James a contortionist and not in a flattering way when he saw James act out on stage at a loft space with one of his early bands, Flaming Youth.

★ ★ ★

I had started dating Anya Phillips, if you can call it dating. She and Diego lived together, and I'd go over there to play house with Anya and see what Diego was up to. Diego landed in New York from the Art Institute of Chicago and worked as assistant to the artist Vito Acconci. He was a renaissance man, directing videos for Blondie and Suicide, writing and curating. He had a lucky penchant for coming across dark and discarded treasure troves. One of his first shows was a box he'd found of medical films of surgeries. He projected the films on walls and on televisions at loft gallery spaces.

When I first went to their place, Diego pulled out a box of photographs of Elvis he'd found in Berlin. The King was stoned or on booze or, judging from the droopy eyelids, on smack. He posed with a revolving carousel of German showgirls and hookers draped all over him, smiling too wide, some with rotten teeth. These are can't-turn-away-from-the-car-wreck photos. The great idol, now the glassy-eyed emperor, a seedy GI too high to care about anything aside from the next shot of whatever was robbing his soul of expression. The photos were exclamation marks to the hypocrisy of pop culture, and the price paid by those it lionizes.

And then there was Anya. Anya Phillips was strikingly beautiful, a small but formidable woman – an extraordinary being in a scene with few people of colour. This lack was not due to racism; it had more to do with how people learned about what was happening downtown, the geographics of the city and its various segregations, and which people were drawn by the predominantly white music and cultural generation of cool preceding us (the Warhol set and the surviving beats like Ginsberg and Burroughs). Most of the Asian musicians in the scene were Japanese: Contortions members Reck and Chiko Hige, and Ikue Mori, the drummer for the band DNA.

The downtown scene did not discriminate against gender or race, and the racial makeup of the art and music scene would morph into a potent mix in the 1980s with the addition of hip-hop, graffiti culture, and the Afro-futuristic abstractions of artists like Jean-Michel Basquiat and Rammellzee.

Anya stood out, and not only for her physical beauty and Chinese origins. A force of nature, charisma dripped from her pores; you felt her coming before she entered the room. Being a Chinese woman meant coming up against stereotypes like Suzy Wong, the China Doll, the Geisha, the prostitute. All the mad clichés of subservience spun on Asian women. She had grown up in Taiwan in a military world where American soldiers sorted Asian women into clichéd containers, thanks to the fetishism personified in American films and an exotic Orientalism created in the West. This dyad of Asian women as infantilized and submissive – always available to the white man – or dominant and mysterious were tropes Anya despised. Yet she knew a tough persona was obviously the best fit, so she based her mask on the latter, curating her No Wave Dragon Lady with an insatiable will to conquer the scene. Hers was a glamour girl stylistic dominance predicated on an essence of negation, a contempt for the ordinary, the boring, and the passé. Her attitude mirrored the nihilism of No Wave perfectly.

Anya's mother fled China's Communist revolution and moved to Taiwan with Anya, whose father is rumoured to have been a general in Chiang Kai-shek's army. Her mother married Wade Phillips, a military attaché stationed at the American Embassy in Taipei, and she became an important presence in the Taiwanese television industry. Her mother was a very ambitious woman, and Anya rebelled against her control. She attended the Taipei American School where she met her best friend Sylvia Morales, daughter of an American serviceman. Anya dreamed of being a fashion designer, sketched prolifically through her teens, and showed tremendous talent. She and Sylvia moved to New York in 1974, and both attended Pratt Institute – Sylvia for painting, Anya for fashion design on a full scholarship. But Anya dropped out after three days, drawn to the downtown scene and its wild possibilities. She continued to design spandex dresses in wild colours, ripped, tied, knotted, and pinned; S&M Flintstone fashion for the punk and No Wave elite.

Anya and Sylvia shared an apartment on St Mark's Place next door to Terence (Terry) Sellers, New York's infamous dominatrix, also known as Mistress Angel Stern, the reigning queen of the BDSM scene. The three were friends, often pitting one against the other in juvenile rivalries – but the actual fracture would occur when Sylvia met Lou Reed in 1975. She soon became Sylvia Reed, Lou's wife, manager, graphic designer, and all-around art and intimate partner. This would cause a falling out between Sylvia and Anya; Anya was the one who had vowed to marry a rock star. And she felt abandoned by Sylvia but worried for her. Lou wasn't exactly a choir boy in 1975.

Like Lydia, Anya wanted you to believe she dined on razor blades. The Anya I met initially was bashful and sweet, and extremely gentle. People who knew her in the scene might laugh in disbelief at this description, but she was vulnerable and easily hurt beneath the facade.

Anya had a faux band with Diego Cortez called the Esoterrorists, a play on the word 'esoteric'. The two approached Steve Maas to open a club in artist Ross Bleckner's Tribeca building. Anya's brainchild, the Mudd Club was a stark black box inside 77 White Street where the decor consisted of its darkly clad denizens: downtown's elite ruffians, musicians, rock stars, art stars, and celebrities.

I was dating Anya when the Mudd Club first opened. There was the night a doorman had taken a bribe from a couple of young Wall Street poseurs, which is the only way they'd ever gain entry. These suits would buy their way in and slouch around the club doped up, trying to appear decadent and louche. Anya and I had been dancing (she was a fantastic dancer), and my arm was around her shoulders when one of the creepy Wall Street duo laughed and asked if she was a hooker and if we were 'lesbos'. One guy was five-foot-nine; I'm five-foot even. When they tried grabbing our asses, I leaped into gear and cold-cocked one of them. His hand flew to his nose, face blanching in astonishment. My pal who worked behind the bar, the stunning Edwige Belmore, helped me tag-team the handsy bankers. She was quite tall, maybe six foot, and I was a shrimp, so it must have been quite a sight to see her leap over the bar to my aid, us punching and laughing while the baffled suits fled the club.

Anya adored these pugilistic shenanigans. I was intensely attracted to her, but she wanted to be a couple, and I was a cad. I had just arrived in town on a narcissistic cloud of reinvention and it was an exciting, dangerous, and precarious time in my life. But it would extend way too long, more than a decade of playing the selfish drunken rake, the mad outlaw. I wanted the heat of sexual encounters and hormonal lust, the physical and the dreamily romantic and beyond that, I hardly knew what I felt emotionally from moment to moment. As a love-starved kid, sex was the closest feeling to love I could experience. Sex was physical warmth, aliveness, release, excitement. To touch and be touched. A biological stand-in for literally caring about someone and being cared for. Understanding that form of love as an abandoned kid seemed nigh impossible. I loved the broken spirit of the world's outcasts in an abstract way and didn't understand how to channel the feelings into art. Love, real love for another personally, required empathy and trust, and both were beyond my comprehension. Emotional intimacy terrified me. I was afraid I'd be discovered as the broken-hearted, unloved girl lurking inside my skin, that she would in turn send any truly loving human running for the hills. If someone I'd laid with wanted more closeness than the physical act, I'd vanish. I was not alone in being a No Wave narcissist. Sex was, most often, free and easy, with no strings attached.

★ ★ ★

Anya knew Debbie Harry, and the two designed the iconic hot pink dress Debbie wears on the cover of the Blondie LP *Plastic Letters*. They starred as 'Nazi Dykes' in a comic strip for *PUNK* magazine called 'The Legend of Nick Detroit'. Their emblem was a swastika inside the circle of the women's power glyph. Of course, it was the 'dykes' that were labelled Nazis, not the punk rockers in *PUNK* editor Legs McNeil's band Shrapnel who wore swastikas on stage and were deemed asinine for it by critics Lester Bangs and Robert Christgau. This Nazi punk fetish was absurd teenage posturing. Hardly antisemitic, yet disgustingly offensive.

Sylvia and Anya were inseparable for a long time. Sylvia is half-Mexican, and when they hung out together, white people assumed Sylvia was also Asian due to her exotic, non-white appearance. Railing against the fetishistic infantilizing of Asian women, Anya was provoked to adopt these harmful stereotypes fully to a laughable extreme. As a stripper, she was called China Doll. Dragon Lady was her dominant person, the Chinese dominatrix her primary mask. She flipped the script to its extreme with the credo, *I will incite your need, but I'm so empty I have no need and your need means nothing.*

The dominatrix, the tough girl-hoodlum. That was Anya and me. Both hiding behind cloaks of the invulnerable; you can't shatter emptiness. There are myriad ways to conceal loneliness and the feeling of never being seen or understood, a longing that runs deep in most of us, unless you're made of concrete.

Even though I did not understand the world of sadomasochism intellectually at the time, I found the coldness, the perfection of the dominatrix stance as overtly sexual yet oddly sexless. Sex utterly devoid of heat, predicated on pain, cold dominance and humiliation always struck me as a disguise for a deep insecurity and vulnerability.

Several women I knew worked as phone girls or dominatrices at Terence Sellers' headquarters, the Dungeon, New York's home for the elite with a taste for sexual abjection. Most likely it was Terence who taught Anya the 'art' of verbal humiliation, which she'd pass on to James Chance. He already had a penchant for verbally abusing the audience when they met. Funnily enough, when Anya first encountered James, she treated him like a mosquito, a pest to be waved away. James was obsessed with Anya from the very beginning. When Anya decided to take him on as a lover and manage him (and the Contortions), she was working for Terence as a dominatrix.

In the early 1980s, a few friends I knew worked at Terence's dungeon; lesbians, for the most part. Some had heroin habits to support and worked part-time as in-person dommes or phone dommes. Intrigued, I asked for a tour. A striking visual I recall from that visit was a glass museum case; the kind where ancient manuscripts and smaller archaeological treasures and jewellery might be displayed. Inside the case on a black velvet bed lay a perfectly arranged collection of primitive gynaecological implements of torture. An ancient enema piston-and-cylinder device that resembled a huge hypodermic needle with a tube made me shiver. (I've always had an interest in European history, especially the pomp and perversity of Versailles. From what I'd read, cleanliness wasn't exactly germane to the court, hence my surprise when my guide related that during the reign of Louis XIV, upper-class Parisians couldn't get enough of their 'clysters', sometimes taking up to four enemas a day!)

NO NEW YORK

Terence's (Mistress Angel Stern's) anachronistic treasury included assorted devices like medieval thumb screws and nipple clamps, cast-iron handcuffs, and a creepy metal thing called a choke pear. (My tour guide explained the pear-shaped device as a type of speculum with four sharp metal leaves. Once inserted in an orifice, it was cranked open for purposes of mutilation.) The most insidious and unnerving of all was the case's final object of cruelty: a red tomato pin cushion perforated with a halo of straight pins.

When my attention drifted toward other objects of desire, Anya didn't act that bothered. She was more surprised in a quizzical sort of way – or maybe hurt, but it was hard to tell. I was terrible at reading people's emotions unless it was delight or outrage. I started to avoid Anya. Shortly after we stopped dating, she began to project her severe persona onto the scene with impenetrable perfection. Downtown's favourite fascination, she was the most compelling subject of every photographer. And I was about to discover the funny and tender Anya as a woman you did not want to mess with.

★ ★ ★

In early December 1977, the first Contortions gig at Max's Kansas City was a blur of speedy noise, served up to an audience of downtown artists. There was plenty of nervous pacing backstage, with Chance cursing about how the audience didn't deserve us (we hadn't even played a note yet). A frenetic version of 'I Don't Want to Be Happy' started the set. We played slashes of noisy polyrhythms to Chiko's tom-tom drumming, timing dropouts to sonic holes for Chance to rage-scream his Dada nihilism: 'I prefer the ridiculous to the sublime!' The next song was a Bo-Diddley-on-crack number called 'Roving Eye' (which seemed to fit my persona) that ramped down into a blues crawl while Chance soloed, then ricocheted back into Diddley speed. James Nares' guitar was tuned to a key in another galaxy. Pat's sliding squeals were well timed with Reck and Chiko, wildly fast and vicious, while Nares and I were slashing our clusters of noise in between the beats Chance had dictated. Chance had counted the songs off so fast, we could hardly keep up.

At our very first gig, I realized James was a dazzling frontman. Totally weird and fascinating. Matching Lydia in his contempt for the crowd, he punctuated his crabby barking with high-pitched scream-bursts as if he were being pinched repeatedly by a mean lobster. On the instrumental bits, he'd launch into utterly insane sax runs, then do his little dance with eyes closed, lips pursed in a pout, wiggling his tight little butt-cheeks across the stage in his contorted version of James Brown meets Mick Jagger.

James had written the dirge 'Jaded', which called for me to play the Catholic martyr on Thorazine. I'd start at the top keys of the Ace Tone, playing a steady, pulsing rhythm, slowly making my way down the keys and octaves. I played to extremes. Got down on my knees, laying on the keys first with fingers, then whole hands, then entire forearms, staring up into the stage lights in agonized supplication to the god who never answers, my version of Renée Falconetti in Theodor Dreyer's *The Passion of Joan of Arc*.

At the end of the last song, 'Bedroom Athlete', James shrieked, threw the mike on the ground with a sonic boom and we fled the stage. The crowd went bananas, pounding on the tables for an encore that would never come. Backstage, I tried to help Pat Place mop up the blood on her hands and the red streaks on the cream-coloured pickguard of her Fender Mustang. Her fingers were lacerated. Broken strings wisped in the air while only two remained taut and intact on her guitar. She'd been playing violently with her knuckles trying to keep up with Chance's tempo. Pumped on adrenaline, I jack-rabbited around the cramped backstage area while the audience continued to bang and howl. Chance said they should 'eat shit and die'. That's all they were getting. This would become the signature of the band for the first year of gigs; short, rapid-fire sets of sonic theatre. The Contortions quickly became the misfit darlings of avant-garde New York. Crowds lined up to see us at Max's, and after performing our first set, the club had to empty the room to fill it again for a second set; sets that would soon include bloody fisticuffs as part of the act.

Grandma's Hands

When the Contortions performed, I raged on that Ace Tone organ. I didn't think of it then, but a ghost – or was it an army of ghosts? – used me as a vessel, interacting through me on the keys.

My grandmother Joan played stride piano but never explained how or where she learned to play, or should I say, swing. Her roots were Irish, dating back to the emigrants who'd fled Ireland for Nova Scotia during the Great Famine. The enigma of my mother's paternity remains as much a mystery as my grandmother's musical skills and her own paternity. This was the norm on the maternal side, a trail of girls with sires unknown; invisible husbands and fathers going back three generations. From Ireland to Halifax and on to French Canada they came, to Maine and Boston, finally settling in Cleveland to be shamed as fallen women. Fallen, yet floating on music.

Grandma Joan eclipsed her own pain through the notes of an upright piano. Striding up and down the octaves with a bouncing left hand to rival Fats Waller, her right fingers improvised melodies as capricious as Art Tatum's. I'd sit next to her on the piano bench, watching and listening. Feeling the bounce while mesmerized by hands tap-dancing and stomping across the keys. Her hair was dyed black in a curly bob with bangs, like Édith Piaf. She smelled of the fragrance Joy by Jean Patou, and of music. If you'd ask where she learned all this, a cryptic grin curled around the sides of the ever-present unlit cigarette dangling from her ruby lips.

'I play by ear, darlin'!'

She played stride and crooned standards in the speakeasies along Lake Erie in Ohio during the Great Depression. Mostly mid-tempo songs sped up with her own kick; songs like 'It Had to Be You'.

She made just enough in tips to get by, and who knows what manner of man or bathtub gin in the speaks resulted in the birth of my mother, Kitty, who burst into life dancing in 1933 – the worst year of the Depression and the year Hitler was declared Chancellor of Germany. When the speaks closed at the end of Prohibition, Grandma worked the bars up and down the west side with her toddler parked in a basket beneath the piano. Kitty hung on to the piano leg bouncing and twisting to Grandma's rhythms. One day the child would become a chorine, her mother's tempos coursing through her system.

Worn down by the Depression and its scourge of poverty, Grandma finally gave in and married an über-stern German named Oliver Tong. They married in 1946 when my mother was thirteen – one year after the Nazis surrendered. All red-faced Sturm und Drang, Tong hardly resembled his chosen surname, which I'd learn was an alias cover for the surname Weiss. Certain to throw hunters off a scent.

Grandma taught me the fundamentals of rhythm at her kitchen table on summer evenings. I was nine years old playing gin rummy with her until late at night; she, clapping out a rhythm on the Formica tabletop with her hand of plastic cards, throwing in a shuffle here, a slide there. I picked up quick, playing counter rhythms to hers and off we'd go on and on, switching beats and creating wild tempos.

I learned how to sing harmony to Boswell Sisters songs like 'Crazy People', we two rocking the piano bench. She guided me over the notes, the high harmony above her alto voice. Watching her play piano like that and sing yet another counterpoint rhythm of words over those two gifted hands was hypnotizing – she became three distinct marchers, each heeding the beat of a different drum. Her coordination was effortless, her joy, supreme.

Then Tong would come home. First, we'd hear the huge clumsy feet crossing the threshold and there he'd be, sneering from his grey garage attendant uniform while vacuuming every particle of joy from the room.

'Joooaaan! Quit that racket, will ya?'

Her hands would still. There went Grandma's sparkle.

'Stop playin' that coloured music. STOP, you hear? I pay the bills! I need peace!'

Hateful Oliver Weiss 'Tong' never uttered a kind word to Grandma in my presence. Uncle Richard called Grandma a quadroon once. She laughed and shushed him.

'Don't say that too loud, you'll get us all in trouble!'

Much later, while researching a story, I discovered that many African-American slaves settled in Nova Scotia and Halifax had a significant population. I figured she may have had Black in her from the time I caught my first glimpse of a Black man on television, and her voice with a vibrato as wide as the Cuyahoga and just as mysterious. As a kid, I fantasized about her being part Black, ready to celebrate any little twist that might position me outside the punishing lines of white Donna Reed womanhood and its conformity lying in wait to jail my life, my imagination.

One day, Grandma's piano vanished. 'Tong' had replaced it with a tiered Hammond organ, a beast of a thing festooned with coloured levers for different beats and sounds; bossa nova and cha-cha, flutes, strings, and French horns all sounding chintzy and carnivalesque. The organ must have reminded him of German calliope music. Grandma hated that damned organ. She couldn't beat out her joyful rhythms on an organ's ultra-sensitive keys. Keys that felt lifeless.

She was never the same after that. I remember watching her gaze out the kitchen window, her beautiful hands lying still in the sink's sudsy water, all joy having drained from fingers that would never dance again. And I would curse Oliver Weiss 'Tong'. Curse having been born a woman, and vow to break every rule of what a woman should do and be. I had so much rage about the injustices committed against womankind, the invisibility of woman as hero, the broken heart of woman. Rage equalled righteousness as I beat at that organ for my grandmother like 'Thug' Rose Namajunas in the ring, beating away all the hurt I'd experienced as a child, liberating the pain of my grandmother. With the Contortions, I made music out of pain, and art out of internalized violence.

Love in a Blackout

James Nares and I became lovers. Beneath his lightly pockmarked skin and dirty blond hair were the features of a British nobleman, one who'd rejected his past for something new and strange here in the city, the ugly-beautiful aesthetic the downtown artists and musicians were swept up in creating. Until that moment, I'd never had a real boyfriend, and James would be my very first and last boy love. There would be other guys, but they'd never make their way into my heart as James did.

The first time I visited his tenement walk-up I looked around in awe at what appeared to be more of a bivouac than a place where someone actually lived. There were no curtains on the windows, big greasy panes looking out onto Eldridge Street. I'd never have admitted it then, but New York scared and overwhelmed me. James knew how to navigate, treating the streets as a benevolent, tameable beast. I'd imagined New York to resemble films like *The Apartment*, *West Side Story*, *The Pawnbroker*. Far from it. The thought of making a life for myself alone in a city that resembled a bombed-out Beirut was frightening. James made me feel safe.

I stayed with him at his place on Eldridge Street, a one-room apartment with an extension cord running from a downstairs establishment feeding electricity to a hot plate and a bare-bulbed lamp. This was the period of his X paintings, huge red X's of paint slashed over sheets, paper, walls, shirts – the original X-man of the red and black. James came from generations of judges, vicars, and solicitors on his father's side. His father Gordon was a well-respected journalist writing eloquently about England's royal homes and architecture until he died of a heart attack at thirty-one years. James was only four years old. His mother had a career as a model before marrying Gordon. James had an older brother, Oliver, and a younger sister,

Gina. Sometimes he worked on odd jobs, but he never seemed to need money. He was always generous and had an air of elegance about him. Elegant scruff.

I liked watching James. His movements suggested there was another being inside his skin trying to get out. He was very conscious of his hands, always emphatic, curiously gestural. Trying to decide which way to hold the fingers, he'd jerk them through the air in staccato movements or allow them to flow in more feminine gestures. Attempting to grace his words, painting a fluid frame around the thoughts, shaping the air around the vowels, the sounds. Running his hands repeatedly through his hair, he'd place a hand, open palm on his chest and clavicle. Like a lady at high tea.

In 1978, James moved into my apartment on East 3rd Street between First and Second Avenues. We played records, cooked simple meals, played guitars. James had a small Sony tape recorder, and the quality was excellent. The recorder was small enough to sneak into shows undetected. We went to see Television play at the Bottom Line and it remains one of the most exciting concerts of my lifetime. The way Tom Verlaine and Richard Lloyd played off one another felt transcendent. It wasn't poet Paul Verlaine informing Tom's and Richard's style, it was Stéphane Mallarmé. The songs on *Marquee Moon* had the guitars and drums placing notes and hits like Mallarmé placed words on a page; with an esoteric understanding of space. Space influenced Television's music as much as notes did. Sounds positioned with an instinctual feel for where silence breathed a pause of astonishment, of wonder – of love and its sorrows. Billy Ficca and Fred Smith held the songs together with a jazzy solid rhythm while the two guitarists danced off into the stratosphere. I felt their notes like stars shooting through my bloodstream.

LOVE IN A BLACKOUT

When James moved in with me, a padlocked trunk came with him. Not wanting to invade his privacy I didn't ask about the contents of the trunk but, soon enough, my curiosity prevailed. Shyly, he said he'd been waiting to tell me. He sprung the lock on a Pandora's box that opened to reveal the woman he'd been hiding inside his skin: her corset, garter belts, and stockings, a femme makeup case, wigs, and a 1950s-style bullet bra. That was the night I met Jamie Nares. And I was not surprised.

⋆ ⋆ ⋆

Today, Jamie Nares does not want or need to draw attention to herself. There isn't a shred of narcissism about Jamie. I see her now, still somewhat self-conscious. She hunches her shoulders, relaxes, then shifts her long arms, hands together resting on knees. The corset and stockings, theatrical femme makeup and bullet bra have been replaced by a simple scoop-neck sweater, colour of wet earth, beige, wide-legged slacks, brown sandals. Her natural long white hair kisses her collarbone. She holds her thighs together in pants as if she's wearing a skirt. Decidedly feminine, she is physically demure. Modest. Nearly old-fashioned.

⋆ ⋆ ⋆

One night on Stanton Street, on 13 July 1977, it was around 9 p.m. and the air was sweltering when, suddenly, we heard bursts, like little explosions or gunshots. We stared out of the sixth-floor tenement window watching little electric fire bursts, transformers exploding like lethal popcorn, pops easily confused with gunshots, which were plenty since the darkness provoked a free for all. All the power and every light in the city had shut down to black. Confusion, looting, and violence commenced, yelps resounding through the concrete canyons. Fires began igniting; some set by people on rooftops for light and fun, while many entire buildings went up in blazes that night, set by slumlords eager to collect on insurance. Sirens screeched through the wee hours, and Son of Sam must have been giddy with excitement, still out there on the loose. I was not easily terrified, but that night of the blackout felt like the apocalypse had finally arrived.

The next morning, we ventured into the downtown streets. Dazed shopkeepers watched people strolling into their stores and taking whatever they wanted, and I followed suit. It was so easy. I walked into a corner bodega and grabbed a carton of orange juice – the shopkeeper gave me a resigned smile and nod as I walked out. Boys laughed and jumped onto the hoods of cars with destructive glee. Men were boarding up smashed shop windows. And about two hundred of us downtown were just getting started – reconstructing new sounds and visions from the ashes.

Poète Maudit Mischief

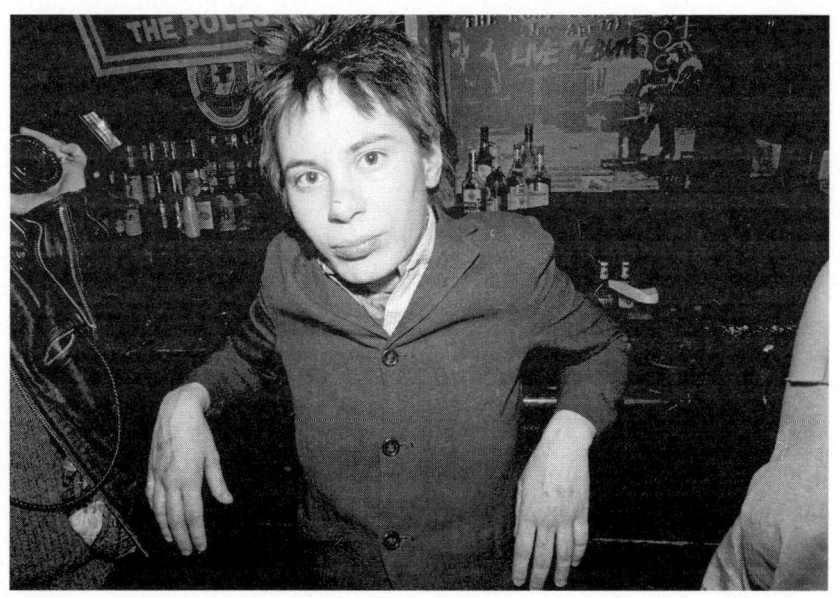

Sometime in late 1977, I told Pat Place I was crashing around and needed a more secure abode and she offered an extra room in her apartment on Sixth Avenue near Prince Street in SoHo for $50 a month. Clean, white, and stark with a minimum of furniture, it was the sanest of the living spaces I'd tried so far. Abnormally, she used her kitchen from time to time – mostly to dye clothes black in a huge spaghetti pot. I moved in and we became pals.

In 1975 Pat had moved to the city from Chicago. She studied art at Northern Illinois University. After a Skidmore summer art programme and seeing Patti Smith in 1976 at the Village Gate, she began wondering if the art world was for her. The work at galleries like Leo Castelli, OK Harris, and Paula Cooper, and their assorted gallery habitués felt uptight, irrelevant, and ultra-snobbish; the antithesis of the rebel heresy concerning who Jesus died for, contained in the opening line of Patti Smith's *Horses*.

New art, words, and noise were being provoked and generated in previously unknown shapes and sounds, coming out of places like CBGB and Max's, and bands like the Contortions, Mars, DNA, Teenage Jesus and the Jerks, the Gynecologists, and Y Pants were exploring a type of musical schizophrenia. Each of these bands included women. Ideas were being exchanged, collaborations born between writers, visual artists, conceptualists, musicians, filmmakers, and photographers in downtown bars like Magoos, Puffy's, and Barnabus Rex. The most striking phenomena of the gatherings were the women; women artists having travelled from the hinterlands of America, from France, Japan, England, Ireland, Germany, and Australia. Patti Smith had provoked a revolution of young women seizing their creative power, seeking new forms and possibilities.

NO NEW YORK

Transcending gendered expectations, we'd moved to downtown New York City. Long-repressed sounds and visions of female desire, eccentricity, and rage provided plenty of napalm, causing fatal injury to patriarchal ideas of what and who we should be. As Poly Styrene of England's X-Ray Spex shouted in 1977, 'Oh Bondage Up Yours!', we girls of downtown New York were slicing through the strings of trad three-chord progressions and minimalist art pretensions with broken glass.

★   ★   ★

Pat Place and I shared an androgynous sensibility in style and stance. We were not each other's type, were too similar. I assumed she was gay, but we didn't want to commodify ourselves. Identity politics, its obsessions and adherence to labelling never crossed our minds. Fluidity and the right to change and morph into whatever and whomever we wanted to be was intrinsic to the nature of so many in the downtown scene. Pat bought her guitars from pawn shops on Third Avenue. There was the monstrous Gretsch with a broken neck – she glued it back together – and a baby-blue Hagstrom. Her main guitar would be a red Fender Mustang. When she wasn't practising guitar to Rolling Stones and Stooges records, Pat took photos of petite toy dinosaurs on primary blocks of colour. The photos played with focus and were whimsical, like Pat, with her idiosyncratic rhythms of movement and guitar-playing and jerky little way of dancing. Sometimes wildly coloured plastic guns would appear in her photos, guns that could never be mistaken for lethal weapons. Toy guns and toy dinosaurs were her thing. Pat was and remains totally unique.

POÈTE MAUDIT MISCHIEF

★   ★   ★

SoHo was desolate in the late 1970s. I recall a large industrial building having caught fire during a snowstorm. Firemen had extinguished the blaze in temperatures of −2°F, and the water froze into ice, encasing what was left of the building, creating magnificent stalactite shapes and shaping the building's bones into a stunning fairytale ice palace. I remember trudging past this vision through banks of icy snow with Pat and James Chance to Johnny Dynell's place to borrow an amp for a show. We weren't fazed by the icy wind. In the early Contortions days, Pat, James, and I hung out quite a bit; we were good friends. Even though the soon-to-be Prince of Petulance never looked us in the eye aside from a quick glance, he laughed with us often, shyly smiling. We were light on gear and heavy coats but solid in our mission together: to destruct all notions of what music and art should be and do, and to laugh about the absurdity of the established New York art and music scenes. And we loved to prank.

Our first gig at Max's Kansas City had ignited our reputation as enfant terribles of the downtown scene, and our infamy guaranteed free admission and drinks at all the clubs. The bands played upstairs while the downstairs backroom was notorious for being a Warhol hangout. Several of Andy's entourage, along with the platinum don himself, could still be found drinking, indulging in drugs, and gossiping at their long-established corner table. I recall a night when Lydia, James Nares, John Lurie, Anya, and I were admitted into the backroom's inner sanctum, where we caused havoc by launching spitballs toward Warhol and his buddies. We thought Warhol and his gang were passé.

NO NEW YORK

Pranking art gallery openings in SoHo would serve two purposes: giving the finger to New York's elitist art scene, and the filling of our hungry bellies with free cheese and wine. The most scandalous art prank happened the evening of Roy Lichtenstein's opening of sculptures at the Castelli Gallery in December 1977. James, Pat, and I marched in wearing our thrift-store resistance outfits and sunglasses, arms locked, wielding dayglo toy ray guns and machine guns. James lived to call out bad art and shallow people with a bark that was viciously damning and antagonizing. The wealthy, black-clad art world denizens turned to us in curious bemusement as we stood there addressing them and Lichtenstein's cartoony, manufactured sculptures.

'This art is shit!' screamed James as we trolled the room insulting each piece.

'A fucking coffee cup! Merde!' We aimed our toy guns at the sculptures while sneering at the moneyed spectators.

'Which one of you rich assholes will take one of these pieces of crap home for your fucking amusement?'

People slithered away like we had leprosy. Some laughed and scoffed, others were beguiled by the spectacle. We made it to the cheese table, partook of all the Brie and baguette we could handle, drank the wine and insulted everyone who dared look at us until a few suit-clad men escorted us to the street.

When I was living in my favourite New York apartment on East 3rd Street between Second and Third Avenues with Jamie, Pat and I pranked the Hells Angels. The gang's New York City headquarters and clubhouse were a storefront and building on the north side of the street, the same as our building, and I'd often pass them hanging out front by their beloved Harley choppers listening to

POÈTE MAUDIT MISCHIEF

Steppenwolf. I'd wave and smile at the bearded scruffy guys, who were hardly monstrous. They maintained a fierce attitude with other guys but to us girls, they were always cordial. Kris Kristofferson-style dudes. Pat and I would occasionally don our bathing suits and hit the roof to sunbathe. One of the tenants had planted a small potted garden and there was a working rooftop hose. As a prank, we decided to squirt a few of the Hells Angels as they roared down the street below us on their bikes, then duck and hide behind the rooftop's lip.

One legendary experience with Pat that will forever shine in our memories happened in the spring of 1978. I call it the Night of the Broiled Chicken. We had just come from Donny Christenson's loft where we'd been rehearsing with the Contortions. Pat and I had taken mescaline or LSD – I'm not sure which, or what the differences may have felt like at the time. Whatever we were on, the effect had us laughing about everything that night; if a rat scurried across our feet, hilarity ensued. We were hungry so decided to stop into the Second Avenue Deli at the corner of 10th Street. We were both broke and wanted ice cream but couldn't afford dinner and dessert. So, we made an executive decision.

Various foods were displayed on top of the deli's long, brightly lit counter, including broiled whole chickens under heat lamps. One chicken seemed to glow, beckoning us to do the unthinkable, and suddenly, mandatory act. Pat and I looked at each other and, without a word between us, grabbed the greasy chicken and ran. We sprinted down Second Avenue with the speed of roadrunners. Tearing the wings and drumsticks off the chicken, we devoured the meat laughing our faces off, tossing the bones behind us at the furious deli employee giving chase. He was no match for our speed.

NO NEW YORK

We ended the night getting ice cream and strolling through Washington Square Park, high on our earlier stunt. Pat and I both looked like boys, but I guess we didn't completely pass because a trio of NYU frat guys dressed in button-down shirts approached, calling out 'Hey! Are you two dykes?' Still enjoying our blissful high, we weren't about to take any bullshit. We threw the ice cream cones at them and ran for our lives. By the time they shook off the shock, we were halfway down 8th Street.

Back when I was in Cleveland, my girlfiend had been Laura Kennedy, but when Peter Laughner died, I decided to move to New York. I was determined to go solo, but Laura wanted to move with me. She had dreams of us being in a band together (she had just started playing bass). When I began living with Pat, Laura would call to talk with me, and I'd never pick up the phone. She'd end up having long conversations with Pat, and one day she turned up at the apartment and moved in.

Kiki

Pat Place and I were roommates when I met Kiki Smith. She had a thick mane of black, wildly wavy hair, dark eyes, and the most expressive, beautiful hands. In her eyes and hands, I sensed what I think of as the witch wound, a magical and intuitive sense carried by women who've inherited ancestral torture or trauma – a burned-at-the-stake lineage expressing itself in the etheric physicality of their woman-ness, and in their work. I remember Kiki's hands then as seeming older than her years, with a wisdom in the long, elegant fingers, the expressive gestures, the lines in her palms. I was by no means a visual artist, but I remember wishing I could draw and capture her hands. Wanting to hold her dark eyes in my own hands, to feel in the ways she could see.

The artist Nancy Spero was an important inspiration for Kiki. Artists involved in the women's cooperative gallery AIR (Artists in Residence, Inc.) and, before that, Women Artists in Revolution (WAR) were our predecessors, fighting to be acknowledged and to create outside of established art world expectations. The chauvinism of the museum and gallery systems is legend. Cleveland-born Spero was involved with both women's groups, and it was her generation of women artists and activists of the 1960s and 1970s that paved the way for women in the downtown art scene later, where we felt free to be authentic, unique to our own visions, and not willing to cater to that time's art world trend of male minimalism and female invisibility.

Much of feminist art was political in the 1970s. The white male imperative at the time was about cold geometric shapes considered beautiful in line and form, whereas women were making work about interior lives and identity, violence against women, and the catastrophes of war. Nancy Spero was completing her *War Series*, and performance artists like Adrian Piper protested in their works; in Piper's case, inspired by the shootings at the Vietnam demonstrations at Kent State University. Millions of people were in the streets protesting Vietnam, for civil rights and farm workers' rights, and for women's rights. In the white male minimalist art world, there was an intellectual imperative toward a perverse purity; entitled male artists didn't feel any urge to be political because they were not suffering under any oppressions (or at least they didn't believe they were). The sole political actions were Robert Rauschenberg and Carl Andre withdrawing their work from the Venice Biennale in 1970 in protest at the invasion in Cambodia. They staged their own biennale-in-exile back home. Not a single woman artist was invited.

★ ★ ★

KIKI

Everything about Kiki felt unique and rarified, including the way she spoke, with a peculiar cadence and accent that was exclusive to her alone. I believe we connected on unknown terrain – that of being in this world, but not of it. Here to try and make sense of what we see and understand. Kiki was able to do this and had the discipline to make manifest her visions. She attended art school in Hartford for a year and a half and was mostly self-taught. I was mesmerized by Kiki; thought she was the most beautiful and curious woman I'd ever encountered. We'd hang out together – get coffee or go to MoMA – and Pat and I helped her move into her space downtown on South Street. She was drawing cigarette packs at the time, was concentrating on learning to draw, learning perspective before attempting to do abstractions. How important it was, she thought, to learn the basics; a concept foreign to my feral thinking when it came to any artistic discipline. She quickly graduated from cigarette packs to guitars, most likely due to her boyfriend Jody Harris, our guitarist in the Contortions, and she painted a mural of guitars inside Tier 3, another downtown club hosting No Wave bands, readings, and performances. The downtown scene provided a kaleidoscopic array of personalities and collaborations, and events were happening at such a pace that we eventually ended up drifting apart, into other people and fascinations.

Kiki became a formidable artist whose invocation to work was partially inspired by our New York place in time, and by the support of artists a generation before her like Nancy Spero and Leon Golub. Decades later, her Brooklyn Museum show told me so much about Kiki, the woman and artist. I sensed a quiet, esoteric wisdom in her when we met but was too young to understand and investigate. When an artist has learned their craft, has the discipline and the ability to channel the most painful and illuminating insights, wisdoms that can only arrive with age and empathy, loss, and love, the most moving work manifests. Kiki lost many people to AIDS, including her younger sister Bea and friend and collaborator David Wojnarowicz. For me, no other work will ever capture the fragility of life as much as her sculpture *Heute (Now)*. She'd built a coffin from unfinished knotty blonde wood. Peering into the coffin from above, one gazed at the most exquisite filigree glass dandelions growing from the coffin's floor. The flowers, gone to seed. Like the white fluffy orbs that children blow into the wind.

In retrospect, Kiki was unlike the rest of the artists in the scene due to her sense of delicacy. She possessed a type of compassion in her work that wasn't visible in others working at that time. She was certainly nothing like Lydia Lunch or Kathy Acker, Cindy Sherman or Jenny Holzer, who all worked with different aspects of anger, oppression, irony, and humour, and who all became under-and-overground celebrities. There remains a huge space for rage from women artists in all its manifestations. Kiki's approach always reached back to nature. Fame was never her aim. Even when addressing oppression, you see her delicate magic, the blessedness of life, of fairy tales, of flesh and blood womanhood. Kiki is an alchemist with a will toward a transcendence capable of creating an experience of stillness in the gaze, of what lies beyond the veil. She continues to bring us into that space. In the absence of anger – with grace.

As recently as the 1990s, artist Lynn Hershman Leeson took a camera to the Whitney and asked passers-by to name three women artists. Stumped, most could only think of one: Frida Kahlo. I'll add a few more here:

KIKI

Nancy Spero   Joyce Kozloff   Judy Chicago   Adrian Piper   Mary Beth Edelson   Joan Jonas   Yvonne Rainer   Howardena Pindell   Faith Ringgold   Lynda Benglis   Faith Wilding   Suzanne Lacy   Lorraine O'Grady   Ana Mendieta   Eleanor Antin   Louise Bourgeois   Carolee Schneemann   Magdalena Abakanowicz   Martha Wilson   Lynn Hershman Leeson   Suzy Lake   Hannah Wilke   Valie Export   Miriam Schapiro   Leslie Labowitz   Renate Eisenegger   Karin Mack   Ewa Partum   Renate Bertlmann   Helena Almeida   Annegret Soltau   Penny Slinger   Judith Bernstein   Lorna Simpson   Lili Dujourie   Alexis Hunter   Katalin Ladik   Sanja Iveković   Birgit Jürgenssen   Ketty La Rocca   Annette Messager   Rita Myers   Orlan   Gina Pane   Jane Dickson   Letícia Parente   Margot Pilz   Ulrike Rosenbach   Suzanne Santoro   Louise Lawler   Francesca Woodman   Nil Yalter   Nancy Wilson-Pajic   Cindy Sherman   Jenny Holzer   Barbara Kruger   Kiki Smith   Yayoi Kusama   Betye Saar   Méret Oppenheim   Lee Miller   Dorothea Tanning   Leonora Carrington   Remedios Varo   Claude Cahun   Ithell Colquhoun   Mona Hatoum   Dorothy Cross   Lee Lozano   Susan Rothenberg   Simone Leigh   Laurie Simmons   Sarah Charlesworth   Lezley Saar   Cheri Gaulke   Lili Lakich   Christine Wong   Terry Wolverton   Karen Finley   Martha Rosler   Johanna Went   Jerri Allyn   Sheila Levrant   Sue Maberry   Mary Woronov   Annie Sprinkle   Marina Abramović

Contortions Part II

The Contortions' bass player Reck's US visa was expiring. He'd arrived from Japan with his girlfriend Ikue Mori and Chiko Hige, our drummer. Arto Lindsay, the front man of DNA, convinced Ikue to play drums in his band. For so many of us, including the men in the scene, playing an instrument had nothing to do with technique or 'chops'; it was all about primitivism and feel. Ikue's only experience with music was her childhood piano lessons, very strict lessons that she happily did not continue. She didn't speak English at the time, but words were unnecessary. Arto coached her in the tight rhythms he wanted with his wild, percussive gestures.

The third member of DNA was Robin Crutchfield, an intriguing young performance artist who worked at the Strand. Robin played keyboards and since DNA didn't have a bassist, he held down the bottom on keys. Robin lasted through the recording of *No New York* but soon after started his own band, Dark Day. He was replaced in DNA by one of the Cleveland tribe, Tim Wright, who'd been the bassist of Pere Ubu.

When Reck returned to Japan, George Scott III joined as replacement. A corn-fed, bass-playing transplant from Iowa, George instinctively knew what the Contortions needed to anchor the cacophony. The extremely adorable George loved beer as much as girls loved him, and his strong stage presence was just enough not to undermine Chance. George had been playing in a band called Jack Ruby and may have been one of Lydia Lunch's sexual conquests, since he came to us via her. He was now the boyfriend of photographer Beate Nilsen, a beauty who happened to be everywhere that mattered with her camera.

I remember playing a gig with George on bass and Chiko on drums at Max's in January 1978, a double bill with Teenage Jesus and the Jerks, and possibly another show with this line-up – there was definitely a show at CBGB by February that year. James Nares was still on guitar, along with me, Pat, and Chance. We performed at an *X Motion Picture Magazine* benefit. *X* was edited by Betsy Sussler, Eric Mitchell, and Michael McClard. It had a punk cut-and-paste aesthetic and an obvious distrust of mainstream media and culture. The three issues that ran from 1977–78 featured the voices and images of Kathy Acker, Tina L'Hotsky, Terence Sellers, photographer Jimmy DeSana, Rene Ricard, Lance Loud, Charlie Ahearn, Jean Genet, Diego Cortez, an interview with Pasolini, and conversations between Lindzee Smith and Berlin filmmaker Rosa von Praunheim. Under Betsy Sussler's leadership, it became *BOMB* in 1981.

From the sound of the recording of us playing at that benefit, George was clearly drunk. His bass sounds like loose mud, which was so unlike his tight playing. This was one of the first instances I recall Chance getting slap-happy at a show, accosting someone in the audience with the rest of us members having to defend him when the blows were returned. We became his protectors and, in doing so, provocateurs. It was also our first gig with the drummer Steve Moses filling in for Chiko. Chance had played in a trio called Flaming Youth with Moses and jazz bassist David Hofstra. Moses didn't fit. He was more of a trad drummer and didn't understand the brutalism we were going for, or the funk. He kept dragging the tempo – anathema to Chance. Plus, he had a mullet.

Sometimes James wanted me to play rhythm guitar on 'Contort Yourself'. I'd leave the Ace Tone and strap on the 1957 Fender Duo-Sonic that Peter had given me to play manic funk guitar. A highlight of the benefit show was playing guitar with one of my

CONTORTIONS PART II

heroes, fellow Ohioan Bob Quine. Quine was a bit older than most of us, and in direct contrast to his musical taste and style of playing, dressed like an unkempt bank clerk. He played lead guitar in Richard Hell's band the Voidoids, and although the band also featured the great Ivan Julian on guitar, it was Quine shredding the most diabolically fresh and outrageous solos. His playing stood out as absolute genius on the first Richard Hell LP, *Blank Generation*. Everyone said he was a grump and perpetually angry, but whenever I'd see him around, at Magoo's or other downtown haunts, he'd always flash a smile and buy me a drink. That he'd share a stage with me trying to play rhythm guitar to his leads was an honour I didn't take lightly.

The Contortions did another show with Steve Moses on drums at CBs in April 1978. We shared a bill with the Cramps, featuring the stunning Poison Ivy on surf-a-billy guitar; Ivy was another woman in the scene with an idiosyncratic guitar style and iconic presence. They had just released their debut single, 'Surfin' Bird'. Lux Interior was from Cleveland, but we never met until he and Ivy moved to New York. After this show, it was clear that we needed a more appropriate drummer for our fractured sensibility. Around this time, James Nares decided to leave the band to pursue making films and painting.

Guitarist Jody Harris and drummer Donnie Christensen stepped in to complete what would become the definitive line-up of the Contortions. (Harris and Christensen had also played with Moses in an R&B-flavoured band called Loose Screws with Dave Hofstra on bass.) With the addition of Jody and Donnie, the Contortions began to cook. We became tighter, musically more dynamic, and Chance's histrionics escalated as a type of violent performance art. Chance, George Scott, Pat Place, Jody Harris, Donnie Christensen, and I began rehearsing in earnest at Donnie's loft on Warren Street, rehearsal headquarters for many of the downtown bands.

This quintessential group of Contortions debuted at Max's Kansas City. Based on the notoriety of earlier outfits and gigs at Max's, we were filling the upstairs space to capacity. Max's would clear the club after the first set and a new audience would rush in to claim front tables for the second set. James had initiated his physical antics in previous shows, yet I remember the debut gig at Max's as extremely wild. It was our first performance together as the 'classic' unit. Jody's funky rhythm guitar and warped leads complemented Pat's well-timed rhythmic slide squeals, and Donnie had a very clean, funky style of drumming that anchored the musical and physical shenanigans. The rhythm section was now tight as a fist, courtesy of Donnie, Jody, and George Scott's pocket bass playing.

CONTORTIONS PART II

After the first set, we were all backstage when someone told us that Clive Davis of Arista Records was in the audience, and he'd fled for the exit during the first song. We howled our approval. It was during the second set in the middle of one of the more frenetic songs (it might have been 'Dish It Out') when we busted off the edge of sanity. The instrumental section started with James playing a sax run but he quickly abandoned his sax and crawled out onto a table at the lip of the stage front, where a jock-looking guy and his girlfriend were sitting. Chance barked something at the guy and proceeded to grab his girlfriend and kiss her. The guy went ballistic and shoved him away. Chance began slapping the guy. Knowing he was provoking a total beat-down, George and I nodded at each other, abandoned our instruments, and dove from the stage and into the crowd to defend James. It was a comedic free-for-all. More audience members jumped in, and hits mixed with hilarity as George, James, and I punched and wrestled the crowd, while Jody, Donnie, and Pat kept the soundtrack going on stage with a fierce rhythm. The crowd went berserk, getting off on what became bloody theatrics. Chance had a gash beneath his eye, but the violence had adrenalized him even more. We jumped back up on stage, and finished the set with 'Contort Yourself' to what sounded like a football crowd cheering and screaming bloody murder. It was shocking how people could get off on a show of violence. No one was hurt aside from Chance, who loved it, and the rest of us went along with it, nerves in high gear.

★ ★ ★

NO NEW YORK

With this version of the Contortions, I began to think of what we were doing in No Wave as a mix of musical Brutalism, Dada, and ideas expressed by Antonin Artaud. In 1938, Artaud spoke of attacking the sensibility of the audience, predicting the invention of musical instruments capable of producing 'sounds or noises that are unbearably piercing'.[1] Many artists and filmmakers who evolved during the No Wave period in New York embraced the idea of counteracting the spectacle of America's mass media culture. I feel many of us were embodying an essentially Marxist idea of revolution as a necessary means of change, knowing that art can, and sometimes should, be dangerous. We avoided anything that could be seen as marketable and felt the need to provoke, to bring an audience to physically experience an antidote to consumer capitalism via convulsive explosions of noise, of visuals and bodies. We reflected and exalted in the urban decay of New York City. A Contortions performance was a psychic sledgehammer exposing the angst we felt running through network of nerve and vein. Where punk and new wave had become commercial, No Wave was an anti-movement; the negation of every wave previous.

Many of us were reading Artaud at the time; he defended his idea of theatrical 'cruelty' as different than violence and spoke of his theatre in the 'gnostic sense of a living whirlwind that would devour the darkness' and 'a passionate and convulsive conception of life'. For James Chance, what began in Artaudian ideas of a convulsive shock theatre would soon take a very dark turn.

★ ★ ★

[1] From *The Theater and Its Double* by Antonin Artaud, trans. Mary Caroline Richards, Grove Press, 1958.

CONTORTIONS PART II

Brian Eno was in New York in April 1978, mastering the second Talking Heads LP, *More Songs About Buildings and Food*. While in town, he met Steve Mass of the Mudd Club through Diego Cortez. Hearing rumblings about the warped brilliance of the downtown scene, he wanted to stay for a while and needed an assistant. Eno sublet a loft-like apartment from Steve on 8th Street off of Fifth Avenue. Steve knew me via Anya and from being a regular at the club, and suggested that Brian hire me. The reason remains a puzzle. Eno was a hero of mine and Peter Laughner's; together we had played his solo LPs incessantly, as well as the Roxy Music albums, always with a keen ear for his wild synth lines and textures. Everyone I knew idolized Eno for his experimental approach to music and his legendary persona. I met him at the 8th Street apartment where he made tea and we talked about No Wave, subverting conventional rock music, and the downtown scene. I was shy yet we had an easy rapport. I was hired.

NO NEW YORK

I'd show up at his apartment in a Boy Scout uniform, and he'd greet me with a list of errands to run and an envelope full of $100 bills – a lot of money for a feral girl to be running around the city with. He was soft-spoken and lovely; his errand lists, erratic and bizarre. For instance, in one day I might be required to procure the following:

Olivetti Lexikon electric golf ball typewriter
French voile socks – black, grey, and brown
Graph paper notebook
Carrots
Porn magazines

Hitting the porn shops on 42nd Street as a tiny androgynous person in an army-green raincoat was like volunteering to be the world's least believable secret agent. Leering goons kept trying to inch closer, with one creep literally fondling a magazine I'd just touched as if I'd blessed it. My credo in accomplishing each mission was to impress Eno, as if scoring unusual requests was just another day at the office.

Sometimes we'd sit and talk about the downtown scene, me describing my thoughts about the music we were making – noise as extreme rebellion against the mainstream. I talked about Artaud and Burroughs and the downtown bands he might want to see and hear, including the Contortions. I remember playing around with water in drinking glasses, hitting rhythms and the pitches changing according to the amounts of water. He showed me his deck of cards, prompts meant to unstick frozen moments in the process of artmaking when a new idea was needed. To be drawn randomly, his Oblique Strategy cards featured prompts like 'mechanicalize

CONTORTIONS PART II

something idiosyncratic', 'do something boring', or 'play the tape backwards'.

Eno played music that I'd never been exposed to: an LP, *Le Mystère des Voix Bulgares*, by a female choir from Bulgaria who sounded otherworldly. He was the first person I'd meet who owned a juicer, the first to practise yoga. He hung out at the Mudd Club quite a bit, and sometimes brought along a mini-cassette recorder, a novelty in those days. Women loved to hit on him. He'd ask them to speak their names and phone numbers into the recorder, which they all did with breathless enthusiasm. When I'd show up for work, Brian would play the tape from the previous night, and we'd listen and muse on which woman's voice sounded most alluring. The winner of the competition might score a date with Eno that night.

Along with Tony Visconti, Eno had been instrumental in Bowie's LPs *Low* (1977), *"Heroes"* (1977) and *Lodger* (1979) as producer and co-writer during the recordings at Hansa Studios in Berlin. Bowie was influenced by Eno's *Discreet Music* and *Another Green World*, and Bowie's Berlin trilogy of LPs are some of his most experimental, evocative music, including the unlikely pop hit 'Heroes', co-written by Eno and sandwiched within all that avant-garde goodness. Although Eno declined a spot on Bowie's world tour of 1978, the two remained friends and collaborators.

The Bowie tour closed with three nights at Madison Square Garden on 7, 8 and 9 May of 1978. Eno was now living full-time in New York and in attendance for at least one of these Bowie shows. The performances that provoked Brian Eno to produce *No New York* happened at Artists Space on Wooster Street in SoHo. For five nights ending on 6 May – one night before Bowie's concert run – ten

No Wave bands played in the gallery space. While working for Eno, I told him about the upcoming shows and although I can't be sure of Eno attending every night, he was in attendance on 5 May, the night of one of the most notorious Contortions performances. We appeared on a double bill with DNA.

It's likely that Eno bent Bowie's ear about the explosive No Wave music he'd just experienced. Sufficiently intrigued, Bowie must have seen at least one Contortions show or the other bands. It is abundantly obvious that James Chance's masochistic streak influenced the cover of Bowie and Eno's next collaboration together, *Lodger*, which features Bowie dressed in a rumpled suit à la James Chance, wild-eyed with limbs askew, nose smashed against glass and hand bandaged, holding a hair comb. The No Wave scene's biggest influence on Bowie (at least what he thought of the scene) was more evident in many of the songs on the LP he'd record in 1980, *Scary Monsters (and Super Creeps)*.

On 5 May 1978, the Contortions played that double bill with DNA at Artists Space. It was a particularly frenzied performance. The gallery space didn't have a stage, and the band played in front of an audience sitting on the floor. This did not bode well for a Contortions audience. James hated SoHo artsy audiences who refused to twitch a muscle to the music. Our biggest fan and sometimes soundperson, Perry Brandston, was mixing us that night and his mother Marilyn was sitting on the floor with her friend, the *Village Voice* music critic Robert Christgau, and her husband, the painter Bob Stanley. I can't recall which song it was but suddenly James launched himself across the floor and started slapping people, including Marilyn, whose husband pulled James away. A brawl occurred with a bunch of guys jumping in, no

CONTORTIONS PART II

actual punching but kicking and plenty of slapping and shoving. Christgau was livid and ended up sitting on James to contain him. The band didn't join in the fracas. We kept on playing but the set ended quickly. Anya Phillips was there that night, which may have planted the seed in her mind that James's antics endowed him with superstar qualities. Her presence always influenced James, provoking his most theatrical shows of violence. As I said, he was mad for Anya. I don't know what impressed Eno more that night: the band's sound or James's histrionics.

★   ★   ★

NO NEW YORK

Shortly after the shows at Artists Space, Eno wanted to document the scene and proposed recording a compilation LP of ten bands.[1] According to Eno, Jeffrey Lohn and his band Theoretical Girls didn't like the idea of a compilation and wanted him to produce a solo LP for each band. Eno knew he'd never be able to convince a record company to record a coterie of bands whose mission was to destroy music. The plan to record ten bands with two cuts each got whittled down to four bands with four cuts each: the Contortions, DNA, Teenage Jesus and the Jerks, and Mars.

There were other bands downtown whose sound exemplified a No Wave sensibility and most of the bands featured women players. Nina Canal played a Fender Strat in the Gynecologists with Rhys Chatham and Robert Appleton. Guitarist and composer Glenn Branca was a formidable and extremely surly presence amongst the No Wave bands, playing in both Theoretical Girls and in Daily Life (a personal favourite) during the Artists Space shows. Daily Life featured the artists Barbara Ess and Christine Hahn on drums. The choice of the four bands for *No New York* set up a teenage rivalry between the perceived East Village bands and the SoHo bands. Jeffrey Lohn and Glenn Branca had played at Artists Space and felt snubbed by Eno and were quite bitchy about the compilation. To his credit, the bands Eno chose all featured women musicians.

★ ★ ★

---

[1] Brian Eno recently questioned the singularity of the 'genius' concept in relation to movements like No Wave, debunking the anointing of individuals by identifying a different phenomenon – scenius – a fertile ground for collective creativity.

CONTORTIONS PART II

The Contortions played the Johnny Blitz benefit at CBGB in May of 1978, a few days after the Artists Space show. Johnny was the drummer for the Dead Boys and was recovering in the hospital after being stabbed five times during an altercation with a gang in the East Village. None of us had medical insurance in those days. Johnny needed money for hospital bills. A who's who of acts played over a period of four nights, including Blondie, the Ramones, John Belushi, the Dead Boys, Richard Hell, Suicide, and many others. New York was dangerous, yet violence this sinister rarely happened downtown. (Aside from being drugged and raped by a supposed friend, which happens to so many young women that it barely and sadly needs mention, the only true threat I'd ever encountered was walking home alone on the Bowery at 3 a.m. one night. A large man was approaching from the opposite direction and as he came closer, he pulled a screwdriver from his pocket and without a word, aimed it toward me menacingly. I was extremely drunk and started laughing at the absurdity of the screwdriver and at him thinking I resembled anything close to a mark he'd score money or anything else from. He laughed in agreement and kept walking.)

★ ★ ★

We had a meeting in early June of 1978 with Eno at the 8th Street apartment, and most members of the four bands were there. Diego was always around; he served as fulcrum to so many connections. Anya and Arto Lindsay were the two most fascinating to Eno and the most vocal at the meeting. I distinctly recall Arto saying 'No New York' at one point, and everyone thinking it a great title for the LP. Eno suggested we all give him photographs of ourselves to use for the back cover, and somebody in the group suggested the photos be laid out like a Wanted poster, mimicking the poster for the Baader–Meinhof gang whom many of us were fascinated by. We fancied ourselves as art terrorists, like the Brigate Rosse (or the Red Brigades), detonating bombs of sound and vision inside an American cultural death march.

★   ★   ★

James had forgotten about our studio date in June when Pat and I picked him up for our first recording session. We joined Brian at Big Apple Studios. He'd set up an ionizer in the studio, explaining how the machine charged the air with negative ions to create a feeling like the air stirred by oceans. It wasn't exactly the energy we were aiming for, but, *hey*, we thought, *it's Eno*. Although we used individual line feeds, including a live microphone for James that undoubtably picked up the sound of the room, we had agreed to record our songs live without overdubs, playing as many takes as needed until we nailed it in one go.

After Eno and the engineer tested our levels, we needed to warm up. The entire band was strung out on James Brown at the time, so Chance wanted us to improvise on a Brown song, 'I Can't Stand Myself'. Maybe it was the excitement of being in a recording studio together for the first time, listening to ourselves with excellent sound on headphones. Maybe it was the presence of the legendary Eno on the other side of the glass, in the control room listening and watching. We launched into an incendiary version of 'I Can't Stand Myself' and played it like our lives depended on how tight we could

CONTORTIONS PART II

throw down. When James counted off the last four beats, with a Pat Place guitar squeal as exclamation point, we froze into silence, chests heaving, staring at each other in astonishment. We had never played that song before. Eno and Anya walked into the studio with eyes wide. Eno was more than pleased. He had recorded our warm-up.

For the other three tracks, Eno let us play exactly how we played the songs live. I believe this was his theory for all four bands. Even if he'd wanted overdubs, our instruments were bleeding over each other on the live track, and not recording live would have betrayed the authenticity we were going for. The Contortions were a live phenomenon, and no other track captured that more than our unrehearsed version of 'I Can't Stand Myself'.

Paradise Lost

By the time we played our second most infamous show at the Paradise Garage, Anya and James were an established couple on the scene. James announced to us that Anya was the official manager of the Contortions, yet it was becoming clear she was grooming him as a star apart from the band. Their effect on each other was immediate – to push to the extremes of outrage, on stage and off. Billed as 'Hell in Paradise', we played the grand opening of the Paradise Garage, then advertised as a rock 'n' roll club, on a bill with Richard Hell and the Voidoids headlining. Teenage Jesus and the Jerks, the Stimulators, and the Senders were also on the bill, the last featuring the handsome Parisian emigré Philippe Marcade on lead vocals. The Stimulators and the Senders were far more punk than the rest, but the bookers may have thought a good mix would bring in a large crowd. They were wrong.

Located at King Street and Varick – a no man's land at the time – the club was cavernous and dark, and no one was aware it existed until after this horrendous night. Afterwards, the owners were convinced they should make it a full-on dance club and never look back to the horrors of punk. There were perhaps 100 people there at most, and the size of the club made it appear empty. We felt at odds from the moment we arrived, but I recall us having a guarantee in terms of pay, so we played a full set, and played well. James and Anya took off after the set, then returned to get paid after Richard Hell's set finished. We were backstage in a hallway when Richard told us the owner refused to pay us for the show.

James snapped. He began screaming at one of the club managers while a completely dazed Anya looked on. Philippe and I approached the manager to argue our case, but the manager was flanked by two bouncers and kept refusing to pay. James smashed a beer bottle, ripped his shirt open, and began slashing at his torso with the broken glass. Blood spurted as he screamed 'Pay us or else I die right here!' Philippe, George, and I grabbed and restrained him before he could do more harm. The bewildered bouncers, clueless as to what to do, walked away slowly. The manager had fled but returned with the money. Pat, Jody, Donnie, George, and I were completely spooked. James's masochistic performance streak was now teetering over the edge of a violence that felt unmanageable and dangerous.

★ ★ ★

This incident led to my decision to quit the band. It had been coming for a while. Anya had started paying me less than the other members. There was also the night I sang 'Chain of Fools' at Max's, which was a surprise for the audience. No one downtown knew I could sing and sing like *that*. James was threatened by my soul voice, a wild contrast to his feral screeching. He never invited a repeat of the song. There was only room for one star in the Contortions, especially with Anya in the Svengali seat.

My questioning what I wanted to do as an artist was not matching the antics of James and Anya and the hubris that had set in. I was secretly longing for a lyrically heart-centred music. I wanted to act in film and was also torn between experimental noise and my desire to write melodic songs about where I'd come from, what I'd experienced growing up as a working-class kid. Listening to chanson réaliste Piaf, Lotte Lenya singing Brecht and Weill, and Jacques Brel was inspiring, and completely antithetical to the sounds I was making in No Wave. When I left my job as assistant to Eno to travel to Europe and play my first solo sets in Germany and the

Netherlands, I suggested he hire Nina Canal to replace me. Nina was a friend who lived in my building on 3rd Street. She played brilliant noise guitar and was one of the women involved in the forefront of No Wave, with her all-girl trio UT. At our last meeting, I asked Eno where he thought the future of music was headed after scenes like No Wave. He answered in a word – 'melody'.

★ ★ ★

I'd show up for another Contortions show which turned out to be yet another fiasco. The Contortions and Teenage Jesus drove up to Toronto to play a show at the Horseshoe Tavern. By this point, Bradly was hanging tight with James and Anya. He was demonic when drunk, but when drunk and also high on whatever was available, he became possessed. It was embarrassing to be around him in public. After the show, outside the club, James and Anya were yelling bitchy diatribes about how ugly and boring Canadians are, egged on by Bradly in a punky exhibition of juvenility. The trio started shouting racist epithets at a few Black guys down the street. The rest of the band members and I backed away, knowing this would end badly. Bradly was riled up and continued with his manic insults until the guys surrounded him. James and Anya fled. I stood by with the rest of the band and watched the insulted guys kick his ass. We returned to New York. I quit the band. Again.

★ ★ ★

The last time I'd ever play with the Contortions was after Anya christened the band as James White and the Blacks for the ZE

Records LP *Off White*. The Svengali motivator behind this project was Michael Zilkha, the son of Iraqi–Lebanese entrepreneur Selim Zilkha, founder of the British store chain Mothercare. Michael grew up and was educated in England where his early music obsessions were film soundtracks and Bob Dylan's *Blonde on Blonde*. The Velvet Underground's debut LP was Michael's lodestar, and meeting John Cale was a major turning point in his artistic trajectory.

He'd been part of the team for John Cale's label Spy Records, a company John started in 1977 with Jane Friedman. Jane was Cale's girlfriend at the time, and Patti Smith's manager. Parisian Michel Esteban was designing graphics for the label, and he and Michael formed ZE Records, with Cale producing a dance record as their first release for Michael's wife, the singer Cristina Monet-Palaci.

PARADISE LOST

Although Cristina certainly had physical star quality, the record and 12-inch remix 'Disco Clone' was thankfully the only dance record Cale ever produced, and a short-lived success. Featuring a male voiceover originally recorded by Anthony Haden-Guest (who was erased in favour of Kevin Kline) and its chorus of 'I'm a disco clone', this first outing set the ironic tone heard throughout the majority of ZE Records' releases. Michael's musical taste always tilted toward cleverness, and cleverness required distance. It was also the beginning of ZE's relationship with producer and engineer Bob Blank; the majority of ZE Records were recorded at Blank Tape Studios.

* * *

Michael Zilkha appreciated the confrontational spirit of punk. He'd watched the Contortions perform on a rooftop in early 1978 and was intrigued by the band and James Chance's antics, as well as by the fractured brutalism of the Contortions' sound. He liked the way Chance confronted the audience, the irony of his lyrics, the distance in the sneer, and the lack of sincerity. Michael approached

Anya about producing the Contortions. Because his company didn't have a track record, Anya turned him down. When he re-approached with the idea of the Contortions recording a disco LP, also offering Anya $10,000 as an advance, the deal was on.

Michael had been thinking about how disco records were not the kind you'd want to bring home and listen to, they were for dancing. The concept for ZE Records evolved from these ideas: take a disco rhythm track as bedrock and, on top, mix a confrontational clever and ironic vocal with non-disco musical textures, like heavy rock guitars, or Albert Ayler-inspired sax riffs. Michael would find his vision coalescing in ZE Record releases by Don Armando's Second Avenue Rhumba Band, August Darnell/Kid Creole and the Coconuts, Was (Not Was), Lydia Lunch, Alan Vega/Suicide, the Waitresses, and Lizzy Mercier Descloux. Ultimately, ZE's hybrid of punk, funk, and dance would be referred to as mutant disco, best exemplified in records like 'Wheel Me Out' by Was (Not Was) and 'Bustin' Out' by Material with Nona Hendryx. The lyrics for 'Bustin' Out' were pulled from revolutionary activist George Jackson's prison letters.

★ ★ ★

ZE Records had an inimitable style. Michael Zilkha also worked with Lydia Lunch in 1979. He saw her in Teenage Jesus and witnessed the irony of her performance; thought she was 'sexy, fun, and damaged', raging about brutality and abuse. Her lyrics and subjects were scathing yet a childish vulnerability lurked just beneath the surface.

Michael wanted to turn this fierce and fragile twenty-year-old into a No Wave torch singer. The project became *Queen of Siam*, produced by Bob Blank, who had the genius idea of bringing in the *Flintstones'* orchestral arranger Billy Ver Planck. In a totally unexpected twist, Lydia takes a crack at being a chanteuse with her dark, dirgy lyrics supported by lush, sometimes campy orchestrations, entirely foreign to the fascist beat of the Teenage Jesus assault. The LP is classic irony, surprising in its brilliance. You can't stop listening.

★ ★ ★

By the time we were recording the ZE LP, Anya was in full control of the band's management and was angling to separate James as the star. She was the creative brain behind James on the ZE Records project, wanting to groom him and the band into a type of No Wave soul revue in dress and sound. Renaming the project as a play on racist tropes, James White and the Blacks was born. Michael signed James Chance/White as a solo artist, and the LP *Off White* was recorded at Blank Tape Studios on West 20th Street in the fall of 1978.

King Heroin had begun his insidious creep into the scene and James and Anya were paying homage, with money that should have been going to the band. Their attitude grew pompous and ugly. They were constantly tossing around racist epithets while their entire gimmick for this LP was a supposed play on race, the white boy as Black funkster in what would be called today, appropriation on steroids. James hated punk and adored Black music, and he valued Black players above white. He'd never have dared utter the ugliest of racial slurs in the presence of a jazz giant like David Murray, a player he admired. If anything, James really did wish he could have been born Black, and this desire may have fuelled the resentment toward what he saw as a life that in essence he could only aspire to. One that would surface in white-punk-only gatherings as juvenile, insouciant racism.

James asked me to do some recording for *Off White*. Most of the songs were supposedly ironic takes on the theme implied in the band's new name: 'Almost Black', 'White Savages', 'Off Black', 'White Devil', 'Bleached Black'. I played keys on 'Contort Yourself' and was directed to follow a script written by Anya and talk 'Black' on 'Almost Black'. Anya and I were the two warring voices; she in James' defence, and me as Little Willie Feather (they wanted people to think Little Willie really was a Black guy commenting on James White's appropriation). As Little Willie, I followed the lyrics to call out James by saying 'that n–ah's white'. My casual use of this word in the late 1970s stemmed from being referred to as a little honorary n-word, christened as L'il Pimpin' by Black girl reform school colleagues. In the historical context of that world, Black girls found calling a tiny white girl the n-word funny. The culture of Blossom Hill 1970 was unfathomable to the white people I knew, little girl gangstahs being as bizarre a concept as alien life on the planet Mars.

My experience growing up as a working-class white girl in a closed Black society was unique and utterly foreign to the experiences of all the white people I've met to date. These important coming-of-age friendships made me intolerant of racism, but somewhat blind to the entitlement my white skin granted me on first visual impression. I grew up poor and, due to familial trauma, never felt entitled to anything. As a child, my singing voice was the only thing that could not be taken away from me. But we live in a world today where the immediate impression of a person's skin colour signals a complex history distilled into being either the oppressor, or the oppressed. The politics of language is wrapped inside the context of history and a multifarious web of racism, colonialism, entitlement, segregation, and a longing for dignity and for unity, however naive. Words have power. The way James, Anya, Bradly, and a few others in the scene were using certain words came off as poisonous, the essence of casual hate. Self-indulgent existential posturing hardly defuses the ugliness of real bigotry.

I was shorted once again by Anya on payment for the *Off White* sessions. I'd had enough of the inane and violent antics, the racist negativity and my second-class-citizen status in the band. The ZE sessions were the last time I'd ever play with the Contortions. Soon after I left, ZE held a launch party for James White and the Blacks at Irving Plaza, where James Chance/White mimed the entire LP.

The Contortions started to unravel quickly after I left. George was the next to go. He and Anya constantly fought due to George noticing the band members being paid less and less, despite the growing crowds. When the band recorded the album *BUY* in February 1979, tensions were escalating. The group quickly fractured into warring camps, with James and Anya in one corner and the musicians in the other. Pat Place was usually caught in the middle, the Switzerland of showdowns. It was becoming clear that James would maintain co-leadership of the band, with Anya as manager and bank. Pat remained when Jody, George, and Donnie walked out, but when James and Anya asked that they return as 'sidemen', Jody and Donnie came back. George refused. Insulted that he wouldn't kiss the rings, Anya and James erased all of George's bass tracks and replaced him with Dave Hofstra's bass.

BUY became a bittersweet coda to the band's implosion – the finished product bore the scars of their feuding. The record tries to sound like the original Contortions but even James's vocal performances lack the intensity of his live shows, as if all the drama, drugs, and fighting had drained him of his petulant rage. In a final twist, the album credits bore no mention of the band members. The credits state that it was produced, composed, arranged, and mixed by James White.

Sore feelings were growing numb. There was another debacle yet to come for the band, and it would prove to be the last. I was long gone at this point, but the story of what happened in Paris travelled fast. Anya had arranged for the band to play a show there, apparently put together by French punk communists/maybe anarchists aligned with the deconstruction aesthetics of No Wave. Before the Paris show, Anya and James did an interview with the socialist paper *Libération*, mouthing off about how they were only in it for the money, to get rich. When the band played the show in a type of circus tent in Paris, political factions in the audience started warring with each other, and a near riot ensued. Dave Hofstra swiftly jumped on a plane back to New York, but the rest of the band were depending on Anya to pay them for the show in order to fly home. Anya and James disappeared, along with the money from the show and a Gallic heroin connection. The rest of the band were stranded in Paris and had to figure out how to get home on their own. The Paris incident was the final act of what remained of the definitive Contortions line-up.

Shortly after, Anya was diagnosed with brain cancer. She was twenty-six years old. Devastated, James sank deeper into heroin addiction, exchanging his habit for methadone while continuing to pull together myriad ensembles, often christening his bands the Contortions. Pat Place and Cleveland bassist Laura Kennedy created the Bush Tetras. Donnie, Jody, and George formed the surf-rock band the Raybeats, along with keyboardist Pat Irwin. Tragedy struck in 1980 when George died from a heroin overdose. Aside from DNA, who stayed together with Tim Wright on bass into 1981, most of the original No Wave bands broke up, with former members pursuing new paths.

As No Wave faded, bands and performers like Swans and Sonic Youth took up the mantle of No Wave's inspired cacophony. My favourite was Sonic Youth. They moved through several players in the early days, and I remember seeing the iteration composed of Thurston Moore, Kim Gordon, and Lee Ranaldo – the blaze of three wildly crazed, slippery guitars – backed by Richard Edson who kept an odd, funk-adjacent beat on drums. The influence of No Wave can be heard in so many of the noise rock, industrial and avant-garde bands and performers through the decades that followed it.

No Wave was never meant to last. Self-destruction was inherent in the DNA of the scene's fierce, combustible resistance to commodification. And outside antagonists like heroin facilitated the scene's demise. No Wave was born screaming as a rejection of new wave and punk, the former (Talking Heads, Blondie, the Go-Gos) being too polished and commercial, the latter (the Sex Pistols, the Ramones) musically predictable and corporate-backed. It began with music as noise, performance, and rebellion, spreading rhizomatically to visual art, film, poetry, performance art, and literature. Patti Smith was the Pied Piper, her gritty, uncompromising poetics a provocation to outsiders from all over the world (especially women) to break our silence, to take up art as electric armament against the status quo.

Many of us didn't see King Heroin coming until he'd dragged us into oblivion. In the late 1970s, our downtown streets were suddenly flooded with smack. This tears-of-the-poppy assisted suicide was compounded by the scourge of AIDS. Some believe the heroin push was political, a deliberate attempt to neutralize all that defiant energy, art, community, and sensuality that was the essence of the East Village and Lower East Side. In 1978, 'Ayds' was still just a chocolate confection filled with benzocaine popped by housewives desperate to lose weight – not a mysterious disease with a new vowel. The awareness of AIDS and its volley of deaths began to spike in 1981, coinciding with the presidential inauguration of Ronald Reagan. As the disease wreaked havoc on the bodies of our friends, brothers, and lovers, the very mention of it was verboten in government. The media called it the Gay Plague. Between heroin and AIDS, the powers that be certainly must have rejoiced as they watched all that rage, rebellious imagination, and joy practically bleached out of existence.

Neglected apartment buildings and lofts populated and revitalized by artists, punks, and No Wavers became enticing to real estate developers, including a family called Trump. Artists not savvy or moneyed enough to buy property were pushed out. Re-zonings, conversions, rising rents, and the gentrification of SoHo and Lower Manhattan began in earnest in 1981.

There is no way a revolutionary art movement like No Wave could have survived the convergence of deadly drugs, a plague that equated sexual freedom with terror, rising rents, and corrupt economic policies targeting our neighbourhoods. The Reagan era prioritized corporate profits over everyday workers, shifting the trajectory of American politics away from the producers of wealth to the robber barons for future unforeseen decades.

The No Wave scene peaked then died quickly like a supernova – a star that suddenly and tremendously increases its light output, then quickly fades away to obscurity. May its trails of light remain to haunt, when darkness is at its peak.

Idlewildly 3rd Street

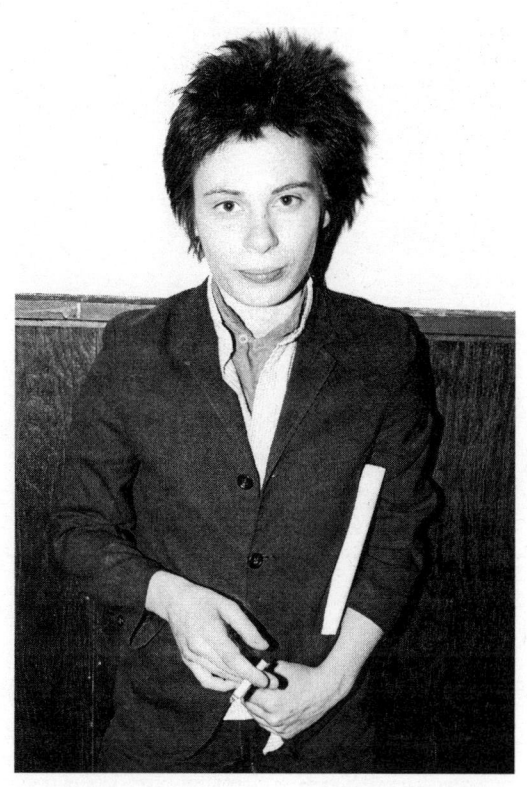

In 1978, I was working at the Strand, still obsessed with Jean Genet's *Our Lady of the Flowers.* Genet's youth of foster homes and reformatories was so like mine, and the erotic, poetic beauty of his writing inspired me to attempt a novel about growing up in juvenile institutions. So much was happening daily and every night, and in such a short period of time, that the idea of sitting still to make work was nigh impossible and felt oppressive. Other tributaries of creative (and carnal) pursuits were constantly calling, and I followed, never considering that the making of sharp, enduring work requires discipline. Discipline as a daily habit felt restrictive and limiting, a shutting-down of the imagination. I didn't understand how the braiding of discipline and imagination must be cultivated to create something capable of moving the spirit. Of making the invisible visible.

I was reading men almost exclusively back then. Aside from Anaïs Nin, Sylvia Plath, Violette Leduc, Djuna Barnes, and Colette, I wouldn't discover the women writers and thinkers who'd have a profound effect on me until much later. I cannot recall many women in the scene downtown writing stories and being published, aside from Lynne Tillman, whose hilarious *Weird Fucks* came out in 1980. Lynne's stories about sexual encounters with guys were graphic, dry, and brave, irreverently punk in spirit. Lynne would become a literary master with her novels. Director Mary Harron was on the scene, writing for Legs McNeil and John Holmstrom's *PUNK* magazine.

And then there was Kathy Acker. We met at a Contortions show when she was living on East 5th Street, in a building next to the police station, with her lover Peter Gordon. I was living with James Nares. If others were sharing our lovers, it wasn't a big concern and hardly discussed. We were in our twenties and many of us were polyamorous.

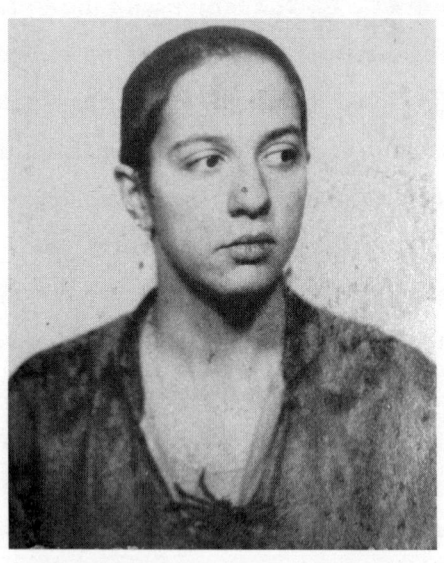

When Kathy and I met, I was obsessed with the story and words of Isabelle Eberhardt, a Swiss-born writer and wanderer who often passed as an Arab boy in the *fin de siècle*. Eberhardt cross-dressed as a boy in her teens and, being obsessed with the more mystical aspects of Islam and North Africa, eventually passed as a man and was accepted into the Qadiriyya (Qadiri) Sufi while living her adventures beyond gender in North Africa, a place that called to her mystic's heart. Her life was a cauldron of political intrigues, mystical insights, love affairs, and tragedies. Eberhardt was accused of being a spy by both sides in the French–Algerian wars. A seer and an outlier who defied all boundaries, her fascinating life ended at twenty-seven years when she died in a flash flood in Aïn Séfra. I came across her biography, *The Destiny of Isabelle Eberhardt* written by Cecily Mackworth, at the Strand; her story coincided with my interest in Sufism, resulting in frequent trips to the esoteric bookshop Samuel Weiser's on Fourth Avenue.

Kathy was working on the 'Persian Poems', handwriting some of the text in Perso-Arabic script, which I found mesmerizing. To see her copying out these calligraphic letters and words, the inked curves and dots, and her soft gentle voice reciting was an intense turn-on. I thought of her as Kathy the Sufi, smoking her bidi cigarettes, eyes like liquid saucers. In 1978, before the curated Acker persona – the Vivienne Westwood corsets, the leather, the Harley motorcycles, and the muscle milk – before the lit cognoscenti hawks descended to feast on her outlier fame, Kathy was tender and gentle. Sweetly ravenous, always directed toward knowledge and love. And for whom sex was freedom, an artistic muscle.

Kathy had built a moat of books around her bed and dared me to cross it. There were birdcages with tiny chirping finches, and many cups of tea, and poetry and more books. I told her I wanted to be a writer and a poet, like Genet. She told me to write about my life, the reform school stories. When I'd leave her house, she'd give me a copy of a book, like Alexander Trocchi's *Cain's Book*, to see how he tells his truth. She'd give me bags of lentils, brown rice, and a warm kiss before departure, saying I looked undernourished and telling me to sit my ass in the chair and write.

I moved around a lot in the late 1970s. One place was a sublet, a first-floor tenement apartment on East 3rd Street between Second Avenue and Bowery, with a bathtub in the kitchen and cockroaches. John Lurie, Becky Johnston, Eric Mitchell, Tina L'Hotsky, and Patti Astor lived in the building next door, and there was a men's halfway house across the street. I recall an early morning there, waking up and blissfully reading Rilke's *Letters to a Young Poet*. Throwing open

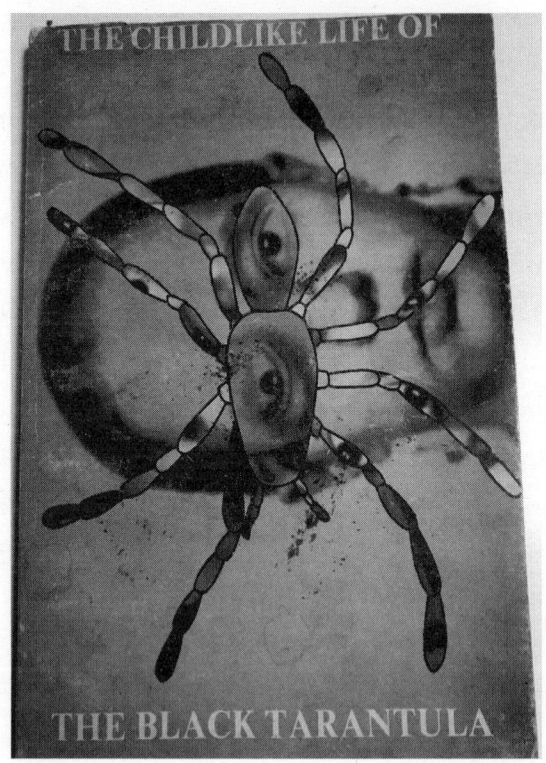

the front window to a sunny day, I peered through the security gate to see a filth-covered man from the shelter gleefully defecating in the middle of the road. This was outside the same shelter that housed the infamous Jack Henry Abbott.

A violent, psychotic criminal, Abbott had been serving time in Utah for fatally stabbing a fellow prisoner during a forgery sentence. Due to Norman Mailer's compassionate stance toward the murderer Gary Gilmore (another Utah prisoner), Abbott appealed to Mailer through letters: he wanted to write a book about the facts of life in prison, what it was really like. Mailer responded, their correspondence culminating in the release of Abbott's memoir, *In the Belly of the Beast*.

IDLEWILDLY 3RD STREET

Thanks to Mailer, Abbott was set free and sent to the 3rd Street Men's Shelter. He often ate at a local restaurant on Second Avenue called the Binibon. Many of us No Wavers and jazz musicians in the neighbourhood often ran into each other there; it was a cheap place for breakfast and meals after the bars closed.

One month after his release, Abbott got into an argument when a young waiter at the Binibon informed him the bathroom was not open for customers. Abbott murdered him, proving misogynist Mailer was no Sartre, and Abbott not even Genet-adjacent on paper or in manhood. Abbott was found two months later in the oil fields of Louisiana. By the time of his capture, *In the Belly of the Beast* had become a bestseller.

★ ★ ★

While I was living in the apartment across from the shelter, I had started my novel about girl-love in reform school, inspired by Kathy Acker's prompt. But all my personal belongings were destroyed by a guy I was subletting from, due to my own negligence in not paying the rent for two months while galivanting in Europe. I couldn't get into the flat upon my return; they had replaced the locks on the door and when I called, the leasor promised when I paid the rent, my belongings would be waiting for me, but that I could no longer live there in the flat.

I got a job at Spring Street Books, worked for two weeks, paid the back rent, and was given the new key to retrieve my belongings. But the apartment had been cleaned out. The first few chapters of the novel, my typewriter, rare photos of my mother, all the books I'd collected, gone. I called the trickster lessor, asking where my stuff went, and he and his girlfriend laughed: *Too bad, you should have been more responsible.* True. But also true; unwarranted cruelty comes easily for some.

I didn't feel terrible about the books, most of which had been stolen from bookstores, like a first edition of Cocteau's *Les Enfants terribles*. But losing my first novel attempt haunted me for decades, it being the second time someone had destroyed my writing. Trying to do the honourable thing by paying the lessor creep, only to be tricked, was salt in the wound. It would take another four decades to write and publish the book I had started on East 3rd Street.

★ ★ ★

Sinister as bat wings, a dual veil of heavy and strange haunted the Chelsea Hotel in the 1970s. The *New York Times* once called it 'the air of a great dame', but like a démodé drag queen on a permanent drunk, back then she was all avant-garde tragedy and no comic relief. I thought of the Chelsea then as a place you'd go to look for inspiration, but instead, a tumble into depression was inevitable. For me, it felt like a place to live out the last days of a doomed love affair alone, to write melancholic songs, do drugs and overdose on drugs, feel cool because your heroes may have slept (and had sad, dark sex) in the bed beneath you.

Some fell into the vortex of the Chelsea Hotel and never escaped. The place has a particular atmosphere, and only the strong survive it. One long-term tenant who trained herself into full shutdown revealed in a documentary about how often she'd hear the thump of bodies hitting the pavement. Of course, as a young nihilist, I was dying to check in. When I walked through its doors in June of

IDLEWILDLY 3RD STREET

1977, the first thing to hit me was the morbid fragrance of Lysol and human misery peculiar to prisons and mental institutions, but I wasn't about to let the miasma dissuade me. My own take on the Chelsea is in part due to a memory of Sid Vicious.

★ ★ ★

I never believed Sid Vicious killed Nancy Spungen. Nancy was a nightmare, the incarnation of Beelzebub with a bad dye job. Whenever she came into any club – Max's, Mudd, CBs – it was time to duck and take cover. You did not want to get caught in Nancy's maelstrom of narcissistic nasty. As for her demise, the Chelsea was always a notorious drug den. Nefarious activity in Room 100 on the night of her murder is well documented.

NO NEW YORK

In the early winter of 1978, I was living in yet another apartment on East 3rd Street, this time between Second and First Avenue in a building filled with musicians and artists. Members of Crass lived there, and Nina Canal of UT as well as the filmmaker Amos Poe. With its ubiquitous bathtub in the kitchen, my one-bedroom tenement flat had a large living room, gated windows, and a penitentiary feel. The gated bars creeped me out, so the living room remained barren of furniture and was never used. I spent most of my time at the kitchen table writing or in a tiny bedroom off the kitchen. I'd later bequeath the apartment to Tim Wright (bassist in DNA and the original bassist with Pere Ubu) and his partner MaryAnne, who I'd known in Cleveland. In turn, they passed the apartment on to Jean-Michel Basquiat.

Jerry Nolan rented a first-floor apartment and had the basement hooked up as a rehearsal studio. I think Johnny Thunders lived at Jerry's when he wasn't at one girlfriend's place or another's. Jerry was a soft-spoken guy, always very sweet, and he reminded me of a sexy greaser girl I knew back in Cleveland. Jerry and I sometimes listened to records, and on nights when Johnny was a no-show at the Heartbreakers rehearsals, he'd invite me down to play with them. I'd sing on their covers of 'She's Something Else' and 'C'mon Everybody' by Eddie Cochran. The Heartbreakers were a quintessential punk rock band. Their guitarist Walter Lure was another friend I hung out with sometimes at CBs.

One afternoon in late October, I was making my way home, shivering (I never dressed properly for the cold – looks always trumped comfort). It was an untypically frigid afternoon for that time of year. No rain, no snow, just a sky the weight and colour of concrete. Turning the corner onto 3rd Street I saw a fellow in a studded leather jacket hunched over on my steps. It was Sid Vicious.

He, Johnny and Jerry shared a habit. Although Jerry was a junkie, he was a junkie gentleman and never offered it to me. Seeing Sid there, I said hello; he whispered back, 'Hi'. He looked as pale as porcelain, and as fragile. As if all life had drained from him. I knew about his troubles. The situation with Nancy had occurred earlier that month; he'd been in jail and attempted suicide by slitting his wrists. He was in terrible shape, not the same cocky punk I saw spitting and roaring from the stage at Max's a few months earlier. He looked so small.

'You alright?' I asked, and he nodded, trembling like me but probably from more than the cold. I asked if he was waiting for Jerry. He barely glanced at me and asked, 'Yeah, you know where he's at?'

'No, but do you want to wait inside where it's warm and have a cup of tea?'

He shrugged, agreed, and followed me up to my apartment. I made him tea. A little smile slipped over him, the only smile I'd see . . . I think he was pleased the tea was PG Tips. We sat at my tiny kitchen table and his desolation and loneliness felt overwhelming. I'll never forget that vision of him, so pale, so shy, picking at the fresh scars there on his wrists. He looked broken, delicate, and utterly lost. It was heartbreaking. I couldn't bring myself to try and engage him in small talk, or bring up his troubles, so we barely said a dozen words to one another. I had a profound longing to make him feel safe, if only for a moment.

'Everything will work out, you know.' He kept his eyes down, didn't reply or even look up. I said it when I knew it wasn't true;

his defeat scared me. I suddenly wished for a brazenly clichéd punk retort, maybe a gruff *What do you know?* or *It's all bollocks*. But he was silent, eyes glued to the table. He drank the tea.

We passed some time together, me playing records I thought he'd like: Burning Spear, King Tubby. We smoked through an entire pack of fags and drank endless cups of milky tea. I watched to see if his foot would tap to the thumping dub, the rhythmic reggae easing our silence. I kept dialling Jerry's number until, finally, he picked up. And then Sid thanked me, thanked me sweetly – then he was gone.

It felt as if I'd been visited by an apparition, one haunting and haunted. A wraith slipping through the time he had left. He'd already died, in Room 100 of the Chelsea Hotel.

★ ★ ★

There was an artist who lived near me. We were friendly. Never close. We didn't hang out or spend time together. Our encounters were run-ins at clubs or events or on the street. I never thought of this man as a threat – he was popular and revered in the downtown scene. He travelled a lot and had a great library. I had only stopped by his apartment once to borrow a book and talk for a moment.

One summer day, he walked up while I was having a smoke outside. He'd just returned from Paris and invited me to his place for a drink. Inside, he pulled out a vial. *Liquid valium*, he said, *from Pigalle. It's a great high, you only need a drop or two*. Never one to turn down drugs, especially from Paris, I said sure. Filling the dropper, he giggled and asked me to stick out my tongue. I laughed and did so, but before I could close my mouth, the drop or two had turned into a dropper-full.

I don't recall anything after that until I woke up on my stomach, my pants awkwardly pulled up over my arse – brutally sore. He was sitting across from the bed, staring at me sheepishly. I looked to the window. Day had turned to night. I knew what he'd done, and he knew what he'd done. Standing up on shaky legs, I pulled up my pants and mumbled that I had to go. Left and walked up the stairs to my own flat and as I undressed to bathe, saw the spot of blood.

I had consented to taking a couple of drops of liquid valium. I had not consented to being doped into unconsciousness and anally raped.

I'll never know why this man decided to rape me. Maybe the sensibility of a revolutionary scene where women were equal progenitors rattled certain men's sense of entitlement. Rape, any kind of violence against women, is always about power: who has it and who can take it away.

Several women involved in the downtown scene during that time have confessed to me how they were sexually assaulted by men, by 'avant-garde' men they assumed were politically conscientious and cool about women. Even the bad boy punks posing as ruffians were, for the most part, gentle. But sexual violence was a fact, and we women had to conceal our wounds, protect our torturers. We knew that if we called out a rapist, we'd be the ones punished and shamed because the guys had ownership of the social safety net. Women were never believed. Even the guérillères of New York City didn't bring it to each other. We learned to live with it. Back then, opening that wound was tantamount to social suicide. We soldiered on, feigning indifference to sexual violence while the men skated away with impunity. We could shout a resounding NO to mediocrity, consumerism, conformity. But the shame, the trauma of physical violence was ours to carry, to bear. It was a different time. Or was it?

The Nova Convention

During the late 1970s and early 1980s in New York and abroad, William Burroughs and his ideas were inspirational to artists rejecting the status quo. The queer, literary outlaw and grand wizard of all arts outré, Burroughs advocated for us to become 'astronauts of interior space' and all that is beyond. He smashed academic etiquettes while appearing like an exhausted accountant – accounting all that is corrupt in society. I had two personal encounters with Burroughs; one at a party, the other when he shapeshifted into a humongous fly.

The Contortions' guitarist Jody Harris and James Grauerholz, Burrough's right-hand man, were friends from Lawrence, Kansas. When Burroughs and Grauerholz were out of town, Grauerholz entrusted the keys of Burroughs's Bowery residence to Jody. The security getting into the building was medieval; several locked gates, a metal door, and, finally, entrance into the 'bunker', an ancient YMCA where Burroughs lived, wrote, and practised shooting his guns. I imagine it must have been soundproofed due to a paper cut-out of a human body, a target silhouette numbered and riddled with bullet holes.

The first thing that caught my eye as I stepped inside were Brion Gysin's automatic paintings adorning one wall. A mix of what resembled Arabic and Japanese calligraphy – yet very much their own secret language of signs – Gysin's paintings had a hypnotic effect because of their repetitive, very intricate and masterful strokes. I'd discovered Brion when doing research about the origins of the cut-up technique of writing, where random texts are sliced into pieces and rearranged to create a new text. This method of re-assemblage can be traced back to the Dadaists, many of whom Brion hung out with as a young artist in Paris in the 1930s. Although Tristan Tzara is given credit for inventing the style, Brion would bring the process into cultural significance during the reign of the Beats. Its initial manifestation would appear as the 'First Cut-Ups' in *Minutes to Go*, a book Gysin collaborated on with Burroughs and others. Burroughs always gave Brion his due when asked about his influences and the cut-ups, utilizing the method in *Naked Lunch*, the book that marked the beginning of the celebrity that would eclipse the creative stature of his friend. Burroughs said Brion was the 'only man he ever respected'.[1]

The bunker was sparsely furnished and clean as a crime scene. There was a floor lamp with a rifle as base. A long table with leather mid-century-style office chairs took up the middle of the large open room. Burrough's typewriter sat on a heavy metal desk. These desks were office cast-offs ubiquitous in downtown New York lofts at the time. The most surprising phenomenon was a pile of stiff, balled-up tissues; a sculpture of Kleenex that rose to at least a four-foot-high peak at the foot of the bed, a conical form as neat and pristine as the rest of the space – William Lee's minimalism as a big rock candy mountain. It was an extremely male space. In a corner sat a strange wooden box-like closet; an orgone generator, based on a model by Wilhelm Reich. When Jody slid aside the front wooden panel and I saw the lone chair sitting inside facing the back wall of wood, I laughed. Burroughs must have been listening.

Discovering urinals in the old YMCA locker room, I ceremoniously pulled down my trousers and underwear, stepped out of them, and, standing with legs spread and pubis jutting forward, peed like a boy. I was able to pull off a good stream until a humongous horsefly came buzzing in. The thing was gargantuan, circling my head

---

1 Video tribute of Burroughs speaking about Brion Gysin, recorded for the Dublin 'Here to Go' show, 1992. beatdom.com/go-back-lives-art-brion-gysin/

with the angriest buzzing sound I'd ever heard. I was convinced this was Burroughs himself, teleporting into the horsefly to chase the fake boy out of his bathroom. How dare I imagine desecrating the sacred space of real flesh-and-blood wild boys? I tried being defiant, daring the fly with my fist but it wouldn't let up its furious circling, growing closer until finally I fled, point taken. It would be the first and last time I'd run from an orgone-pumped fly capable of playing William Tell.

* * *

I had the great fortune of meeting Brion Gysin and briefly hanging out with him while covering the Nova Convention for the *New York Rocker* in 1978, my first official writing gig, which I owe to the editor Andy Schwartz. Andy hired photographer Marcia Resnick and me to cover the action-packed convention, a stellar gathering of avant-garde artists brought together by Columbia professor Sylvère Lotringer and the poet John Giorno. Patti Smith performed, as did Timothy Leary, John Cage, Laurie Anderson, Merce Cunningham, Frank Zappa, and many others. Burroughs was the nexus, declaring from behind a desk onstage what the Nova Convention was all about: 'This is the space age, and we are here to go.' Prescient, in that the No Wave avant-garde as a vital cultural force would soon disappear from the American landscape in the early 1980s.

* * *

I met Brion Gysin the first night of the three-day convention outside the Entermedia Theater on Second Avenue and East 12th

Street. I was sporting a headscarf and suitcoat, what I called my Mouchette/Eberhardt drag, when I spotted Brion and decided to introduce myself by asking if he knew about Isabelle. I was obsessed with Isabelle and with Sufism at the time. Someone had slipped me a rare cassette tape of Sufi qawwali and ghazal music, mystical calls to God as Supreme Lover. One of the singers was Nusrat Fateh Ali Khan and I fell immediately in love with his voice and the music of devotional call and response. The singers were accompanied by a large group playing various percussion instruments and harmonium. I was also reading Paul and Jane Bowles and the writer Mohamed Mrabet at the time, thoroughly intrigued with Tangiers, that avant-garde hub for writers and artists in the mid-to-late 1960s and on, including Burroughs.

I heard about a workshop for writers that Paul Bowles was teaching in Tangiers and had sent Bowles a short story about a djinn, a supernatural spirit in Islam. He'd written back accepting me as one of five workshop participants. I would have had to pay for my own airfare to Tangiers, and a $500 fee. I couldn't afford tuitions or air fares so missed the opportunity.

But here was an artist that represented my pull to Morocco and the mystic – Brion Gysin in the flesh. Where I often felt tongue-tied and like an imposter among others, Gysin and I shared many fascinations and I felt he'd get me. I'd read interviews with him where he spoke about the mysticism of music, of Sufism, and of radical new ways of creating. We smoked cigarettes and he told me the story of the Moroccan Pan, Bou Jeloud, the human/goat creature who was tricked into teaching the secrets of his enchanted music to the master musicians of Joujouka. To this day, there is an annual festival where the musicians perform ritualistic music for Eid El-Kabir, reenacting the drama of Bou Jeloud by dressing a young boy as the goat god. The boy Pan races and dances through the village as the trance-like music and his movements become wilder, more frenzied in the yearly ritual blessing the health of the village. In 1968, Gysin and his friend Mohamed Hamri brought a Rolling Stone to Joujouka to record the master musicians there. *Brian Jones Presents the Pipes of Pan at Joujouka* was the West's introduction to the trance music of Morocco but it is badly recorded. Jones phase-shifted much of the music, which detracts from the immediacy of the musicianship. And Gysin was not happy that Jones never paid the Joujouka musicians.

Brion certainly knew about Eberhardt, and as we talked about Morocco and the Sufis, I waxed on about how time was not linear, how his calligraphic paintings signalled the idea of time being infinitely circular. He said I reminded him of Isabelle, so of course I asked him to adopt me! He laughed and said yes but I'd have to move to Morocco. It was dangerous for a woman in Tangier, him counselling that if I ever planned to journey there in future, I was passable, and boy-drag was a good bet for me.

As we talked, a crowd of rocker boys surrounded the photographer Marcia Resnick. She revolved in the circle, snapping photos of all the sharp boys. I joined the gang to enact a playful, comedic rendering of the denouement in the film *Suddenly Last Summer*; we became the gang of young toughs surrounding Marcia as 'Sebastian', all us guys laughing and pushing her back and forth, spinning her gently, like a ragdoll. I was the only girl in the gang acting like a little rough-houser. Marcia loved it, laughing and going limp with the spin. Brion enjoyed watching the game, looking on like a proud father, and Marcia captured our father–daughter moment on film.

* * *

Burroughs' most recent novel *The Wild Boys* (1971) was a queer, violent romp. His sci-fi drug-filled novels had an absurdist, obscene sensibility and a non-linear, confessional approach I appreciated. What intrigued me most about Burroughs were his ideas about magic and the occult, especially as it pertained to sound. I'd read a 1975 article in the rock magazine *Crawdaddy* of Burroughs in conversation with Led Zeppelin's Jimmy Page about the ritualistic aspects of rock music. A devotee of Aleister Crowley, Page purchased yet hardly resided in Crowley's Loch Ness mansion, Boleskine House, in the Scottish Highlands. The two discussed ideas about certain frequencies capable of creating actual physical reactions in audiences, reactions that can also turn dangerous. The rock musician as modern-day shaman, the aspects of trance. Many of the subjects, presentations, and people performing at the Nova Convention solidified my interest in the science of sound affecting matter in both physical and mystical ways.

The first night of the convention's programme featured films. The first two were collaborations between Burroughs and Antony Balch – *Towers Open Fire* and *The Cut-Ups* – kaleidoscopes of images with a Joujouka soundtrack provided by my favourite among the artists, Gysin. A repetition of cityscapes, tribal masks, boys masturbating or shooting up, and General Burroughs at the post giving the command, 'Towers open fire!' as pages of Mayan hieroglyphs blow through the streets. The cut-up technique of writing developed through Gysin paintings and Burroughs is employed here in the visuals, super-impositions, and the repetition of key phrases building and swirling into climaxes that can create mild discomfort and disorientation – an altered state of consciousness, which is the point (as in Gysin's Dreamachine).

The rest of the programme featured a film by DEVO and various shorts by a coterie of downtown filmmakers: Amos Poe, Michael Oblowitz, Eric Mitchell, and Tina L'Hotsky. Kathryn Bigelow's first film, *The Set-Up*, was a beautifully shot display of violence in lurid colour; two men beating the hell out of each other. The homoerotic fight turns into a kiss, a split-screen of a sado-masochistic dance. Meant to be a parody of machismo, the two men traded very real blows to a soundtrack of voiceovers on faggotry and fascism by Sylvère Lotringer and Marshall Blonsky.

Kathy Acker read her *Persian Poems* over a colour film of Burroughs, which did not sit well with the filmmaker and Burroughs. The film had a soundtrack, unbeknownst to Kathy. Kathy traded the Janey of the *Persian Poems* with William, resulting in the line, 'William is a girl. William is a child. William's night. The red night . . .', and so on. Last on the programme that day were home movies of Burroughs by Steven Lowe: Burroughs relaxing with friends, delivering playful Chaplinesque dialogues with the camera, doing target practice with his pistol. It's unfortunate he didn't engage in more practice before he delivered a lethal bullet to his wife's head, a crime he paid a mere two years of suspended sentence for. He claimed it was a mistake; he was playing a game of William Tell. In retrospect, you'd think it would be odd how this killing wasn't much of an issue concerning beloved Burroughs' character. There was an insouciance around criminality that seemed to snake through the downtown scene. Danger was romanticized and those who walked its edge, often elevated.

★   ★   ★

THE NOVA CONVENTION

On the second day of the convention, Semiotext(e) publisher Sylvère Lotringer led a panel discussion with Richard Sever of Grove Press and Maurice Girodias of Olympia Press – the small firm in Paris in the 1950s that specialized in erotica and published Nabokov's *Lolita*, Pauline Réage's *Story of O*, Burroughs's *Naked Lunch*, and other risqué books when American censorship and obscenity laws prevented the publishing of works considered offensive to moral standards. Girodias asked his authors to write assorted smutty titles with the directive: 'Three sex scenes per chapter. Anything less and you're fired.'

One of the few but most notorious woman writers published by Olympia was Valerie Solanas. She and Girodias met while both were living at the Chelsea Hotel and Girodias was attempting to relaunch Olympia in New York. One story alleges that Solanas wanted to kill Girodias because she thought he gave her a rotten publishing deal for her *S.C.U.M. Manifesto*, a satirical diatribe about the patriarchy and a call to eliminate men from the face of the earth. She couldn't find Girodias and ended up at the Factory, shooting Warhol instead (who she also believed ripped her off for her film work with him). Girodias published the *S.C.U.M. Manifesto* after Solanas shot Warhol in 1968. In court, Solanas was represented by the lawyer and political activist Flo Kennedy. (Flo played a major role in Lizzie Borden's film *Born in Flames*.) It was Solanas's intention to become famous by shooting Warhol. It worked. She was called the 'Robespierre of feminism' by Norman Mailer. Ti-Grace Atkinson, the feminist president of the New York chapter of the National Organization for Women, said Solanas was a heroine of the feminist movement and was expelled from NOW for her opinion by Betty Friedan. Solanas did not agree with second-wave feminism due to its lack of rage and what she deemed its polite, traditional feminine codes of passivity. She referred to NOW as a civil disobedience luncheon club.

Sometimes I'd see Valerie on Second Avenue in late 1977 with shopping bags and a suitcase, looking unkempt and homeless. During her trial for the Warhol shooting, she had been diagnosed as a paranoid schizophrenic. As much as I wanted to talk to Valerie, my curiosity couldn't override the wild stare in her eyes – vortex eyes you'd rather avoid at all costs.

★ ★ ★

The convention had its ribald moments. There was a theatrical adaptation of an excerpt from *Naked Lunch* featuring a girl strapping on a dildo and all manner of group fuckery ensuing. Lots of humping amid hard-ons and hangman's nooses. The performance artist Julia Heyward, known then as Duka Delight, introduced poet Anne Waldman saying, 'There should be more women out here pissing in the streets.' Ed Sanders of the Fugs followed Anne, and I bristled, since anything hippie-esque was anathema to No Wave sensibilities, and you couldn't get farther hippie than the Fugs. But he caught my attention by the metal rings he wore on his fingers. When pressed together, the rings produced electronic tones, and he sang a chant that was meant to conjure the ghost of Sappho from her Mytilene shores.

Merce Cunningham and John Cage came on with Merce dancing slowly around the stage and Cage speaking into a telephone at a desk. Burroughs returned to talk about brainwash, mind control, religious cults and leaders, Scientologists and the People's

Temple – groups that should be taxed out of existence. 'We must keep our children safe from lunatics.' I'd never seen Laurie Anderson perform but had heard of her experiments with sound. She read a piece about an oncoming plane crash. Via whatever type of chorus or synthesized effect was available at the time, her voice transformed into the most baritone male voice imaginable. Duka Delight performed with a harmonizer that created three simultaneous voices. She read in a Southern-tinged little girl's voice about the extinction of animals, complete with bird calls. Eerie and compelling. I often wondered why Laurie Anderson became such a phenomenon yet despite Julia's immense talent, her work is nearly invisible. At one point in her career, she was signed to Columbia Records, but left quickly, which is understandable when a woman artist in the 1980s refused to compromise. In this regard, Laurie Anderson was an outlier. For a woman to navigate the wicked system of the music business without compromising their work and integrity bordered on the miraculous.

Allen Ginsberg, his partner Peter Orlovsky, and a few other men with an array of hippie instruments, like banjos and spoons, accompanied Allen's poetry, which felt tepid and uninspired. However, I am embarrassed by what I wrote at the time, shaming Ginsberg for being a sham Buddha. I was so invested in being the enfant terrible, the vitriolic critic refusing to be censored, that my disrespect was ludicrous and regrettably juvenile. Shortly after the convention, Kathy Acker gave me a copy of Ginsberg's 'Kaddish'. The poem, about the loss of his mother to madness and his estrangement from her religion, brought me to my knees.

Another panel discussion followed featuring Burroughs, Les Levine, Robert Wilson, Timothy Leary, and Gysin filling in for

Susan Sontag. The subject was the science fiction generation, with Leary sitting up there laughing like the Mad Hatter, most likely tripping his gonads off. Gysin mentioned that Alexander Trocchi once called Burroughs an astronaut of interior space and Burroughs pointed out that a thin line exists between interior and exterior; we are in space every night when we dream. Someone posed the question to Gysin: 'Will there be room for the arts and space?' He laughed and answered, 'No paintings or sculpture – but there will be music.'

★ ★ ★

The closing night of the convention was the night I'd been waiting for. Brion Gysin would be performing, along with Patti Smith, and this was the first event of the weekend where the younger set of punks, artists, and No Wavers filled the auditorium. Terry Southern did introductions, Philip Glass filled the hall with the sound of beautiful trance-like modal structures. Music to evoke UFOs. Music to evoke Gysin himself, who walked on stage as a huge projection screen descended.

In preparation for the convention, I'd read the book Gysin had written and recently published with Burroughs called *The Third Mind*, describing their cut-up method of writing, and ideas that can rise unconsciously when two minds are in synch and working together, manifesting in a type of third mind or presence. Cut-ups were not a new concept. Various Surrealists used the device, and the Dadaist Tristan Tzara wrote a manifesto in the 1920s on a poetic technique of cutting up words from newspapers, placing the pieces in a bag, and pulling words out randomly. But it was Gysin who introduced Burroughs to the concept, which Gysin would also employ in film and with tape recorders, the two men developing the idea in the 1950s into the literary device we know today, and that Burroughs would use in works like *The Nova Trilogy*.

Brion performed along with calligraphic slides and taped echoes. His poetry was mixed-up lines turned incantations: 'Kick that habit man', 'Junk is no good baby' and so on. A sound piece of his called 'Tears Set to Music': very surreal with bells and cymbals, like the ocean. Celestial voices. 'I am that. I am.' John Giorno followed and Burroughs returned, reading about the ridiculousness of political systems and life in general, followed by Frank Zappa reading an excerpt of *Naked Lunch* called 'The Talking Asshole'.

Patti Smith appeared, wearing a couture olive-green trench coat, and would change into a fur coat during the evening. The crowd went wild as she blew a few notes on her clarinet and was joined by Lenny Kaye on guitar to recite/sing her poem 'Fire of Unknown Origin'.

The convention concluded with a party at Mickey Ruskin's restaurant at One University Place, where assorted members of the cast held court at the centre table. Pink punch spiked with a mild psychedelic was being served out of a huge vat. Timothy Leary giggled in a corner with Gregory Corso while Lizzy Mercier, Kathy Acker, and I hung at the bar making fun of aging hippie men.

Gysin and Burroughs remained far removed from anything hippie-adjacent.

The convention had been a huge success toward illuminating the work of both men, who wrote and spoke presciently of a world overcrowded with images and poisons, a world that escalates ever more into danger and transhumanism. For Brion Gysin and William Burroughs, the cut-ups method wasn't only a literary device. It was textual alchemy, a means of divination. As Burroughs declared, 'When you cut into the present, the future leaks out.'

Le Faux Garçon

I met Luc Sante while working at the Strand bookstore in 1977.[1] The Strand's eagle-eyed owner Fred Bass parked me at the main desk in the basement to handle phone orders and help people with inquiries in non-fiction. I loved working at the Strand, surrounded by dusty hardbacks harbouring all the most fascinating ideas of science, antiquated maps, European histories and philosophies. I imagined myself as a sailor and the Strand basement as my own nautical Library of Alexandria. When the phone lines weren't busy, I'd spend hours studying the sections, memorizing where to find literary criticism, dictionaries, languages, biographies, skimming through all the books that caught my eye. If a customer asked for a title that I wasn't familiar with, one of the ship's able-bodied seamen was always eager to help navigate the maze.

I liked Luc right away. He oversaw the paperback department that never had its own section, which made him a roving presence; pricing, shuffling and rotating, feeding displays, running all over the store's many floors and to the $0.25 racks outside on East 12th Street. We'd roam aisles above and below deck talking about titles we'd discover hidden between neglected volumes of forgotten lore; rare copies of Gérard de Nerval's *Journey to the Orient*, Oscar Wilde's 'The Decay of Lying', or the prison letters of Fidel Castro. I'd often tuck a rare book into my knapsack and waltz out with it at the end of the day, even though Fred's scrutinizing gaze was nerve-wracking. I'd have to pass him upstairs on my way out and there he'd be at the big library table, perpetually appraising and acquiring books and more books, his eyes flickering up over the bifocals perched on the tip of his nose to follow me with suspicion. Fred was a good guy. I

---

1 For the purposes of this recollection, until the year 2021 and her transition, I knew Lucy Sante as Luc Sante.

felt guilty about these petty thefts, but the Strand's eighteen miles of books, and the justification that knowledge should be free always trumped my guilt. Many other Stranded sailors carried dubious backpacks that no one ever searched, so maybe benevolent Captain Fred must have known what was happening all along.

Luc put together a 'zine called *Stranded*, publishing aspiring writers employed at the Strand and various downtown artists like Kathy Acker, Jean-Michel Basquiat, and Jim Jarmusch. My output as a writer was very slim in those days due to the 3rd St wipe-out, but I did contribute one solitary poem to *Stranded #3* under my pen name of Pierre Mouchet, Isabelle Eberhardt's pen name.[1]

I had a nerd-crush on Luc. A Belgian romantic who also loved all things French, Luc wore small, round-lensed glasses like Bertolt Brecht, always had a book tucked under his arm, and walked with a loping style that was kind of jaunty, as if the world were at his feet. It felt delightful walking and talking beside him due to his contagious gait and his obvious joy over words, words he'd use like *tumuli* and *chorine* in effortlessly musical sentences. Words I'd pretend to understand and would send me to the nearest dictionary whenever I left his company. In the instance of chorine, I happily found the word a qualifier for my mother, who worked as a chorine before her marriage to an Italian wannabe gangster.

The low self-esteem I'd inherited from my lack of education would dissolve when someone as smart as Luc made me feel seen and valued. We'd hang out after work at his place. He'd put on a Françoise Hardy record, and we'd lie around talking and writing

---

[1] Isabelle Eberhardt used this name when travelling incognito as a boy, eventually changing the name again to Si Mahmoud Saadi in Algeria on her quest to join a clandestine Sufi sect.

LE FAUX GARÇON

little snippets of French symbolist poetry in East Village idiom, piecing shards together in the style of Brion and Burroughs' cut-ups.

Luc had interviewed Burroughs for a magazine, and having made his acquaintance, was invited to a party being given in Burroughs' honour by the filmmaker Howard Brookner. Luc asked me to come along. I bit my nails into bloody stumps in nervous anticipation and donned my best boy's suit.

When we arrived at the party, a sweep of the room revealed no other women in attendance. Lots of good-looking men, elders and juniors, and their companions; bits of French conversation. I was asked what I'd like to drink, then handed a glass of Scotch decorated with pin-up girls just as a young buff dude was vacating a seat next to the guest of honour. Gulping down the drink, I took courage and sat. Burroughs checked me out through narrow eyes. I was miserable at making eye contact, afraid I'd be seen for the uneducated guttersnipe I was at the time. Ironic, since many in our scene aspired to be streetwise, not knowing how hard it might be to have come from nothing, which was often stressful and shame-inducing. A tough veneer worked to mask the shame. Or so I thought. Maybe sensing me adrift in the charade, Burroughs unsettled me even more with a hard-boiled, 'So, who are you?'

I imagined he might think I was a boy, so I went with my alias, Pierre Mouchet. I thought he might get a kick out of the name, probably not knowing the Eberhardt reference, but possibly familiar with French filmmaker Robert Bresson.[1] (*Mouchette* was a

---

[1] I knew of Bresson through Patti Smith's mention of his film *Au hasard Balthazar*, another Bresson tragedy, both films commenting on the cruelty of supposedly Christian people toward the girls in the films, and the beloved donkey Balthazar, a Christic figure in Bresson's transcendental style.

Bresson film about a ragamuffin girl from an abusive home who goes through absolute hell and finally ends her own life.) After identifying myself to Burroughs with the semi-confident alias, I received a smirk in return. Then silence. I had to think of something to say.

'I liked *The Wild Boys* a lot.'

'Thanks, Pierre.' More silence. My face flushed red.

'Have you ever done time in jail?'

I wanted an opening to let him know I'd been to jail – juvie jail – which I thought might impress him. I certainly didn't want to have sex with Burroughs, but sometimes imagined myself as a gay boy, a wild boy, a boy who wrote outrageously beautiful work that the venerable William Burroughs would respect.

Another twitchy-lipped smirk. Another question as answer.

'Well, what about you? Have you ever been in jail?'

'Reformatories mostly. In Ohio. Good times.'

I nodded my head, acting all tough and gangster while he just kept that half-grin, eyes like slits, checking me out. I was a nervous wreck.

'I need another drink. You want something?'

'No, I'm fine.'

And with that I escaped the hot seat, silently thanking every Italian saint for the respite of watching a starry-eyed Burroughs fan slip into the chair I'd fled. I poured another glass of Scotch and slunk away to avoid further scrutiny.

A little later, I spotted Luc chatting with Burroughs. When their conversation ended, I grabbed him.

'Can we get out of here?'

On the street I reiterated my uncomfortable conversation with

LE FAUX GARÇON

Burroughs. Luc said I'd amused the old bard. He'd referred to me as 'le faux garçon'.[1]

* * *

Cabell Hardy, sometimes Cabell McLean or Lee Angel Hardy, also worked in the Strand's basement. He had a dimpled chin and thick curly hair, the ruddy looks of a young Irish stevedore in tight T-shirts, newsboy cap, and worsted pants. In private, Cabell liked to dress in women's clothes. Aside from a 1940s thrift store dress, black in the tradition of Piaf, I didn't have any girly clothes he could borrow – but I was happy to paint Cabell's lips red and decorate his eyelids with shadow in my shoebox bedroom. At the Strand we'd flirt between stacks of remainder books and talk literature, usually books about dope and hustling by John Rechy and our mutual idol Jean Genet.

A cross-dressing writer who loved heroin, Cabell lived with a woman who was apparently his lover, but he loved men too. With me, he was happy to call himself a lesbian. His sensual fluidity wasn't the cause of intrigue; shifting sexuality was often a given, but the noms de plume and him going MIA often had me worrying about his criminality not being a fantasy, or maybe his habit taking the best of him. He never did return to the Strand. Sometime in 1978, Cabell simply disappeared.

Jody Harris, the Contortions guitarist during my stint as organ-shredder, also worked at the Strand alongside his pal Bob Quine. Not to demean Jody – a tight bad-assed rhythm

---

[1] Lucy Sante would later inform me that Burroughs had actually called me 'la fausse fille', the fake girl.

guitarist – but Quine was the downtown guitar king. His musical action painting mixed razor-sharp lyricism with a jazz-outlier sensibility that elevated any outfit lucky enough to play with him. Quine had a look, too. Baldheaded in trench coats and fuck-you sunglasses, he resembled an ambulance chaser or a bureaucratic grumpy banker. Jody was way sexier in a lean, boyish way that matched his scorching rhythms on guitar. He and Pat Place had the best behinds in New York City and both knew it – they wore the tightest jeans they could find, proudly showing off their cupcakes.

Luc Sante, Cabell Hardy, Jody Harris, and so many others – the Strand was just crawling with wild boys. In the late 1970s and through the '80s, my hormones were, let's say, highly stimulated. Especially testosterone. During these decades of sexual escapades, the suspicion often entered my mind that I might be intersexed. If not an outer hermaphrodite, certainly an inner one – due to my hormonal sweeps and what were considered untypical and unfeminine desires for a woman at the time. Could it be I was harbouring a pair of undetected testes, or did one lonely testis get lost in the tangle of female anatomy? How could a girl possibly have this much testosterone running through her veins? My only perceived crime as a woman in a body was being as ravenously free as a man in my sexual pursuits. Beneath the shabby thrift-store suit, newsboy cap and that lone black Piaf dress danced a carnival of shifting sexual personae.

My imagination was often provoked by whatever I was reading at the time. Thanks to Genet and company, I elevated myself to a creature beyond the binary; twisting man and woman, whore and saint on beds of blood roses. A revolutionary spring of emerald poetry and sorrow, a sorceress drag king criminal waif, lonely and longing for love without a clue of how to find or give it. The girl-Narcissus gone lonely-wild.

Although I was gay in heart and romantically longed for, courted, and fell in love with women, sexual trysts were so much easier with boys. An easy snap of the fingers; hot, fun, and leading to nothing other than sex, pure and simple. You meet a cute balloon boy riding a bicycle cart with a helium tank and balloons while leaving Puffy's on a summer night. You flirt. He asks you to jump in, he wheels you to the docks for a quick tryst on a blanket. You never see him again and you couldn't care less. After you've just played crazed music to a packed house, you're high, laughing, and strolling past Grace Church on Broadway with a musician pal when the church courtyard shrouded by trees and the possibility of sacrilege beckons. To touch and be touched.

Most women I was drawn to were either straight or wanted to be courted, and long-playing seductions weren't my game at that age. Nor was I adept then at solving the mysteries of women's bodies. When alcohol or drugs and a dancefloor with a DJ playing some wicked groove was involved, my chances were best. I could also be aggressive with straighter women friends, would try making out with a few but understood 'no' meant 'no'. Some expressed not wanting to be 'that way' but didn't abandon our friendship over my clumsy come-ons. It's hard not to imagine most straight women getting off on the idea of another woman desiring them, even when they don't have the courage to act on it – afraid of it being good enough to turn them toward what they think of as an oppressed lifestyle and identity. The simple truth; although it's much better in many ways, politically and culturally it's still difficult to be a woman without adding the stigma of lesbian to the equation. And it was so much harder back then. Yet I ignored society's cultural norms, understanding them as antithetical to life itself. Not understanding how there might be a price to pay for such freedom.

My erotic fascinations were extremely visual; it was the picture that sent my blood rushing. They say men get off more on visuals, but the more I live and desire, the less I believe in sexual absolutes. A Cuban girl I dated had the most beautiful feet, slopes and curves of a young ballerina. I sat next to her on a park bench watching her dangle a flip flop from her brown toes in rhythm to her own internal guaguancó, and me feeling her beat beneath my skin. The image meaning more to me than the sex or even the kiss; the arch of her foot like the curve of a vase begging for a carnation to slip in there, sex clenching at the vision – how the exquisite sensuality of life can be contained in the burn of one afterimage.

★ ★ ★

When I was nine years old, I'd hole up in my grandma's walk-in closet, extension cord juicing a small record player where the Stones revolved endlessly with Brian Jones' jangly guitar on '19th Nervous Breakdown' and a Christmas tree colour wheel making its orbit, bathing me in condensed, coloured light. Pouting my lips with hair slicked back into a duck's ass, I'd pose and strut in place while singing 'Time Is on My Side' into a broom handle to my imaginary audience, who were full of multiple Hayley Mills clones. I wanted to be her (in the movie *Tiger Bay*) and simultaneously be her boyfriend. Or I wanted to be Mick Jagger. He felt like man and woman with no demarcation. The greatest rock stars have been hybrids of the two, masters at climbing the double-helix of DNA's twisty ladder.

LE FAUX GARÇON

Many of the downtown boys I knew had a homoerotic aura around their friendships. Lots of touching, wrestling and hair-rustling, giggling and mutual flirty admiration. For the ones who didn't dare act on their impulses, there were a few of us girls who had a certain agency we expressed physically by dressing like boys, signalling we were unafraid to be sexual in a spontaneous rough-and-tumble way that felt *Querelle*-and-Cocteau-gay. Boundaries were blurred. If you wanted to get with someone, you did it without needing or having a label slapped on your ass. You appreciated the girl in the boy and vice versa; it was fascinating and seductive. Where clothing was anti-fashion, fluid sexuality *was* fashion, even for those who didn't choose it.

Anti-Fashion

Gender is a costume. In No Wave, anti-fashion ruled, it being anathema to dress even remotely close to the reigning culture's fashion dictates. By 1973, I had morphed into one of Bowie's androgynous Moonage Daydream kids, but the style was petering out by 1975 (you can only sport an orange mullet and green glitter platforms for just so long). Although I loved the look and music of the Warhol and Velvet Underground set, its women were too feminine for me, except for the seemingly sexless Mo Tucker. Although she was a female musician I admired, I could not be moved to imitate the style of someone who foreshadowed *Saturday Night Live*'s Pat character. And I was just too puny to pull off Gerard Malanga's black leather uniform. Clueless about where to seek out my true tribe in the industrial hellhole of Cleveland, inspiration finally appeared in the form of an album called *Horses*.

Patti Smith broke the world open for me on that album cover – her 'I dare you' expression dressed in a man's white shirt, a skinny black tie and a suit jacket thrown casually over her shoulder. What's more, she rattled off a prose that would singe your scalp, dropping names like Jimi Hendrix, Edie Sedgwick, and Jean Genet in the same breath. Patti taught me that fashion was equal parts art, romanticism, and rebellion. Most of the women I knew in the gay scene of Cleveland dressed like disco bunnies in glittery spandex or like granola dykes in Birks and flannel shirts, or pimpy glam dykes in garishly coloured bell-bottomed polyester suits (me). And I knew my look was tired.

It has been well documented that Richard Hell birthed the 'punk' look that Malcolm McLaren and Vivienne Westwood made iconic. When his tatty wardrobe left much to be desired, Richard painted drunken triangles on a ripped T-shirt and used safety pins to cinch holes together. Back then, Richard was a poet and bass player high on French symbolism, broke and living in a tenement apartment on a heroin block with a bathtub in the kitchen. Inspired by the detritus around him, he was merely taking advantage of the resources at hand and would begin the East Village trend of wearing the distorted geometry of your inner life on your sleeve. Richard was also known to wear a floppy black scarf as tie with a blousy white shirt like the Parisian poètes maudits. Style had everything to do with mood, poverty for some, and whatever film, book, or music sparked your imagination.

When Brit purveyor of punk McLaren returned to New York toting Westwood's Seditionaries line, trying to sell it back to its Yankee provocateurs at ridiculous prices, it was like the Boston Tea Party; none of us were having it except for the bridge-and-tunnel wannabes, and Malcolm found himself homeward bound where he kept busy dressing up his very own meat puppets, the Sex Pistols. McLaren also approached incendiary British band the Slits, raggedy wild girls high on rasta who created an utterly unique skank punk reggae hybrid. Rumour has it he tried to woo them into management via ridiculous faux-punk posturing, telling them he hated music and hated women. Surprise – they turned him down.

Where McLaren and his Pistol gang were the essence of punk fashion, post-punk New York was the quintessence of anti-fashion. The costuming of renegade post-punk misfits had more to do with words and music, film, art, and unspoken visionary gender politics than it ever had to do with fashion or feminism as anyone knew it. Post-punk was a slap in the face to commercialism and when the ugly-isms happened to rear their little pinheads, the more idealistic among us ignored them as idiotic.

ANTI-FASHION

One of the things I initially admired most about the way the new breed dressed was their penchant for black, which was, is, and will always be supremely sexy. Although the black leather jacket remained a staple of rebel uniformage, everyone in the post-punk scene had their own individual take on style. The Brit punks had our initial inspiration regurgitated up into a very specific uniform of mohawks, safety pins, and Seditionaries – we took our style cues from actors in the films of Pasolini, Fellini and Godard, Marlene Dietrich, Jean Seberg, *Barbarella*, from Antonin Artaud and Anaïs Nin, Monique Wittig's *Les Guérillères*, *Valley of the Dolls*, Bertolt Brecht, kabuki, the Zulus, Kerouac, Jackson Pollock's paint splashes, and terrorist groups like the Brigate Rosse and Baader–Meinhof gang.

Girls felt free to express their inner animas in their thrift-store choices. It was exhilarating to dress like Catherine Deneuve in *Repulsion* one day and a black-and-blue Artful Dodger the next – and to be a No Wave filmmaker on Friday and a neo-surrealist poet on Saturday night. The boys all looked gay even when they were trying to ape Jean-Paul Belmondo's machismo, rubbing their 1950s-panted ass cheeks against a brick wall while dangling a Gitane from their bottom lip, a Borsalino cap cocked over one eye. Girls worked this French gangster look with equal heat. There was definitely a French thing going on then. Even Stiv Bators of the Dead Boys, a true bad-boy punk, wore a boat-necked striped T-shirt and a little fey French sailor scarf around his neck on occasion.

My hair was buzzed to half-an-inch short, kept that way until a Wall Street cretin, having paid a bribe to gain access to the Mudd Club, ruined it for me.

'You remind me of a French prostitute!'

Just as I was tensing up a fist, he fell all over himself exclaiming, 'The Nazis shaved French women's heads because they worked for the Resistance! It's sexy, no kidding!'

He and his buddy laughed at their inside joke. I slugged him and ran off. I discovered it was the just the opposite – French patriots shaved French women's heads and marched them through the streets to shame them for sleeping with the Nazis, which many did to save their own lives and those of their children. And I wondered, did they physically shame the French Vichy men who colluded in the occupation of France by the Nazis? Why was it always the women who were pushed forward as public examples to punish and humiliate?

★ ★ ★

The freedom to express our inner animas by acting out characters through clothing was exhilarating, and lucky for us, a panoply of used clothing stores and shops run by the Eastern European émigrés who came before us were everywhere. We could dig through treasure troves full of riches. There was a shop on First Avenue where the vendor sold deadstock, items untouched and waiting in their plastic wrappings for twenty or thirty years. Boys clothing from the 1940s and '50s, great shirts and little jackets and pants in striped mattress-ticking fabric, boys' laced dress shoes, suspenders, neatly stitched shirts with long collars.

We girls were skinny for the most part, but our eating habits stemmed from poverty more than compulsion. Our scene preceded the age of huge billboards with emaciated models in haute couture underwear imploring us to join their ranks. (Decades later in the

1990s, fashionistas and advertisers searching for their new sartorial designs went into frenzies over Nan Goldin's photos, perverting the essence of Nan's visions and seizing on the concept of 'heroin chic' like piranhas to a bloodbath. They sure thought they knew what and how to exploit and what to ignore when it came to women, culture, and fashion.) Not that advertising ever would have swayed us. Even though we were hungry, the comfort of food as nutrition just wasn't a priority. We preferred to live by our arrogant, independent wits than to sit down to formal mealtimes, work a normal job in the 'Piss Factory',[1] or wear generic styles.

There was also the well-positioned bruise or cut – as anti-fashion as you could get, stemming from some type of performative violence. It could be from a fistfight provoked by the lead singer in your band, or in some instances, strenuous forms of love-play. Or out-and-out abuse via a love feud and a drunken, drug-fuelled squabble. And if you sliced up your fingers while playing your guitar on stage or got smashed in the lip by a swinging microphone, the blood was all the better and stayed on whatever garment or cheek fortunate enough to be spattered by it – until it flaked into dust.

---

[1] 'Piss Factory' was the B-side of Patti Smith's first recorded single, 'Hey Joe', released on her own indie label Mer Records.

Where Have the Gazelles Gone?

I met Lizzy Mercier in 1977. Infatuated with Africa and hyped up on her own hormonal ecstasy, Lizzy played rhythms on her guitar that no master musician could follow; fingertip percussion guitar solo licks uniquely her own, teased into life by her love for African music, jazzy film scores, and No Wave brutalism. She'd pick out rhythms that sounded like she'd grown up in a dusty alley in Soweto. I'd try to match her on my Fender Duo-Sonic as she danced crazy note clouds into circles above my head. Lizzy was an inimitable visionary, never fully recognized in her lifetime for her musical innovations and startling presence as a singer, player, and performer.

Immortal girl Martine-Elisabeth Mercier Descloux was born in Paris in 1956 to unmarried and underage Christiane Mercier. Christiane was impregnated by a much older man named Descloux. Abandoned by her mother and not recognized by the father, Lizzy was raised by great-uncle Roger and his wife Mauricette Gaire (born Mercier). They lived at 10 rue des Halles, an apartment they'd lived in since 1938. The three were close. Mauricette died in 1988 from a blood transfusion contaminated with AIDS. I remember Lizzy telling me about Mauricette, but she never spoke of her lost mother. Many of the letters I'd receive and send to Lizzy usually bore the rue des Halles address; she moved around constantly but always checked in when she stayed with Roger when in Paris.

Lizzy had style. She also liked to wear boys' suits, and she had a mop of crazy brown hair. Hair with buoyant natural waves, sometimes matted and dreaded, or standing up in shock like a startled cat. Sometimes she'd tie it up in rags or a cap but most days she allowed it to go where it might, this way and that. It bounced over perfectly arched eyebrows and played peekaboo over her eyes. She'd shake it from her vision to look at you, eyes and hair loaded with mischief. You couldn't meet Lizzy and not be affected by her unique presence. She hit me in the pit of my soul. Motherless girls can have that effect on one another.

I remember us in the aisle of the Bleeker Street Cinema revival house with Melville's *Bob le flambeur* flickering on the screen and the seats packed, our inner animals wrestling on the carpet. She bit. Lizzy was a poet with teeth. She wasn't afraid to use them, to devour life by the mouthful. Richard Hell rightly called her a carnivore. Laughing and gleefully wrestling, we'd create a ruckus until an usher pushed us cursing into the streets of our downtown New York to meet up with shadow figures painted on the walls. Hollowed buildings sprayed with new alphabets, echoing sonics of art-gangster noise and hip-hop and trysts on the docks – our cinematic playground.

Lizzy was my friend, sister, brother, and lover, another girl whose mother had abandoned her as mine did. She would drift in and out of my life, filling me with wonder and love every time we came together. Her laugh, the space between her front teeth. That crazy brilliant way she played guitar and loved music. And it was her very own music, idiosyncratic and as formidable as any New or No Wave man-boy that ever made a mark.

Her debut record on ZE was a musical collaboration with Michel Esteban's brother Didier – the mini-LP *Rosa Yemen*, a masterpiece of No Wave guitar innovation. Lizzy shone with the fire of ecstatic life. She demanded to make music her way, yet she'd always be financially dependent on men, never able to seize control and ownership of her own music and work. She often complained how her

WHERE HAVE THE GAZELLES GONE??

royalties and performance monies never made it into her pockets, that Michel controlled the money.¹

Lizzy's passions took her to Johannesburg in 1983, breaking the boycott during the height of apartheid to record the brilliant masterpiece LP *Lizzy Mercier Descloux* (later renamed *Zulu Rock*) with South African musicians. I'll hazard a guess that Paul Simon must have heard this album, was inspired by Lizzy as well as the music of South Africa and followed suit, recording his own masterpiece *Graceland* in 1985 with the hegemony of the male-dominated music business in full support of him.

We'd write to one another through the years, with most letters exchanged while she lived alone for a time in La Plante at Happonvilliers in the Loire Valley, in an isolated country house with her dog Harpo and cat Bébert. The house belonged to the family of her ex-boyfriend, Charlot. She was diagnosed with ovarian and colon cancer in 2002, and began travelling, staying with friends. Toward the end of her life, she was in care at the Hôpital Broussais in Paris, where ex-lover Richard Hell visited her.

I spent an afternoon with Lizzy's cousin in 2015 while staying in Paris. He recounted being with her at the hospital and running into Richard at the Porte de Vanves flea market where Richard had just emerged from a patisserie, his face covered with creamy cake. Lizzy's friend Samira was with her throughout her illness, and along with

---

1 Michel Esteban was Lizzy's boyfriend when they moved from Paris to New York together in 1976. After partnering with Michael Zilkha at ZE Records, Esteban became Lizzy's manager and signed her to ZE. When he and Lizzy separated, Esteban's next wife was Portuguese-Belgian singer Lio, popular in the 1980s. She became his partner, he managed and produced her music, and had a child with her. Sometime after Lio left him in 2018, she reported his alleged counterfeit record sales and royalty thefts. Michel is now living in Brazil.

Richard, they took Lizzy out to lunch. Sadly, she said the food had no taste because of the medication.

Lizzy did not want to die in the hospital in Paris. She was counting on money from a cover of her song 'Mais où sont passées les gazelles?' to come through. According to Samira, Esteban allegedly took the money, a final heartbreak. When Richard Hell sold his papers to a university, he sent Lizzy money to help with her health expenses. She also appealed to Michael Zilkha for help. Michael was also kind and generous to the artist who dazzled him in 1977.

Lizzy travelled to her beloved Corsica and spent the last ten days of her life there, where she died in April of 2004. According to her wishes, she was cremated, and her ashes were scattered in the bay of Saint-Florent.

* * *

On a certain night in the month of April, I light a candle for her and ask, *Mais où est passée la gazelle?*

No-llywood

In the late 1970s and early 1980s, you couldn't turn the corner in downtown New York City without running into a young cineaste wielding a Super 8 camera. Many women were shooting and directing films: Lizzie Borden, Vivienne Dick, Becky Johnston, Coleen Fitzgibbon, Kathryn Bigelow, Sara Driver, Sheila McLaughlin, Lynne Tillman, Bette Gordon, Ericka Beckman, Aline Mare, Pat Murphy, Gail Vachon, Kiki Smith, Jeanne Liotta, Susan Seidelman, Tina L'Hotsky, Edit DeAk, Beth B., and others. Many of us were directing, appearing in, or scoring music for films. People usually shot in Super 8, sometimes 16mm if you had a bit of money and means.

Making movies has always been prohibitively expensive, but that didn't stop any of my friends from picking up cameras. Most of the downtown filmmakers went to Rafik on Broadway for equipment and film. The saint of downtown filmmakers, Rafik would often give out short ends or sell film for pennies on the dollar. He rented cameras, Steenbecks and assorted production gear dirt cheap.

On Canal Street, Super 8 projectors and assorted used film gear were acquired for practically nothing at one of so many stores selling a jumble of assorted electronic parts. The bemused vendors would watch as we scavenged through piles in their bins on the sidewalk, and they'd often throw in freebies just to get rid of their excess. Their junk became our treasure. Downtown New York screamed location as character, a place filled with wild girls and boys moving through a fairytale ruin of the greatest city on earth. We integrated internal and external torn beauty, creating the sets and costumes we needed and scoffed at the idea that hefty budgets were fundamental to filmmaking.

I acted in underground movies from 1978 into the early 1980s. When I wasn't working at bookstores, I worked the ticket booth at the Carnegie Hall Cinema, sister theatre to the Bleeker Street Cinema, both repertory houses where I could catch all the European films I loved in my time off. While working at the Carnegie, the amazing character actor Lawrence Tierney would come in to see noir films. I loved him in *Dillinger*. People said he was nuts, a very violent drunk, but he was gentle as a lamb with me. We'd talk, I'd tell him about wanting to act, and he'd take me out for coffee at the Carnegie Deli after my shift. He was sober when I knew him, wouldn't touch a drop. His off-screen gentle gangster vibe felt familiar, having grown up with an Italian made man, Uncle Caesar, and the working-class Italians on my father's side. Larry talked in his tough, fatherly way, saying I should just be myself and not let the bastards get me down. That if I ever needed advice, I should come to him.

I also met the goddess Sophia Loren at the Carnegie when she was promoting a series of films. Anna Magnani and Sophia were my favourite actresses, and I'd read that Sophia's husband and producer Carlo Ponti was being indicted for smuggling art and money out of Italy. I'd rehearsed what to say if I met her. As Sophia posed on the balcony at the top of the staircase, surrounded by an entourage with cameras clicking, I climbed onto a table below and pulled myself up to the railing, calling her name, '*Sophia! Mi dispiace tanto che Carlo sia in prigione! Ti amo!*' Her eyes grew wide on seeing the ragamuffin with the smart mouth talking about her husband being jailed. Raising her finger to her lips in a hushing motion, she laughed, bent down, and gave me a kiss on the cheek. I was walking on clouds for weeks afterwards.

NO-LLYWOOD

★   ★   ★

There were many downtown indie filmmakers active during the late 1970s and '80s, writing and directing films in the No Wave spirit of aesthetic rebellion against conventional narrative cinema. I must mention the guys too: Ivan Král, Amos Poe, James Nares, John Lurie, Edo Bertoglio, Charlie Ahearn, Richard Kern, Nick Zedd, and so many others. Michael Oblowitz directed films featuring a favourite downtown actress of mine – his partner, the iconic Rosemary Hochschild.

I'll cut to the chase here, focusing on my own first experience of acting on film. With Lizzie Borden at the helm, none of us involved imagined this scrappy, defiant film would become a cult prophecy of feminist resistance.

Screenwriter Becky Johnston introduced me to Lizzie Borden in 1978. Lizzie was a sexy academic, intimidating and exciting. I was writing agit prop poetry and making dissonant music. Lizzie was involved in the New York art scene, writing art criticism for *Artforum*, assisting Richard Serra, seeing Vito Acconci, and beginning to discover her sexuality while shooting her first film.

Shot in 1976, *Regrouping* was a documentary experiment filled with second-wave feminist tensions. The film was Lizzie's attempt to capture the discussions and trajectory of a feminist collective but proved as problematic as second-wave feminism. There were breakdowns in communication, contradictions around approach resulting in chaotic jump-cuts and mismatched voiceovers, and various acrimony toward Lizzie as an exploitative filmmaker. The film featured many downtown women artists: Nancy Arlen and Connie Burg of Mars, Kathryn Bigelow, Joan Jonas, Barbara Kruger,

Julia Heyward, Judy Pfaff, and Edit DeAk among others. The first of Lizzie's feminist trilogy of films (*Born in Flames* and *Working Girls* would follow), she had to shelve the film for forty years due to the initial group of four subjects picketing its first screening at Anthology Film Archives.

Although *Regrouping* knighted Lizzie with a reputation for controversy, it did not stop her from pursuing radical visions in her work. She began formulating what would become *Born in Flames* soon after we met. With *The Battle of Algiers* by Gillo Pontecorvo as inspiration, she wanted to make a film that felt like a documentary, about a time in the future where America has a socialist-democratic government that continues to oppress women. In her futuristic political scenario, what would it take for women to fight back? The answers came out of dialogue with women friends and artists. In the tradition of Ingmar Bergman's later films and the work of Mike Leigh, Lizzie never handed her actors scripts. She conceptualized the premise of the film and the scenes, and how the story should unfold sequentially. Several scene ideas were collaborative, and most of the dialogue was improvised based on the actions Lizzie needed to drive the plot forward.

Honey, lead radio announcer of Phoenix Radio, kept her real name as character, writing her own dialogue, contributing ideas and suggesting friends to act in the film. Radical feminist lawyer and activist Florynce (Flo) Kennedy played a role as a revolutionary coach and improvised a powerful scene with Jean Satterfield, who plays the character Adelaide Norris. Head wrapped in a Palestinian keffiyeh, Flo schools Adelaide on the agency and power of women taking up arms. Becky Johnston, Kathryn Bigelow, and Pat Murphy also brainstormed scenes as the three women journalists committed to telling the truth about the government's involvement in Norris's death.

I wanted to create a character who actually had an arc. One of the very first right-wing radio personalities of the time, Bob Grant, had a show on WABC in New York. Grant was the equivalent of the 'shock jocks' we know today. Then there was the character of Howard Beale in the 1976 film *Network*, railing against the hypocrisies of our time. So I created a feminist street version of Howard Beale: shock jock and radio announcer Isabel of Radio Ragazza.

I was reading a lot of revolutionary works at the time: Vladimir Mayakovsky's poetry, Emma Goldman, Malcolm X, and the prison writings of a young Fidel Castro. The chip on my shoulder would not prevent me from self-educating, seeking truths about history, class, colonialism, racial and gender oppression. I blamed so much of my childhood on what I thought was a particularly American system of harm that traumatized my mother – a system cruel to women, to the working class, to Black citizens, and to immigrants like the family of my stepfather. I had so much fury, amplified by a compassion that taught me to see through the hypocrisy of the American dream, and it filled me with a longing to publicly uncover these harms and fight against them. In Isabel, I created a character based on these feelings hyped to the max (and occasionally fuelled by alcohol). Back then, my punky distrust of feminism's passivity and lack of revolutionary agency came through Isabel. Rap was starting to emerge from the South Bronx in the late 1970s, and I found it to be the perfect rhythmic and performative vehicle for Isabel's style of agit-prop poetry. The band I sang lead in, the Bloods, also appear in the film. During one of my most radical on-camera speeches, Isabel states the number on the dial for Radio Ragazza is 2016; also the year *Born in Flames* would be restored.

Malcolm X once stated that the media is the most powerful entity on earth, and no political maxim seems truer. If women interested in revolution wanted to push messages out to the public, they'd need to do it through the media. In *Born in Flames*, the two radical feminist radio stations are eventually destroyed by the government after broadcasting revolutionary messages. I'd been reading Marshall McLuhan's *The Medium Is the Message*, and I had travelled to England for the first time, learning about Radio Caroline and loving the idea of pirate radio. My research revealed that radio signals in motion could not be traced (at the time), which resulted in

Lizzie filming our two radio stations going mobile via stolen U-Haul trucks. There was no internet back then; we had radio and television, wheat-pasting, newspapers, 'zines, and word-of-mouth. Blowing up a transmission tower at the end was the ultimate radical act for the army to broadcast the hypocrisy of the supposed revolution.

In *Born in Flames*, Lizzie was committed to bridging a gap in feminist reality: that of the very real tensions that existed between Black and white women in second-wave feminism. The issues that Black women faced positioned them outside of white feminism, which was reluctant to learn about race and be inclusive. Lesbian women also felt discriminated against by the mostly middle-class white women at the helm of the movement. The failure to integrate the women's movement signalled weakness to the patriarchy, ultimately opening the door for the backlash in years to come. Lizzie knew these issues would be fundamental to her story; unless women of colour and white women could unite across class, colour, and sexual identities, the possibility of a women's revolution was nil. Black women and lesbians became integral to a feminist story that walks a line between dystopia and a utopian dream. Isabel softens up substantially in her understanding that rage is not enough and that revolution will never be accomplished in the face of racial divides, the bridging of which requires an empathy of spirit.

The New York art and No Wave scenes were starkly white with few exceptions. Lizzie frequented gay bars, like the West Village's lesbian bar Bonnie and Clyde's, looking to meet Black women who might be interested in appearing in the film. She approached Jean Satterfield when she saw her playing basketball at an uptown YMCA. Jean introduced Lizzy to Honey, who in turn brought other Black women to the film.

Lizzie took tremendous risks to make the film when she did. Not only were its ideas and guerrilla style radical, but it was a true labour of love. It took her several years to complete the film. She'd shoot when she was able, with small grants, the generosity of Rafik, or an extra $200 that would arrive here and there. Most actors appeared for free or for dinner or lunch, or maybe the occasional small compensation. All in, the film's budget was roughly $40,000. Lizzie shot on reversal film, so she could immediately see what she'd shot instead of having to pay to develop negatives. A wheelchair served as a dolly. She'd call people to see who was available to shoot, pile them into her old Lincoln Continental, and we'd shoot a scene mostly with available light, one camera person, and one sound person. Bare bones, and all shots were stolen – no permits necessary. You could shoot practically anywhere in New York without interference.

Lizzie had a Steenbeck in her loft on Howard Street and was her own editor, piecing the story together from the hundreds of hours she'd shot over a period of five years. The film is truly revolutionary and remains relevant today. Those who think it's rough or poorly acted are missing the message in the medium, a message that is not lost on culturally diverse audiences who do understand what it's like to be under-represented, especially on film – those who continue to long for, and fight for change.

★ ★ ★

There was a time when acting felt as if it could be a serious pursuit, with study. Enamoured of actors with duende, like James Dean and Marilyn Monroe, I wanted to study the Stanislavski method at the

Actor's Studio in midtown and was granted a preliminary audition. I chose a monologue by tomboy Frankie in Carson McCullers' *The Member of the Wedding*, applied myself, rehearsing diligently, and was surprised when they invited me back for a second audition. Nerves got the better of me and I never showed. There were numerous projects pulling my attention at any given moment, and it was impossible to commit to one for a dedicated amount of time. Beneath it all was the anxiety that without a safety net or family, I lacked the foundational support to follow through on such an opportunity as the Actor's Studio. Yet I would try, in my own feral way, to pursue acting.

When the filming of *Born in Flames* ended, Kathryn Bigelow wanted to do a short film adaptation of Georges Bataille's story *Ma Mère*, with me playing the seventeen-year-old boy involved in an incestuous relationship with his promiscuous mother. Kathryn set up a photo shoot with me dressed in suit and tie as the French boy posing with a sultry red-headed German actress as la mère. I recall the astonishing stills from that shoot having a greenish patina, similar to the look of Christopher Doyle's cinematography for Wong Kar-wai's films. I don't know why the film never happened; perhaps because Kathryn couldn't raise the money. Her cinematic eye demanded a decent budget, and it's hard to imagine any financier wanting to produce a film in 1978 with a lesbian playing a boy involved in a sexual relationship with his mother. Or a lesbian playing any role, for that matter.

Which brings me to the director of the film *Times Square*. The Canadian filmmaker Allan Moyle must have seen the Contortions and heard me sing or heard rumours about my feral side. He began following me around sometime in 1978 saying he was writing a film about two runaway girls and wanted to cast me as the wilder of the two, a punk singer. Would I like to play her? I was flattered and thrilled to imagine a buddy film for girls, a kind of film that had never existed, and thought Allan must be very brave and smart to attempt it. I was thrilled, told him I'd love the character to be called Nicky. Allan would visit my apartment across from the men's shelter, and what started as genuine interest in my life turned into him goading me to get drunk and talk about the darker aspects of my childhood. I wanted to talk about French symbolist poetry, Italian neo-realism, and the artistic socialism of our scene. He'd taunt and tease, accuse me of not knowing what I was talking about until I'd get angry; if he wanted to use my life experiences for his film, he'd have to start paying, and he eventually paid about $150 for several of these visits. It was obvious he was slumming it, peeking into how downtown art evangelists lived and thought.

I liked Allan's girlfriend at the time. Leanne Ungar was an audio engineer, and we met when she was working with Laurie Anderson's producer Roma Baran during a vocal session for Lizzie Borden's soundtrack of *Working Girls*. Leanne engineered. She suggested I write a memoir and should read *The Things They Carried* by Tim O'Brien and *Dispatches* by Michael Herr. Via Allan, she knew I had war stories of my own and encouraged me to write, which is why I was disappointed to find out she'd co-written a script debasing a young rebellious woman – the script that eventually became the film *Times Square*.

Allan introduced me to an eccentric acting teacher named Bob Brady. His loft on Union Square was always filled with a motley crew of friends, students, low lifes, and aspiring actors. I liked Bob. Scruffy and handsome, fun and generous, and wildly improvisational, he was a charmer – charismatic with a beautiful speaking voice and a grace in his body language that could flip into boyish mischief. One day I walked into his loft to find him and John Cale high as kites messing around on the piano. I practically begged Cale to play 'Buffalo Ballet' from his *Fear* LP which I had listened to relentlessly when I was nineteen. I wanted to sing with him on the choruses, but it was folly; they were both tripping on acid.

Allan asked Bob if he'd be willing to coach me, and if we could do a sort of screen test for *Times Square* there at his loft. Bob had a huge lug of a video camera and would tape his students doing improvs and scene work. When I showed up for the audition, Allan had paired me with a young actress named Amanda Plummer.

★ ★ ★

Amanda was mesmerizing – an eccentric with doe eyes, dropped from a far-off planet into a world inhospitable to wild girls. We immediately connected on the etheric plane of those who are 'in this world, but not of it'. Her parents were Hollywood royalty – Christopher Plummer and Tammy Grimes – which made for a crazy childhood and not my story to tell. Bob and Allan wanted us to improvise a scene where Amanda, playing the rich girl Pamela, is in the passenger seat of a car being driven by the street girl Nicky (me). *You are running away together. You're helping Pamela escape her oppressive family. You are getting to know to each other.* Amanda and I had never met before that moment, but our energy together at that audition was electric. We sat on a couch, Bob placed a single spotlight on us, and we started our improv. I can't recall a word between us during that test. I only remember a chemistry capable of melting steel.

Allan and Bob were speechless. Allan couldn't wait to bring the test to his prospective financiers. As Amanda and I ran around cemeteries and the Chelsea Piers, living out the ecstatic New York romance of a script that Allan should have filmed, he was approaching the mega-producer Robert Stigwood (the man behind *Saturday Night Fever* and *Jesus Christ Superstar*) with our screen test. Amanda and I were dancing on starlight, as we imagined Robert Stigwood watching us set fire to video tape.

I had one final meeting with Allan at my apartment on 3rd Street, thinking he'd be bringing good news; that the producers loved our improv, the film would be financed, and he wanted help with the script. I'd be paid well, and it would all start now! Instead, he delivered the news that Stigwood – a known homosexual – watched the test and declared that Amanda and I looked 'unfuckable'.

Allan would have to cast much prettier, sexier girls if he wanted a green light.

'I'm sorry,' said Allan. 'I'm disappointed too.'

When hurt, I raged. To hear this outrageous sexism was painful enough, but that Allan needed to spell it out to me felt doubly cruel. I flipped open my switchblade and stuck it menacingly into the wood of the front door, demanding he leave my house. I never saw Allan Moyle again.

Robert Stigwood did produce *Times Square* with Allan directing. The film was released in 1980 and starred two young actresses, Trini Alvarado in the role Amanda Plummer should have played and Robin Johnson as Nicky. When I saw the film, I was heartbroken. What could have been a profoundly compelling and entertaining film about two young, rebellious women wanting to live outside of society, a buddy film with a music score like no other, turned out to be trash – a film about two 'mentally disturbed' young women with cotton wool for brains. It was always the same: women rebelling against the societal expectations of their gender somehow had to be nuts. The one highlight of the film is its soundtrack, featuring luminaries like Talking Heads, Patti Smith, Chrissie Hynde, and Bryan Ferry. The original songs composed for the character Nicky summed up everything about the film that felt like a disgrace. Her theme song's chorus has her begging to be fed because she's a *damn dog*. Nicky sings the song dressed in a plastic garbage bag. In fact, her fans all follow, dressed in garbage bags, joyously singing about being damn dogs.

Roger Ebert wrote in his review: '*Times Square* rarely comes together into anything more than a good idea that fails, but there are times when it seems on the brink of wonderful things. Of all the bad movies I've seen recently, this is the one that projects the real sense of a missed opportunity.'[1]

★   ★   ★

Irish filmmaker Vivienne Dick was living on East 9th Street when we met. She shot experimental Super 8 films, short, documentary-style vignettes without narrative storylines. She was a good friend of Nan's, and one of many women artists who relocated to downtown New York from Europe. She emigrated from Dublin and was immediately immersed in the downtown scene. Vivienne was seeing

---

1 https://www.rogerebert.com/reviews/times-square-1980#google_vignette

the songwriter and musician Alex Chilton at the time. She was extremely kind, and I related to her Irish side due to my maternal ancestry. I'd often stop at her apartment to chat about filmmaking and writers like Monique Wittig; she was always generous, sharing fresh baked bread with Irish butter and strong coffee.

We formed a salon with several other downtown women artists and named it after Wittig's book *Les Guérillères*, about a women's army in a war against men. Vivienne shot us hanging out in our apartments or in the rubble of the Lower East Side, talking ideas or personal obsessions. The portraits included Vivienne, Anya Phillips, Lydia Lunch, Pat Place, Beate Nilsen, Ikue Mori, Nina Canal, and myself. (Other guérillères who didn't appear in the film included Nan Goldin, Lizzy Mercier, and Claire Pajaczkowska.) The film was a series of edited portraits, each portrait a fifty-foot Super 8 roll, shot and printed as it spooled to its end, lasting anywhere from two and a half to four minutes. *Guerillere Talks* screened at Club 57 in 1978. Nan also premiered her slide show *The Ballad of Sexual Dependency* there. Where movie theatres, museums, and galleries were not open to women artists and underground film, clubs were eager to show and support experimental art and films.

Vivienne made three films in 1978 – *Guerillere Talks*, *She Had Her Gun Already* and *Staten Island* – and all three focused on No Wave women. She said to the writer Maria Elena Buszek: 'I'd never seen anything like it. They were very androgynous, and to see women who looked like that and have that kind of energy . . . they were completely self-sufficient [and] weren't running around looking for husbands.'[1]

---

1 https://disband.us/wp-content/uploads/2022/03/Buszek-LadiesAuxiliary-2020.pdf

NO-LLYWOOD

★ ★ ★

In 1979, Vivienne made what would be her longest film and the first to feature men, *Beauty Becomes the Beast*. The brilliant Klaus Nomi makes an appearance, and there's a scene where an eleven-year-old Harley Flanagan (then the drummer in the band the Stimulators) and I wrestle and drench each other with squirt guns. There's also a dance between Nan's roommate Janet Stein and me to the Marvelettes song 'The Hunter Gets Captured by the Game', and Nan and I dancing at her Bowery loft where she is dressed in a leather dominatrix outfit (the scene appears in the more recent film about Nan's life, *All the Beauty and the Bloodshed*). Now back in Dublin, Vivienne continues to make experimental and documentary films. Along with Pat Murphy, director of *Maeve* and *Anne Devlin*, she is considered one of Ireland's most important filmmakers.

★ ★ ★

Many people involved in the group Collaborative Projects (COLAB) were friends and collaborators of mine, for instance Scott and Beth B, yet I never attended their meetings. Although the group was left-wing and politically motivated in their work, there were a few members who used an academically coded lexicon I did not understand, one purposely meant to exclude working-class people. My imposter syndrome would often flare up in the presence of this breed of intellectual and sometimes I'd act out, imagining myself a snotty Arthur Rimbaud in the presence of the elite poets of fin-de-siècle Paris; poètes maudits were highly critical of bourgeois values, even though some came from aristocratic backgrounds. For the most part, COLAB artists had revolutionary and counter-cultural impulses, and they embraced No Wave aesthetics. I admired the Ahearn brothers John and Charlie, James Nares, Kiki Smith, Tom Otterness, Robin Winters, and Jenny Holzer.

Possibly with funding from COLAB (who seemed adept at getting grants), a few COLAB members rented a fifty-seat storefront at 12 St Marks Place and called it the New Cinema. Films were transferred to video and projected on a four-by-five Advent screen. Why is a puzzle, since the quality of Super 8 was not great to begin with, and the transfers degraded the images even more. Maybe that was the aesthetic the filmmakers were looking for. James Nares and John Lurie processed their films and screened video at New Cinema along with Vivienne Dick, Eric Mitchell, Becky Johnston, and others.

★ ★ ★

Jim Jarmusch, another Cleveland exile, made his first film *Permanent Vacation* in 1980. Like many of us, Jim wore several creative hats and played in a band called the Del-Byzanteens with several mutual friends. I knew Jim Jarmusch and his partner Sara Driver from the scene and liked them both immensely. Jim's first film featured performances by many people in the scene including Sara, and John Lurie. Jim was decidedly underground and auteurish in his approach. His impulse to make films was never a reach toward any commercial success in the conventional sense, and if a potential financier's money even had the hint of a puppet string attached, Jim would vanish. With his aesthetic of stasis and downtown cool, he was determined to work without interference from the suits.

NO-LLYWOOD

I continue to respect Jim immensely for staying true to his aesthetic. It takes resolve to raise production money and steer true to your vision, especially when you're not following the paradigm of conventional narratives and Hollywood beauty aesthetics. This integrity is also true of filmmaker and producer Sara, who remains as fiercely independent as Jim. She co-produced his first two films, *Permanent Vacation* and *Stranger Than Paradise*. Her first film as a director, *You Are Not I*, was an adaptation of a Paul Bowles story – a mysterious tale about a woman who, having left an asylum, wanders onto the scene of a car crash, and an identity is exchanged. Filmed in black and white and exquisitely shot by Jim as cinematographer, the film featured many downtown collaborators in acting roles, like Nan Goldin and Luc Sante, with a score by Phil Kline (Phil also played guitar in the Del-Byzanteens).

Jim's first feature utilized many locked-down camera shots. He did move the camera occasionally in the beginning; his was not a complete lock-down like in the films of Bresson or Carl Dreyer,[1] but it was close. Not surprisingly (because she was a woman), some reviewers complained about the stillness in Sara's work and the long takes, but I imagine the slow-pacing in editorial and use of locked-down camera shots were about not wanting to manipulate the viewer's eye or pander to Hollywood narrative trends. It was a style that felt like a purer form of storytelling, where actions unfold naturally in front of the lens. Like Sara's, Jim's characters often seem somewhat adrift. He frames the characters with a loose story, then allows the proceedings to unfold in front of the camera

---

[1] Published in 1972, Paul Schrader's book *Transcendental Style in Film* features Ozu, Bresson, and Dreyer as the masters of filmic stasis. Chantal Ackerman's *Jeanne Dielman, 23 quai du Commerce, 1080 Bruxelles* is a masterpiece of the form.

without attempts to manipulate the viewer into specifically feeling anything. Both Jim and Sara worked with a slower pace in scene length and editorial style that invited (without demanding) a more meditative gaze. One of my cineaste friends called Jarmusch's style a 'junkie' aesthetic, a term one would never use for Bresson or Ozu. But, then again, Bresson and Ozu didn't live in junkie town.

When Jim was first brainstorming *Stranger Than Paradise*, he approached me about playing the female lead. Jim said he wanted to do a 'screen-test' of sorts and shot Super 8 footage of me as we wandered around Little Italy late one night, walking down Mulberry Street beneath the carnival lights strung for the Feast of San Gennaro. My hair was shorn in those days, and I was going through my Piaf dress phase. I imagine he saw me like a No Wave version of *La Strada*'s Giulietta Masina, one of my favourite actors.

He gave me a few rough pages of notes, what he'd written for *Stranger Than Paradise*, and shortly after we met, I went to a screening of *Permanent Vacation* and sat there entranced by a female character in the film played by Leila Gastil. Leila played a girl who simply hung around the periphery of things, a ghost in a slip, more wallpaper than character. Jim hadn't given her any dialogue; she seemed to exist as set dressing for the lead character of Aloysius played by Chris Parker. Chris was a sweet kid with a nasally voice that sounded like he got stuck on the cusp of puberty. I wondered why he'd chosen him, rather than Leila, as his focus, and guessed at how Jim might work with women based on this first film.

I assumed wrong. I turned down the role and Jim cast Eszter Balint, a unique and charming presence. She was the perfect choice. Although her dialogue was sparse, she made the part her own with her strong, quirky attitude and a face that Jim's camera found impossible to downplay. Eszter is the daughter of Marianne and Stephan Balint, co-founders of the Squat Theatre company. The troupe had emigrated from Budapest to New York in 1977, having been censored and banned by Hungarian authorities from performing in public due to their revolutionary politics and aesthetics. Squat's headquarters was a large storefront conveniently situated next to the Chelsea Hotel. Squat was the pinnacle of avant-garde theatre in NYC. Nico often appeared in their plays, as did Shirley Clarke, Mark Boone Jr, August Darnell, and many others, including an eleven-year-old Eszter. Squat was Sun Ra's favourite place to perform in the city, and Jean-Michel Basquiat was a habitué.

Eszter Balint is now a performing singer-songwriter and occasional actor. She played a recurring role in the limited streaming series *Louie* as Ellen Burstyn's niece and Louis C.K.'s Hungarian love interest. Eszter is an über-talent and No Wave royalty, a fact not lost on Louis C.K.

★ ★ ★

With a script penned by writer and raconteur Glenn O'Brien, Edo Bertoglio began shooting the film *New York Beat* in 1980, starring Jean-Michel Basquiat. Glenn and Edo gave Jean-Michel studio space and his first art materials to begin painting on canvas, which helped him make the transition from street art. The film was abandoned for a time, renamed and released as *Downtown 81* in 2000.

French-born artist, stylist, producer, and photographer Maripol was the original film's art director and was in charge of post-production on the 2000 release. Maripol's Polaroids of downtown scenesters are classic documents of the personalities who made that time legendary. She was responsible for dressing the young Madonna in the black stacked rubber bracelets, lacey tops, mesh gloves, and crucifixes she became known for. Maripol helped create an icon. Madonna's initial fashion aesthetic was copied by hundreds of thousands of young girls and women globally as her pop star ascended.

Charlie Ahearn's film *Wild Style* was pivotal in precipitating the melding of downtown and uptown underground cultures. Chris Stein of Blondie was a composer and music supervisor for *Wild Style*. Through meeting Fab 5 Freddy, Charlie's collaborator on the film, and inspired by the phenomenon of rap, Debbie Harry and Blondie released the song 'Rapture', integrating the downtown scene musically with the rap and hip-hop scene uptown. Charlie started hanging out as spectator at the new rap, graffiti, and beat-breaking parties happening in the South Bronx and began shooting the film in 1981. Artists Fab 5 Freddy and Lee Quiñones were actors and collaborators, and the film starred Patti Astor as the journalist who Freddy invites into hip-hop territory to document the South Bronx scene. Wildstyle is kind of graffiti that feels like action painting in its dynamism; it's dense with a vibrant flow of colours and interlocking letters. Cryptic and decorative. Twisted and stretched letters with 3D effects visually lift the letters off their surfaces.

Due to her role in *Wild Style*, Patti emerged as a fundamental player who shaped the downtown scene of the time. Recalling Oscar Wilde's words about life imitating art, Fab 5 Freddy convinced Patti that owing to her enthusiasm for the scene (and her looking as good a 'Queen of the Art Scene' as he'd seen since disgraced Mary Boone), she should open a space downtown to show graffiti artists' work in a gallery setting. Patti had acted in several No Wave films: Tina L'Hotsky's *Snake Woman*, James Nares' *Rome '78*, and Eric Mitchell's *Underground U.S.A.* She lived in the building next door to me on East 3rd, between Bowery and 2nd Avenue, across from the men's shelter. John Lurie and Eric Mitchell also lived in that building. I'd often run into Patti on the street and admired her femme fatale star quality.

Shortly after starring in *Wild Style*, she opened the FUN Gallery (named by Kenny Scharf) on East 11th Street in collaboration with Bill Stelling; they then moved the space to East 10th. FUN was her bid to 'get away from that whole white people, white walls, white wine Soho scene'.[1] Soon Patti was presenting shows by Fab 5 Freddy, Kenny Scharf, Jean-Michel Basquiat, and Keith Haring.

Aside from Basquiat's ubiquitous aphorisms in black letters as SAMO (making everyone wonder, *Who is this SAMO?* when the tag started appearing) and being influenced by graffiti, I don't believe he or Keith Haring and Kenny Scharf were involved in elaborately painting subway cars. Kenny was more of a pop-culture surrealist, psychedelic, cartoonish, and into sci-fi, whereas Keith usually drew on subway walls, simple pictograms of human figures, dogs, babies . . . always playful yet often political. Those three artists were among the first to show paintings at FUN.

I see Patti as the bridge-builder and integrator between the No Wave and punk sensibilities of Lower Manhattan, and the breakbeat hip-hop scene of the South Bronx. FUN Gallery and its street artists became the catalyst for a new and vital art movement, breaking away from the elite societal definitions of what art should and could be. Art dealers, buyers, and connoisseurs rallied through the

---

[1] Michael Hixon (5 June, 2018), 'Patti Astor revives New York's Fun Gallery in Hermosa Beach', *Daily Breeze*.

garbage-strewn streets in stretch limos looking for the next art star as a host of new galleries (inspired by FUN) popped up all over the East Village and LES: Pat Hearn, Gracie Mansion, International With Monument, ABC No Rio, Cash Newhouse, and many others. The influx of wealth marked the beginning of the gentrification of downtown. The artists living south of 14th Street and in SoHo who were making art, music, film, having created a new dynamic culture and revitalized decrepit neighbourhoods, would see developers rushing in to take advantage of the excitement generated by all that talent. Along with the scourge of AIDS and the evaporation of affordable housing, both the vibrant artistic and queer communities downtown would suffer massive losses – replaced by corporate interests, rising rents, and a pasteurized cultural landscape that erased the very spirit that once defined these neighbourhoods. Yet, the ghosts remain.

Patti hosted a solo show for Jean-Michel in November 1982. I didn't visit FUN very often, but this show blazes in my memory. I knew him as SAMO (he would take over my apartment on East 3rd Street), but I wasn't truly aware of his incendiary work until that show. Paintings like *Equals Pi* and the triptych *Portrait of the*

Artist as a Young Derelict were astonishing. His work reminded me of my mother's schizophrenia (his mother was also schizophrenic); it was mind-blowingly alive and wild, as if he were standing there creating the work naked and on fire. The opening was packed and everyone was mesmerized. I also remember Jean-Michel's date at the opening – Madonna throwing shade at me, she having just signed to Sire Records and I to Geffen Records. (The beginning of our rivalry.)

Another actor who never got enough oxygen as a key player in the graffiti scene is artist Lady Pink. At seventeen years old in 1981, Pink was on the rise as a prominent artist in the 'yards', where graffiti artists were wrapping entire subway cars in the Wild Style. I recall watching the trains, being mesmerized yet curiously perplexed by what I saw; the visuals often felt hallucinatory, a *Fantasia*-like fairytale parade of secret alphabets dancing on LSD. Graffiti artists didn't seem to have any interest in being understood by spectators and subway riders. They were talking code, secret alphabets, among themselves, but it was no less dazzling a spectacle. The magical visual layer created by these artists was fundamental to the dystopian landscape we moved through, the collective junkyard dreaming of our altered reality.

Lady Pink had street credibility, mad skills, and her own unique visual signature. If at any point her work was on view in Charlie's film, it was not linked to her character. She portrays Lee Quiñones's love interest, a promiscuous yet respected player and mural director in the yards. In real life, Lady Pink called herself a blood writer and was not alone as a woman. Her best friend in the yards was the writer Lady Heart, and graffiti artists like Barbara 62 and Eva 62 were tagging cars in the early 1970s. Initially the boys would not take Pink to the yards; she had to fight to get in. Pink dressed like a boy, considered herself a feminist, and thought of graffiti as radical, bringing social and political messages to the people.

★ ★ ★

Susan Seidelman isn't considered No Wave, but *Smithereens*, the narrative film she directed in 1982, featured many downtown personalities in the scene. An adorably endearing narcissist moves to New York longing to be a 'punk'. Seeking her fifteen minutes of fame, she beds Richard Hell, and becomes a petty criminal. It was shot on 16mm and captures what downtown felt and looked like in the early 1980s. Susan Berman plays the captivating lead character Wren. Susan worked as a waitress at a favourite restaurant on St Mark's Place called Dojo's. Along with a slew of other customers, I had a crush on her. *Smithereens* was the first American indie to be shown at the Cannes Film Festival.

I appear in a jail cell next to Madonna in Susan's next film, *Desperately Seeking Susan* (apropos to where Madonna and I would ultimately land; she gets sprung while I remain behind bars). If you blink, you'll miss me. The film helped launch Madonna to superstardom and Seidelman to get more green-lit films in an industry hostile to women directors. Susan isn't given enough credit for the feminism of her characters, which many male reviewers objected to, especially in *Making Mr Right*, a science fiction romantic comedy starring Ann Magnuson and a young, adorable John Malkovich. The indisputable Queen of Club 57, Ann Magnuson was magnificent in all her various roles on film and off, an outrageous glam-punk version of Shirley MacLaine in *Sweet Charity*. *Making Mr Right* places

Ann's female protagonist in charge of finding the perfect man (that he happens to be an android upset many male critics!). Seidelman's female characters are not your passive sex objects or dangerous femme fatales, as was the norm for women on film in the 1980s. They are reminiscent of Susan Hayward's roles in the 1940s and '50s, fast-talking intelligent women unafraid of adventure.

When I was hanging out with Seidelman, we went to a show at the stand-up comedy club Caroline's to see an up-and-coming comedienne with buzz. I'd heard she was gay. The lights went up on stage, illuminating a woman stretched atop the grand piano sound asleep. The pianist played 'To Sir with Love', and Sandra Bernhard woke up singing. She talked about high school in Arizona – 'They treated me worse than Carrie!' – and had the crowd roaring with laughter as she skewered celebrities and heckled the audience. I was wearing an apple cap cocked over one eye, and she pointed to me.

'Shouldn't you be on your way to your audition for the Dead End Kids?'

I shot back with 'Shouldn't you go back to taking your nap?'

The rest is history; we have been fast friends ever since. Besides being iconic for leading the way in comedy as a gay woman, she has never shied away from telling the truth and is one of the warmest and kindest I've known.

★ ★ ★

Speaking of the *Dead End Kids*, we started filming *The Offenders* in early 1979. Scott and Beth B had a rough storyline about a street girl (me) being kidnapped by a creep (John Lurie) for ransom money from her dad (Bill Rice). The film was a collaborative effort, and practically every downtown personality made an appearance. We shot the film episodically, each episode running at about fifteen minutes. Max's gave us a Tuesday-night residency. Each week, we'd shoot scenes, Beth and Scott would cut the film together on an ELMO 8mm/Super 8 viewer and editor, and we'd screen it on Tuesday nights, with one of the actors doing a performance. (John Lurie, Lydia Lunch, and many others also performed solo and band sets.) Max's took the bar money and the B's took the door money, which would be used to film the next fifteen minutes. This went on for six weeks. When the shooting and editing were finished, we scored the music to picture while projecting the scenes at Scott and Beth's loft on Crosby Street. One night while standing in the back by the bar at Max's, I was standing next to Robert De Niro while he grinned watching scenes of the girl gang in the film (Lydia, Pat Place, Laura Kennedy, Cynthia Sley, and myself) torturing John Lurie.

The Offenders is nuts. We scripted on the fly, us actors mostly writing our own dialogue. As the expression goes, I'm chewing the wallpaper. The movie's cast of characters, and the fact that we pulled it all off for basically nothing, says so much about the fun we had downtown in the late 1970s. I loved doing a scene with Judy Nylon where she plays a sort of guardian angel in a trench coat, and I'm crying fake tears about the plight of working-class people and the American dream. It's so bad, it's kind of good. At the end of the film, after my character's dad has been killed, our friend Kristof Kolhofer made a life-size model of Bill Rice (my father in the film), sat the dummy in the driver's seat of Scott and Beth's old Chevy Vega hatchback (with the dying clutch), and dumped the car into the East River. Not a soul batted an eyelash.

NO-LLYWOOD

As I recall, we created the soundtrack for *Vortex* mostly with Scott B. I remember screening the scenes on the wall with the B's Super 8 projector, composing the score, and recording directly to picture; Richard Edson, Brenda Alderman, the bassist in the Bloods, and myself, with guest appearances by Angel Quiñones on percussion and John Lurie on sax.

Both *The Offenders* and the B's capture of me reciting an original agit-prop poem 'The Ragazzi Manifesto' at Club 57 are now in the Museum of Modern Art's permanent film collection.

<u>The Ragazzi Manifesto</u>

For those listening who hunger
        for a taste
of the brave new soul of today

     we are the ragazzi
          the true children of fire

we alone are the image of our time
we spit on that self-consciously
          artsy era the 70s
we turn around and crush the nihilism
        of this wretched decade
with the heels of our shoes
        we have come to know
and ceased to fear
    murder
        death
            poverty

NO NEW YORK

and the loss of God

it is out of this mire
        that we uphold
            the pure innocence of our dreams
                  for we are young and thirsty for life
and naivete
                      is not spineless.

we will create a magic theater!
        we will create new languages!
                the proportions of which Antonin Artaud
could only muse upon

we extol a love of danger
but do not condone acts of
                          violence
against the audience
our weapons will be   slick pink tongues
armed with truth
            sharper than any double-edged razor blade

we proclaim our God as truth
        our goal as
                outer space
that is our place

if you must call us anything
        call us
            Star Brats
but never punks

NO-LLYWOOD

        stop.

                for the last few years
    the ragazzi have brazenly
        smashed and screamed our way
through the
        valley
                of the shadow of death

        look back.
as we march
        our fingers perched at the back of
    our throats
vomiting up the ungodly poisons that a society
            bent on destruction
insists on trying to shove down
        our throats

        listen.
the kings of the earth
        are closing their ears
to the thunder of keys
                coming on like cannons

the ragazzi will sing and shout
                'til all that they believe in
and all that they perceive
    to be true
        is through
yea it will come tumbling down

we deceive deny and

NO NEW YORK

      defy you
             we are the untouchables
                  we have slipped on leprous
skins
so that they may not touch us
              with the filthy hands
of greed and self interest

         for the spirit of ragazzi
  is like that of
     a bird

and all of the cloudscapes they darken
         cannot hinder
its flight

for all those who harken to the call
     of the spirit of
         ragazzi
I say to you
        if the shoe fits,
           dance in it.

join our procession.
the main elements of
       our theater will be
   courage
      audacity
         rebellion
and that dreaded word of words

NO-LLYWOOD

love

yes brothers and sisters
        I say
love

the ragazzi have been blessed
                with the secrets of alchemy
that will reinvent the meaning
                of the lost word

la guerre est finie
          the war is over
masculine/feminine
                yin yang yahweh
        alchemy
in the   USA

Dancing the Wild Step

James/Jamie Nares and I were together when he began brainstorming *Rome '78*.

At the time, he was on fire with ideas but also wanted support and someone to brainstorm with him. As a couple, I found myself falling into that age-old trope of the woman behind the man. The imbalance ultimately broke us up. Our last few months were all about *Rome '78*, and I went along until I couldn't any longer. He asked me to play the boy-companion of David McDermott's Caligula, which resulted in an enchanted evening spent at David and his partner Peter McGough's anachronistic apartment reading *Alice in Wonderland* by candlelight. The artist couple lived entirely in the 1920s, from the spats on their shoes to their disdain of electricity. I turned down the part; another regret. James moved out soon after the film was finished.

In my relationship with James, I realized how unaware certain men are of their entitlement; how they take their privilege for granted. Men don't often act this way with malicious intent; at least not the men I am close to. But it is wired into the male DNA of history. I sincerely believe many men don't realize how their behaviour might feel diminishing and oppressing to women. I know James never would have intended this. If I'd had the emotional intelligence to speak to him about the dynamic at the time, when she was in her male form, I'm sure she'd have been embarrassed and would have corrected, tried to be less self-involved. Our best relationships are medicines, sometimes only in retrospect. Jamie is, and always was as James, a gentle soul. Back then, trapped in a body that never felt like home.

James would shoot *Rome '78* in various stolen locations like Grant's Tomb and assorted neo-classical buildings, Central Park,

and any place in New York that might pass for ancient Rome albeit comically. The funniest shoot story is when he took a few of the gang to the American Thread Building pretending they were looking at a potential rental and, while there, unlocked the windows. Hours later, they broke in from the roof, in costume, and shot the scene. An anachronistic gender-bending comedy starring Lydia, Bradly, John Lurie, Anya, Pat, and others, *Rome '78* is genius – alongside *Born in Flames*, the best of the downtown No Wave films.

★ ★ ★

I've fallen in love many times. With *The 400 Blows*. The church bells of Pisa. The books of Jean Genet. A twilight blazing slices of pink through the cables of the Brooklyn Bridge. The music of LaBelle. A 1957 Fender Duo-Sonic guitar, candy-apple red with a cream pickguard. A leather motorcycle jacket from the 1950s. Mourning doves landing on a rooftop. A playbill from Paris featuring a black and white photograph of a couple engaged in La Danse Apache. Pasolini's *The Gospel According to St Matthew*. A 1930s fountain pen from the Salvation Army. A postcard of a nun smoking a cigarette. And a dance on East 3rd Street with James and John.

James Nares and John Lurie were both incredibly tall and skinny. James stood up straight at six-foot-eight and John hunched at around six-foot-four. I stood between them at five feet exactly. For a brief time, we three were inseparable. James and John were best friends and I was the in-between who adored their wild hearts and found comfort running around with the two of them as gigantic bookends in a city I was sometimes fearful of.

One summer night in 1977, James, John, and I marched through the desolate streets of the East Village high on our own crazy rhythms. We tap-danced down the middle of East 3rd Street beneath the streetlamps through pools of shimmering light, pantomiming our own film musical, playing off one another's rhythms while singing Leonard Bernstein's melodies from *West Side Story*.

Moments in time can show up in the memory like beautiful ghosts. That night, we created a bond that flew free of all definitions. James and John weren't anything like the macho punk or rock 'n' roll boys I knew from Cleveland. They could be playful, refreshingly childish, feminine, and unguarded. Affectionate to each other without shame, with a robust love. John and James accepted me as an androgynous creature, not expecting or projecting anything other. I imagined the men I had affairs with – especially those not brave enough to explore their homosexuality – liked me because I sometimes passed as a teenage boy in my movements and looks. We danced, every muscle like living embodiments of Descartes' 'animal spirits in the blood'. Expressing the life force of music animating the spirit through the body, dancing became a nightly practice of how I moved through the streets, in the clubs, with a vitality I could not physically suppress.

★   ★   ★

The most exciting dance moment of my life happened at the Mudd Club. I think it was Johnny Dynell on the turntables that night. Talking Heads' LP *Fear of Music* had just been released. I ran into an old friend from Cleveland on the dancefloor. I'd taken an African drumming class from Linda Thomas Jones when I was nineteen. She was majestic, an extraordinary drummer and dancer in Cleveland's Black theatre company, Karamu House. We saw each other in the crowd at Mudd and wordlessly moved toward one another as the track 'I Zimbra' came on, and we started to dance. We did not speak one word to each other, but our movements signalled every rapturous move we'd made and every word we didn't speak since our last connection. We danced . . . and we danced. The DJ segued into a Fela Kuti track and we improvised movements that I never dreamed my body could make. I've never felt the power of dance as ecstatically as in those moments.

Decades later I'd learn how much Linda Thomas Jones and I had in common in one particularly pleasing respect. She too had answered the call to adventure, taking her away from Ohio into transportive experiences across the world. Linda is now known as Mama Fasi, a Yoruba priestess and a community arts educator, splitting her time teaching drumming between her homes in the USA and Ghana.

Berlin to Rotterdam

I had left the Contortions and started performing solo shows of original songs, poems, and covers with my guitar and with backing tapes I had recorded on a Tascam cassette deck, playing the taped music from a 'ghetto blaster' miked on stage.

Scott and Beth B were organizing a short tour in Europe to show their experimental films *Black Box* and *Letters to Dad*. Brainstorming their next project, they were interested in me playing a role and invited me to join the tour, playing solo, along with Teenage Jesus and the Jerks. Lydia had replaced Bradly with her then-boyfriend Johnny O'Kane, and Jim Sclavunos was playing bass. The shows would expose Berlin and the Netherlands to what was happening in the New York No Wave scene.

We began the ten-day tour – and my first trip out of the country – in Amsterdam, playing a venue called the Melkweg. The B's projected their short films, I did a set of music and poetry, and Teenage Jesus played. It felt as if I'd landed in an anachronistic fairytale; Amsterdam was dreamy and the crowd enthusiastic, but we were in and out quickly. We travelled to play a small venue in Nijmegen, the oldest city in the Netherlands and a mere seven miles from the German border. Something strangely dark occurred between Johnny and Lydia after the Nijmegen show; we woke up the next morning at our bed and breakfast to find Lydia being carried off to a local hospital in a wheelchair. Not my story to tell, but Lydia was able to continue with the tour.

★ ★ ★

Next stop was Berlin. It was early winter 1979; Bowie and Iggy were still around, and Bowie was wrapping up his third work of the

Berlin trilogy, *Lodger*. I found Bowie's Berlin LPs *Low* and *"Heroes"* addictive, and the LPs he produced for Iggy – *The Idiot* and *Lust for Life*. I will never tire of playing the Berlin-inspired LPs. The city's stark and depressing atmosphere spoke to the reality of World War II, which had ended only thirty-four years before our visit. I was moved by the place. The incredible art nouveau Bülowstraße Station in the Schöneberg district, the Church of Memories. Many structures had not yet been rebuilt, and some shop-fronts were still riddled with bullet holes. When I asked our new German acquaintances if their parents had been in the war, the question was casually but always dismissed.

The artist Martin Kippenberger was our sponsor for the Berlin show. While the others stayed with Kippenberger, he introduced me to the formidable fashion designer Claudia Skoda who offered her home. Inspired by a mix of Weimar Berlin, punk, constructivism, and fertile imagination, Claudia's designs continue to be cutting edge and incomparable.

Kippenberger and Claudia were at the apex of Berlin's new avant-garde, and I had the honour of meeting many of the artists at its epicentre. Berlin was much more of a sister city to New York than London, London's scene being primarily about punk music and fashion. Claudia introduced me to Rainer Fetting, Salomé, and Luciano Castelli, painters dubbed the Neue Wilde. I was travelling with my Fender Duo-Sonic in a burlap sack and Rainer painted me large, running with the guitar alongside the Berlin Wall. I met the director Rosa von Praunheim and the stunning actress and costume designer Tabea Blumenschein. We started a brief affair; once the lover of Patricia Highsmith, Tabea was both partner and muse to the brilliant avant-garde filmmaker Ulrike

BERLIN TO ROTTERDAM

Ottinger. She played lead characters in many of Ulrike's films and designed costumes for such dazzlers as *The Enchantment of the Blue Sailors, Madame X, Ticket of No Return,* and *Dorian Gray in the Mirror of the Yellow Press.*

We performed at Kippenberger's club S.O. 36 in Berlin's Kreuzberg district. The club was a spartan box with two long fluorescent tube-lights in green and red which, when combined, turned the club into a glowing white cube. The scene there was amazing, with a crowd that felt like the German version of our Mudd Club back home. Based on the success of the show at S.O., I was asked to do two songs at the popular club Dschungel, famous for its mix of celebrities, intellectuals, and avant-garde artists, and a frequent hang of Bowie and Iggy. (Bowie was seeing the transsexual beauty Romy Haag during his Berlin period.) The anti-fashion ethos and the collaborations happening across disciplines in Berlin felt as exciting as downtown New York. I didn't want to leave, but we were due to return to the Netherlands. The B's had booked a show at a club in Rotterdam.

Jim Sclavunos and I decided to hang back for another day in Berlin. Because of our poor language skills, we accidentally boarded the wrong train and eventually found ourselves being tossed from that train and stranded inside East Germany. In terrible broken German, we talked a kind train attendant into letting us board a boxcar back into the West and on to the Netherlands. How we managed our way out of this misadventure and were able to navigate our way to Rotterdam remains a hilarious and confounding mystery to this day.

★ ★ ★

NO NEW YORK

The Rotterdam venue was a frightening experience. I was twenty-three years old, standing at the microphone on the stage of the small, dark club called Heavy in a rough port town, 3,600 miles away from home. Alone with my guitar and a ghetto blaster playing backing tapes of music I'd pre-recorded, trying to get through the songs, I was terrified by the packed-in crowd of Rotterdam punks, stevedores, and prostitutes, some spitting toward the stage, others clapping and yelling in Dutch. Scott and Beth B had started our night by projecting *Black Box*. Billed as a 'terrifying allegory of societal repression', Lydia Lunch brutally tortures a young guy and throws him into a black box to the accompaniment of eardrum--shaving synth throbs. The Dutch audience hurled things at the screen, some running out of the club screaming: 'Hersenspoelen! Brainwash!'

I finished the set and ran offstage where the man who had booked us in Rotterdam put his arm around my shoulder to tell me the crowd liked me; Dutch punks thought spitting on stage was a show of appreciation. Peter Graute ran a one-man record store in Rotterdam called Backstreet Records. His shop was on the Boomgaardsstraat in what was a derelict area called Cool. Backstreet was a mandatory first stop for most travelling musicians playing Rotterdam from 1976 to 1982. Peter was an avid record collector with an uncanny curatorial ear. His shop contained tons of rare releases, bootlegs, posters, and books that only an avid collector could pull from behind his counter, and he made a visitor feel like you were the only one privy to his secret stash of wonder.

★ ★ ★

BERLIN TO ROTTERDAM

It was a shaky time in my life, of feeling adrift and of wanting some type of break in the chaos of my days. Peter, the carillon towers of Rotterdam, the parks, and the fifteenth-century feeling of the Aelbrechtskolk district offered me a moment of reflection and rest.

I fell into inamorata with Rotterdam, found it beautifully evocative. Port cities still capture my imagination and set me to dreaming. Peter had a bedroom/living room and rudimentary kitchen of sorts above the shop. During workdays I'd help him in the shop sorting albums, cleaning, making coffees for visitors. His many friends often stopped by to listen to records and talk. We would shop at the open-air market on Witte de Withstraat and cook scrambled eggs mixed with fresh mussels, drink strong Douwe Egberts coffee, eat Dutch pastries like Bossche bol, and listen to records endlessly. Sometimes we'd play guitars, droney, trance-like jams. I was drinking at the time and Peter loved hash, so we smoked a lot of Lebanese Blonde, hash being legal then in the Netherlands as it is now.

The craziest moment in Rotterdam happened one night when we were strolling a rough part of town called Katendrecht or De Kaap, an area considered Chinatown and which was also its red-light district. Peter had told me about a famous Chinese woman who lived there that dealt opium and we were going to visit her. On the way, we walked past a few sex workers, many of whom were from Surinam. A very petite young woman decided she liked my looks, switched her hips over, and started soliciting me with 'Zin in een avontuur?' She was asking for an adventure. Wearing a boy's suit and my hair cropped, I must have passed, for a moment. Peter was amused as I swaggered toward her, asking whether she liked Americans. I thought she may have known I was female. As she stepped closer, her flirty expression turned to panic. 'Een vrouw! Lesbo!' She was furious, went at me like a ferocious cat, scratching me with her nails – her strength nearly alien as she knocked me to the ground, got on top, and tried to dig my eye from its socket. Peter and his friend had to drag her off me. It was the second most outrageously violent display of homophobia I'd ever experience, but I had to blame myself too, for playing trickster to a stranger. My left eye still bears the scars.

The city was demolishing an old house built during the 1600s directly opposite Backstreet Records, leading to the exile of its residents – hordes of tiny mice who apparently loved music. They'd fled the ruins and skipped across the street to the record shop looking for warmth and shelter. Although Peter was oblivious, when I started waking up to their wee squeals as they danced around on top of our covers, I knew it was time to return to New York.

Poppies and Poets

My flirtation with opiates began during a chaste romantic friendship with a filmmaker, based on our mutual admiration for surreal daydreaming and all things Moroccan, including Paul and Jane Bowles, and Eberhardt. We also shared a love for certain filmmakers, Bresson and Fellini in particular.

Lara and I hit it off immediately. She had a lovely sensuality about her, was beautiful with long hair swept over one eye, a warm, easy smile, and a quickness to laugh at life's absurdities. The city felt both haunted and haunting, begging for its stories to be told, and you just needed the right friend to indulge in the creation of poetic fantasylands. Not a stretch in the ghost town of New York City at the time.

Isabelle Eberhardt smoked kif, a psychoactive hashish, and the Bowles were also kif-smokers. There was no kif in New York but Lara and I were able to score something much better: opium. We convinced one another it wouldn't hurt to experiment with the tears of the poppy. My rooftop at night would be the perfect place and time to light up. Performing the ritual as it had been described, we placed the little tar ball on tin foil, lighting it from below and watching it sizzle, then sucking up the smoke through a rolled bill. The high took its time coming on. We kept giggling, asking each other if the other felt it yet. It was subtle and crept up on me like a caress, made my limbs feel liquid, and sent my head into languid dreams. I tried to kiss Lara – of course I did – and she laughed at me while I laughed at myself. Chastely, we rolled around a lot that night because we felt so incredibly good, the few responsibilities waiting for us in the real world seeming absurd and inconsequential. The drug brought on a sexy, lazy happiness. We spent hours that summer night on my roof, gazing down and across into windows of apartment buildings, weaving stories and interconnecting the lives of the bodies we saw there moving in lamp light, or prone on beds illuminated by the blue flicker of black and white TVs.

Friendships then were usually intense. If they didn't burn out quickly, you sometimes simply drifted toward other lighthouses. It is too seldom we understand or feel the resonance of a moment when we are in it. I imagined heroin would be like opium, but cheaper and more available – a dance into a warm, sensual womb of safety. For the broken running from a world of pain, opiates were too perfect an elixir. The oblivion that opiates bestow on the seeker could be a welcome escape, but I never got along with heroin. When I was high on smack, I vomited constantly and had visions of actual demons invading me. Heroin's embrace felt satanic. Luciferian. While others revel in its womblike liquidity, for me it felt like a portal into an evil I could not stomach, literally and poetically. People love to say drug addicts are spiritually bankrupt, the scum of the earth. But when you see an addict, there is usually some trauma or pain there that they cannot imagine being strong enough to conquer. That, or they are spiritually lazy about reaching a state of nirvana, choosing to take the shortcut into sweet nothingness. The oblivion one reaches through heroin is a dark journey, an existential descent into an eye of a God reversed; the source of an all-enveloping darkness.

★ ★ ★

Janet Hamill and I were introduced soon after my arrival in New York in 1977. She became my mentor. Under Janet's wing, I learned how to feel words in the deepest sense. She guided me into the mystic, coaxing me to follow my imaginings and to visualize words as colour and insight. A genie of the alphabet, like the name of her poem, she illuminated, and I was fortunate to be informed by that light.

She had a first-floor apartment on Vandam Street in SoHo and opened her home to me to live, read, and write, while leading me to a more nuanced understanding of literature and poetry. When I lived with Janet, we both worked at bookstores; she at Cinemabilia, I at Spring Street Books. After work we'd prepare a simple dinner and talk poetry – of words, of film. Poetry of a voile ribbon or the boat-necked shirt of a sailor. Janet would read me a poem she was working on, and I'd painfully eke out a few words on the typewriter, praying for her approval. With Janet I read Yeats, Eliot, Hart Crane. She turned me on to Federico García Lorca's concept of the duende of Andalusian Spain: neither muse nor angel, the duende is a mischievous imp, guardian of mysteries lying dormant in the body. The duende dares you to grant it access to your most secret emotional wounds, to wake and shake. Only the bravest artists allow the duende to wrestle inside the wounds to push and pull and play, then to emerge in an alchemical dance that graces the artist's work with a commanding, blood-fuelled essence.

Janet grew up in New Jersey, and as a little girl spent her time gazing across the Hudson River toward New York City. She majored in English at Glassboro State College, where she met Patti Smith, who would later refer to her as a mentor and has been a lifelong friend and collaborator. After graduation, Janet moved to New York and began her life as a poet; writing, working in bookstores, travelling through Egypt, Ethiopia, Kenya, Marrakesh, Tangier, spinning dreams and visions into poems, into works of deep beauty and mysticism. She began reading her work in New

NO NEW YORK

York City in 1975 when she published her first book of poetry, *Troublante*.

* * *

I did my first public reading of 'The Ragazzi Manifesto' with Janet in 1978 and played drone guitar behind her as she read from her searingly beautiful poem 'Belladonna'. The intensity of her reading is more incantation than spoken word. Electric guitar awash in echo, I'd pick at the strings, attempting to paint a flock of delicate birds around the dark, glittering ship of words she, the grand mariner, creates and creates again.

Janet's work is at turns enigmatic, surreal, alchemical. Her canvas is a deep and breathtaking sea of chance, of shameless greens and blues, 'dark blue stronger than the Flemish blue of hummingbirds'. A place where Buster Keaton turns somersaults in air beneath a butterfly umbrella, where hands brush a chest, coming away with diamond dust, and the night is inhabited by saurian daemons, mendicants, wild dogs. Vermilion tents and altars of alabaster where 'Victorian dark-eyed sleep embraces you with embroidered flowers and the deep song of subterranean waterfalls'.

A poet shawafa, Janet Hamill is a wise woman, a witch, a jinn, and I look back on my time with her as sacred. She inspired me to seek out esotericism, to continue exploring Sufism and various mysticisms. It was during my stay with Janet that I wrote the story I'd submit to Paul Bowles. When I approach her poems, I say 'Quli Taslim!' (I submit to the powers of the jinn), and am unafraid of the fires I discover there, for they never cease to warm me into new dreams, new journeys.

Women musicians and performers,
and bands featuring women musicians in fundamental roles,
playing New York City
1975–1980s

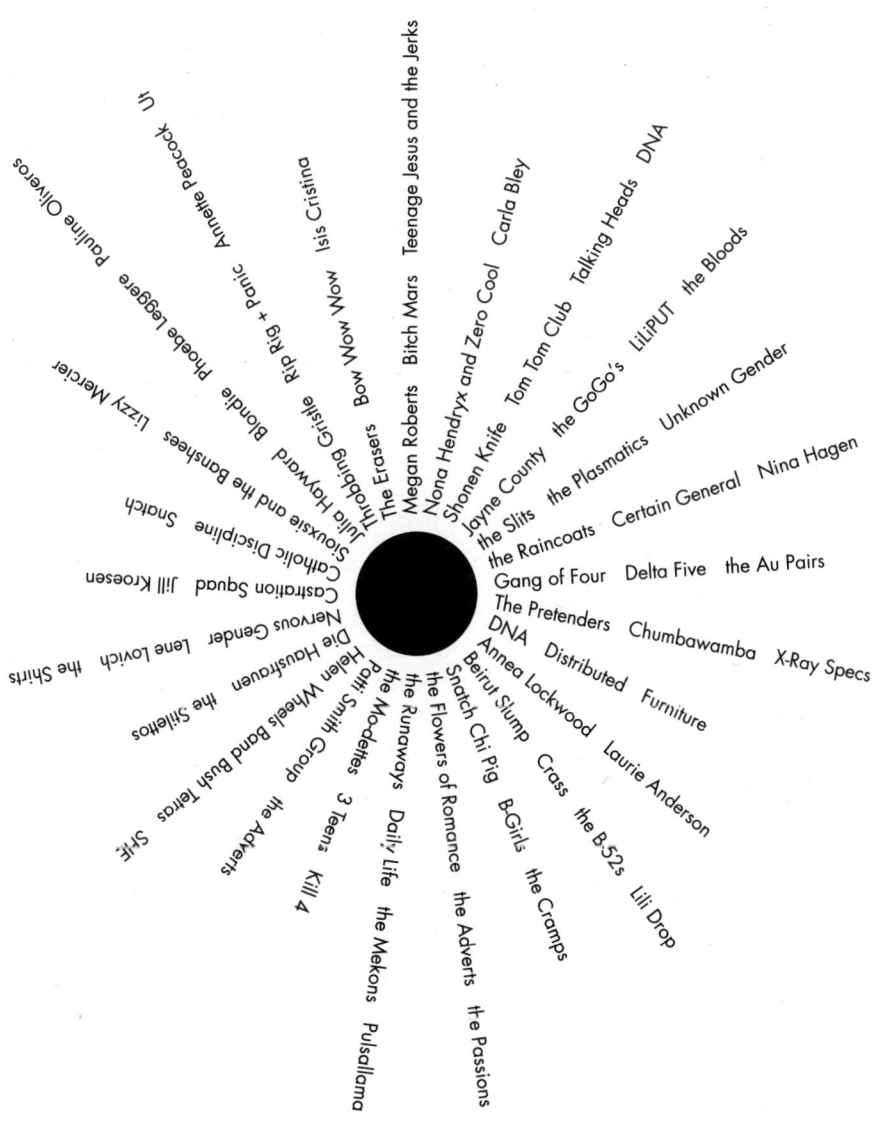

Girl Gang Dreaming

When I wasn't under the poetic tutelage of Janet, I ran the streets of New York. Dancing at the Mudd Club and with the queens at the Pyramid, hanging out at Club 57 on St Mark's Place between First and Second Avenues. At Club 57, I watched the brilliant Klaus Nomi sing arias while John Sex indulged in crazy antics with the fabulous Ann Magnuson, and Dany Johnson played the turntables. And you never knew what might be happening at the Pyramid on Avenue A. So many great gender-f•ck shows took place there: John Kelly channelling Maria Callas (what a voice!), Ethyl Eichelberger breathing fire as Medea, the hilarity of Hapi Phace . . . these weren't just drag shows but high-art performances. Actors Steve Buscemi and Mark Boone Jr were regulars, doing their Buscemi & Boone comedy skits. RuPaul would get his start at the Pyramid in 1984.

All the while, I cannot remember a time when I wasn't dreaming of starting my very own all-girl band.

Goldie and the Gingerbreads were the first all-girl rock 'n' roll band in America, starring Genya Ravan on lead vocals. After having rocked a Warhol party in 1963, they were immediately signed by Ahmet Ertegun to Atlantic but were under-promoted and never had the hit record they truly deserved. The closest they came was their recording of 'Can't You Hear My Heartbeat', a minor hit for them in England, scooped by Herman's Hermits. Their slightly rough and ragged quality felt closer to the great '60s garage bands like the Music Machine or the Shadows of Knight, in large part due to rock organist Margo Lewis, who knew how to beat a dirty groove on the keys. Genya Ravan and Lulu had a similar vibe going on, but Genya was rougher around the edges. She had a distinctive, fierce-kitten type of voice capable of ripping out a perfectly scratchy rock wail with spot-on timing.

NO NEW YORK

In 1964 I was too young to know anything about Goldie and the Gingerbreads, but just old enough and aware when Fanny came around in 1972. Fanny was the second all-girl rock group to confidently stride into the world of man-rock and play as good as the boys. Sisters June and Jean Millington started the band and were both fantastic rock musicians. I had been dreaming of being in an all-girl band since I was ten, and Fanny was my first real manifestation of hearing the dream on wax.

It was Suzi Quatro's '48 Crash' that sent me over the edge – a girl, playing the crunchy glam rock that was all the rage. Playing bass too, sporting leather pants and vest, and singing with sexy rock-star attitude. This confirmed the reality of what once seemed like an impossible fantasy; girls not only rocking but rocking hard.

★   ★   ★

When I left the Contortions, I played solo at places like Tier 3 and Max's. I created my own backing music on a four-track cassette player with a Roland CompuRhythm, which had a poxy little sound, but it kept a cool beat. I found a few wind-up jewellery boxes, a toy piano, and a melodica, and created weird sonic audioscapes that I'd mix down to backing tapes, performing alone with my Fender Duo-Sonic and a digital delay pedal. This was a continuation of the type of stuff I was doing on tour with Lydia and the B's in Europe. At one solo gig at Max's, I performed a rendition of Brecht and Weill's 'Pirate Jenny' from *The Threepenny Opera*, replete with choruses in German (the A&R man who would eventually sign me to Geffen Records was in the audience that night).

I wrote songs that flowed more like poetry, inspired by films like Pasolini's *Accattone*. Aside from the Brecht song, I wasn't really using the larger scope of my singing voice for fear I'd be ridiculed, like when I made the mistake of being overheard belting out a soul tune once by John Lurie, who snarled, 'What, is that what you wanna do, sing *the blues?*'

There really hadn't been an all-girl band of consequence since Fanny, and then came the Runaways – working-class girls without a stitch of art rock sensibility whatsoever. They had the chops to pull off a serious rock sound. Cherie Currie's vocals and Joan Jett's hard, chunky guitar work aside, their hit 'Cherry Bomb' was just another male-manipulated chicken-hawk's dream of young women demanding sex, a predecessor to Madonna's woman-as-sexually-empowered bait-'n'-switch. I kept dreaming of an all-girl band that followed Patti Smith's heretical salvo, the opening of the first track of her debut LP *Horses*, 'Gloria'. About exactly whose sins Jesus did and did not die for.

Pat Place and Laura Kennedy created the Bush Tetras with a very cool heavy-grooving drummer named Dee Pop. They asked me to sing, and I was totally floored by the sound they were pumping out; with her unique and hypnotic sense of rhythm and brilliant distorted sound, Pat's guitar was large enough to fill all the textural sonic space. Add Laura's bubbling bass which always sounded like a sonic underwater boom, and Dee's Scott Asheton-inspired, nut-crushing rhythm, and this was a unique noise. Like the Stooges but funky and mesmeric. I loved their sound but longed to move into other terrain as a singer. After playing skronky noise with the Contortions, a return to melody beckoned. Anything remotely close to a pop melody had no place in the Bush Tetras, and they needed another type of front person to match their sonic assault. It was a scene where being naturally good at something wasn't in vogue. A range of more than four notes, a strong melodic sense, and a vibrato was considered utterly uncool, unless you were Nina Hagen or Klaus Nomi: both had extraordinary voices, operatic to an alien degree, and über-theatrical.

I did one gig with the Bush Tetras where I stood at the side of the stage and wailed into the microphone, straight vowels, no lyrics. High on something at the time, I didn't even step foot on stage, intimidated by the sonic riot of the band who must have been playing out of Marshall amps with so loud of an assault, I had to hold my ears. The size of the crowd was as big and boisterous as the sound. David Bowie was there that night. I always imagined him writing the album *Scary Monsters* based on what he saw and heard in New York between 1978 and 1979.

That night made it obvious that I was not fated to be their lead singer, so I went my way. They took on Cynthia Sley, another girl from Cleveland who'd made the exodus. Cynthia knew how to do the talking thing that was in vogue in No Wave. Compensating for her lack of range, she turned her lyrics and monotone into a repetitive vocal style that worked perfectly for the Tetras, and together they moulded a unique sound with cool lyrical hooks – a perfect fit for the No Wave zeitgeist.

Bloods Light

Kathy Rey was a beauty – she had black hair cut Stones-style to frame her face, and full lips shaped in a cupid's bow with a little bit of an Elvis sneer at one corner. The whole effect was softened by sad brown eyes that slanted down a bit at the ends. And she looked fantastic in leather pants. Her Mexican family had emigrated to Texas and moved on to Minneapolis. Like most of us, she came to New York City following the siren song of Patti Smith, aching for new sounds and sensibilities.

I told her about wanting to form an all-girl band. She played the electric guitar. I had abandoned my usual mental-institution haircut, and we planned for her to cut my hair, and maybe play a bit of music together too.

She was blaring the Pretenders' first album when I walked in the door. Vocally, Chrissie Hynde was more my style than Patti Smith. I loved her vibrato, which reminded me of 1960s singers like Dusty Springfield, Lulu, or Dionne Warwick. Kathy had on her leather pants and a cool vest with a white sleeveless T-shirt underneath and a bunch of leather strips tied around her wrists. An electric-blue Squire guitar lay on the couch, waiting like a patient girlfriend. Every place my eyes landed provided another bolt of excitement; Iggy's *The Idiot* album cover, a leather jacket thrown with just the right casual arc on a chair, a mirror covered in trace marks of white powder, and a colour Polaroid of Kathy recently used as platform for razor-bladed stardust.

She posed like a Fiorucci model while cutting my hair and Chrissie wailed in the background. I shook pieces of hair over my eyes and laughed when she was through. It looked good. Then she plugged in, slung her guitar low on her hip and started playing the chords to 'Ready for Love' by Bad Company. I knew all the words and sang along. I always liked Paul Rodgers' vocals – something I'd never admit to No Wavers.

We fell into the song like we'd been playing together for years and I nearly started crying – it was so thrilling to sing actual notes again. And to have a girl playing electric guitar next to me who liked a good melody as much as I did. We knew what we were doing was old school and we didn't care. We kept stealing looks at each other and cracking up. She showed off to me by playing 'The Wait' along with the Pretenders' recording and we laughed ourselves sick while I tried to mimic Chrissie Hynde's speedy vocal. Kathy lived up to her posturing. She could play the guitar, hard, and a little sloppy, which worked fine for me. We decided to start a band right there and then, celebrating with a line of coke and a tequila shot.

I was twenty-four years old but still an emotionally stunted kid from the streets, and would remain that way for quite some time, due in no small part to the extended use of various unhealthy panaceas. We all tended to operate on automatic when it came to dealing with any past hurts, ramming any pain down into the deep. Drugs became a balm that kept you pain-free and in the present, an often-addled idea of present.

I knew nothing when it came to building any semblance of a smart life for myself; healing the traumas of my past was the furthest thing from my mind. I had no family, and only a few friends. Could barely hold on to a job. What I was sure of, with a shattering clarity that only cocaine can heighten in your heart and head, was that the moment had finally come; I'd found the Keith to my Mick.

Kathy and I started hanging out regularly, playing cover songs, drinking at the nameless gay bar we called The Bar on the corner of East 4th Street and Second Avenue. The mischievous elfin writer

BLOODS LIGHT

Gary Indiana was a fixture at The Bar. I adored him. Gary was often extremely drunk (like me) and inclined to bare his loneliness, weeping openly, and there was a lot of hugging and maudlin boozing and quoting poets like Dylan Thomas and Oscar Wilde and moaning about getting laid often but being perpetually single. When Kathy and I were drunk and coked to the gills at The Bar, it wasn't unusual to see us outside in the snow, jumping on to the hoods of random parked cars, howling at the moon, and provoking giggles from a shivering Gary.

Going out to see bands made us more antsy about putting together our own band. I don't know if the Bloods would ever have been born had it not been for the Festival of October 1980. Lesbian power couple Peggy Shaw and Lois Weaver were touring Europe in the late 1970s with the LGBTQ+ group Hot Peaches, which included Marsha P. Johnson (the trans activist on the frontline of the Stonewall Riots of 1969), when they came up with the idea. Peggy and Lois were inspired by the way Europeans were combining film, performance, theatre, dancing, and socializing into festivals, which was not happening in New York City, especially for gay women. To meet the need, the Women's One World Café (WOW) became a lesbian performance festival created by Peggy and Lois, the regal Pop and Mom of the lesbian scene, along with Pamela Camhe and Jordy Mark. Women from eight countries performed, and European and New York lesbians began collaborating on ideas and practices that would also bring many of us over to Europe.

★ ★ ★

At WOW, Kathy and I met Annie (now Anderson) Toone, as well as women from the Netherlands, Germany, and Italy, some who'd become our girlfriends. We also met the fantastic Minou. Minou was Dutch, possibly part Surinamese or Indonesian, and was based in Amsterdam. She ferried performers back and forth across the Atlantic. Once we were a fully fledged band, Minou arranged for us to perform at the first all-women's music festival happening in Berlin in June 1981 and would also bring us to the Netherlands for a tour. The fact of us being an all-women rock band was novelty enough to get us booked in most New York clubs, and in Europe. Despite the novelty, we didn't disappoint. At first.

Annie Toone was short (like me) with a tremendous overbite (like mine), which made a lot of people assume we were sisters. She had a high-octane personality with a sharp, aggressive edge – quite the opposite of Kathy, who was laid back to the point of being languid. Unlike my own percussive keyboard stylings (I couldn't tell a fifth from a major), Annie knew basic music theory and played keyboards well. She had a good sense of timing and in some ways was more musically competent than Kathy. Yet what Kathy didn't know on the side of music theory, she compensated for with style. Annie's keyboard style skewed more toward Ray Manzarek of the Doors than the Stones. She loved the blues. Her personal sartorial splendour was about hippie scarves and brown leather pants topped with a Flock of Seagulls haircut. Lots of leather pouches and a punky swagger on a five-foot-tall frame completed the picture. Kathy, Annie, and I were boyish to an extreme, yet the three of us wore eyeliner and sometimes lipstick. I often hit the stage in flimsy T-shirts with no bra and a fedora or newsboy cap. Kathy wore her usual black leather pants, a sleeveless tee, and kohl-rimmed eyes.

Annie also played harmonica. When she really got going, she'd wail on a mouth-harp like the crazed progeny of Little Walter and Big Mama Thornton. She was a good keyboard player and a great blues harmonica player but she really wanted to be a lead singer. There can't be two lead singers in a rock band, and we were hardly aiming for the Bee Gees. This misaligned desire would ultimately help sink the band's leaky ship.

Annie was also immersed in the occult; Crowley and his *Book of Thoth*, *The Egyptian Book of the Dead*, the Hermetic Order of the Golden Dawn. Darker arts, lighter elements of alchemy, and plenty of astrology were thrown in for good measure. We shared a fascination for the ouroboros, a mystical symbol of a serpent eating its own tail representing the cyclical nature of time. I was intrigued by esoterism more in the sense of the comparative mysticisms of world religions, philosophies, and alchemy. The idea of Mary Magdalene as Jesus's chosen disciple and her erasure's haunt on civilization, haunted me.

Kathy and I had a friend named Maggie who worked at Samuel Weiser's bookstore. Next to the Strand, Weiser's was my favourite bookstore in New York City. I hung out there discovering books on theosophy and Gnosticism. Maggie hooked me up with real (and sometimes fully nicked) discounts. Mine and Annie's interests in esotericism made for a lot of intense discussion at our hangouts, mixed with spurts of music-making, drug euphoria, and visions of wild girls ruling the world – a new world we were committed to bringing to life.

The band needed a name. We'd heard about the Slits in England and wanted to come up with something equally female and irreverent. The Bloods kind of appalled me, but it stuck and there seemed to be much hilarity when we passed the name around among friends. It was street, it was female. We hung out and rehearsed at Kathy's apartment on East 10th Street across from the Russian bathhouse. We smoked too many cigarettes and took turns buying pizza, coffees, smokes, chicken wings. I was often broke and would mooch cigarettes and food off the band and my friends, which annoyed people to no end. But when I had money, I gave it away without a second thought. The ashtrays were always overflowing, and *The Idiot*, *Horses*, and the Pretenders' first LP blared from the stereo. Annie had a Casio keyboard and both she and Kathy would plug into a small amp. I'd sing loud in the room without amplification while we wrote songs, wanting to have at least five ready for auditions. Initially it was just the three of us, feeling we had the beginnings of something great; not only a girl band but one that played rock 'n' roll with teeth.

We felt we were truly unlike anything that had come before us. Cocaine has a way of inciting delusions of grandeur, yet it was true we were part of a movement that had never occurred previously: women picking up instruments and claiming their voice in defiance of rock's male dominion. A bassist responded to an ad we'd placed in the *Village Voice*, a girl with a Midwestern rock 'n' roll style and a mop of curly black hair that reminded us of the Mott the Hoople album cover. Her name was Ann Phelan and she became our first bass player. Finding a woman drummer proved more challenging but finally someone reached out: a hippie from the West Coast named Kathleen (Leen) Campbell.

Leen is your typical 'granola' lesbian: Birkenstocks, Tibetan undershirts, turquoise jewellery, sprouts, and kale . . . all of it. She was organic before the word ever entered the vernacular, and she had the sweetest disposition. A great drummer, metronome-solid with swing and eager to please, she'd always ask what type of rhythm we were looking for on the songs, and her simple, tasty fills were nothing like the grandstanding most young drummers are prone toward. When she left the audition, we were blown away excited yet got a kick out of poking good-humoured fun at her Woodstock personality – *Mean Leen the drumming machine / Doesn't eat meat, it's why she's so sweet!* Even tough little punks like us couldn't help but be charmed by her. To see the light filling her face when she called us *Hey Blood!* and slapped us each high-five was a moment next to heaven. Kathleen didn't drink or do drugs, but she was definitely one of us, another girl musician who loved girls and always dreamed of being in an all-girl band.

As a lead singer I could hold a crowd by being a hot mess, to put it mildly. In fact, when I look at some of my drunken performances now, I cringe at the macho posturing. I truly thought that drinking and drugs would improve my performances by making me less inhibited and nervous, more open to channelling some type of inner demon-angel in my voice, like, *Hey, it worked for Billie Holiday*, which was a terrible misrepresentation of Lady Day's vocal prowess. It must have been hilarious for some, to see me strutting around in what I thought was a close imitation of Jagger yet appearing more like the type of feckless street pimp I'd automatically run from. I forced my voice into a butch phrasing, a deliberate dumbing-down of range and tone to sound 'punk' while also trying to blend with Annie. She insisted on lots of harmonies and often on doubling the lead vocal. It may have been unconscious, but Annie seemed to think we shared equal 'lead singer' billing. I had to compete with her volume and compromise my singing even further. She insisted on singing lead on a song she wrote called 'Bleeding Culture'. The song begins with her screaming staccato yelps like she was receiving shock treatments. But the fun we were having, the sisterhood and comradery of the band, eclipsed any problems, and we were never contentious with each other in the beginning. I had spent my life longing for a sense of family and freedom as a young woman. Next to the girls in Blossom Hill, the Bloods was the closest I'd come. We were a bona fide all-girl band, a true anomaly in rock 'n' roll. And we were family.

Showing softness in song, lyrically or vocally, was impossible. I was intensely defensive after a childhood of abuse. Traits I equated with femininity (gentleness, vulnerability) were anathema to me. I saw life from the perspective of watching my mother's pain and the roles women played in reality and on film; women as victims of oppression. Instead of seizing agency and fighting against it, women usually gave up, victimizing themselves by subjugating their souls to men. Culturally and politically, being a woman meant weakness; being a tough-boy gamin with attitude was a far better gender to dwell within. And to pull it off, I needed to 'take courage' in drink and drugs. The most vulnerability I managed in the Bloods was in our song 'Puppet', a slow blues disclaiming the role of the controlled woman. The only other humans I trusted in that moment were queer women, and girls who acted like boys. Tough and cool. Gay. Bad boys were the ones who always had the adventures and got the cool girls, so bad boy I'd be. It would take what has felt like lifetimes and the grace I found in certain mystical teachings to allow myself the embrace of being one with my incarnation – in the body and psyche of a woman embracing the spectrum of gender as not bifurcated, but multi-faceted and fluid.

BLOODS LIGHT

I was listening to opera at the time, and we wrote a song called 'Turandot' about a potential lover testing the limits. One of the better songs we wrote, 'Blue Chevrolet', contained lyrics that expressed our predilection for both politics and the esoterics of gender. We created the character Johnny Belinda as stand-in for our internal union of male and female, dark and light, searching for a love capable of uniting the two.

As soon as we had enough songs to do a full set, we were playing back-to-back gigs through 1981. We debuted at the Mudd Club in February that year and played several gigs in our first six months – at Max's, Hurrah's, Club 57. Frank Roccio, manager of the Peppermint Lounge, loved the Bloods. He paid us well and often filled our dressing room with all the liquor we could (or couldn't) handle. For the brief year and a half we played together, the Bloods opened for and played on bills with the Clash, Strange Party, Richard Hell, Adam and the Ants, Question Mark and the Mysterians, the Fall, Van Morrison, the Delta Five, the Au Pairs, Herman Brood, John Cooper Clarke, R.E.M., and the Passions. The Bloods were an anomaly, and probably to some, a bit of a freak show due to our shameless dykey stage presence.

We'd often hang out at Bleecker Bob's, where the downtown set went to buy the newest releases. Bob had seen us play and didn't mince words when he told us that guys in the music industry thought we were a joke. To them we were a bunch of crazed lesbians, and no matter how well we played, no one would touch us with a bargepole. His pitch to get us to record a single with him was bizarre reverse psychology. He wanted to convince us that we were despised and would go nowhere without him. It worked because, in a sense, it was true. Aside from our beloved fanbase, word on the street was that we were out of control. Queer, bad-news psychopaths. Although we played with many boy bands who accepted us, homophobia was ever-present.

Danny Heaps was working for the New Music Seminar and had seen the band and complimented my vocals, but the band being outrageously queer was a joke to him. He'd make snide, condescending remarks, implying that I must be kidding to think anything would ever happen for the Bloods. We knew it wasn't going to be easy for us. None of the women musicians we admired were queer; Patti Smith, Chrissie Hynde, Tina Weymouth, the fabulous Debbie Harry. We loved Debbie for being her effortlessly sexy femme self; Debbie was street-savvy, the first femme pop-punk singer with an authentic street sensibility in look and lyric. She had the subtle curl to her lips, and would often sneer if the lyric required teeth, an ironic flip to the usual female lead singer presentation. Blondie were in a class all by themselves, and Debbie's singular authenticity was magnetic.

I believe a lot of men in the business – bookers, journalists, certainly record company suits – thought of the Bloods as an entertaining aberration because of our brazen lesbianism in song and on stage. However, freak shows sell, especially to carnival barkers. Bleecker Bob took us on and recorded two Bloods songs to release as a single on his own label. He hired Mick Rock to take our picture, a thrilling moment because of his classic photos of David Bowie and Iggy Pop. When Bleecker Bob presented us with a contract, we nearly had a communal heart attack; he was asking for five pints of Bloods. Bob wanted us to sign a Colonel Tom Parker management-meets-record-deal (the Colonel managed Elvis) where we'd have to give him 50 per cent – half of every penny we earned after he recouped every penny he spent on us. We tried to negotiate, but Bob wouldn't budge. The worm turned, we didn't sign the deal, and Bob was livid to the point where we were petrified to step into his store. Needless to say, the record was never released.

With all the macho business and the drugs, Ann Phelan decided to quit. We were left high and dry without a bassist and a show coming up at CBGB, so we put an ad in the *Village Voice*. Brenda Alderman answered.

Bloods 2.0

BRENDA ALDERMAN ADELE BERTIE KATHY REY KATHLEEN CAMPBELL ANNE TOONE

The Bloods

Brenda Alderman was (and still is) a self-professed Black nerd, cute and tall with glasses and a very straightforward demeanour. She blew us away immediately, playing her bass with an effortless funk feel. Brenda lived with her family in Queens and was the only one among us who drove a car. Her father had served in World War II in the Red Ball Express, a predominantly African-American-staffed convoy that brought arms and supplies to American troops in the months after D-Day as they left Normandy to fan out through Europe. Brenda grew up with a stable family life and soul music, a winning combo for an aspiring musician. In essence, she was a good girl and never did drugs, hardly drank. She was gay, kind of boyish, but very low key about it all and not 'out' to her family.

Brenda plays bass better than most men I've heard. She spanks the strings, spanks hard, but can also play deep, bottom-heavy groove when called for. Brenda was the musical elixir that gave us an edge as a band. Her dedication to holding down the bottom with Kathleen was phenomenal, especially considering Kathy, Annie, and myself, aside from rehearsing, didn't practise to save our lives. When we asked Brenda to join, she immediately planned to get together with Kathleen to firm up the rhythm section. By the time we played Berlin, they were tight as a fist.

★ ★ ★

We'd heard about the Michigan Womyn's Music Festival, a women-only Woodstock on acres of land in northern Michigan. Before I moved to New York, when I lived in a lesbian-separatist communal house in Cleveland for a few months, I remember how excited the women were about what would become known as the lesbian-oriented MichFest. The lesbians I lived with were teachers and bank clerks, saving their money for the prospect of taking a summer vacation in the woods with music, with only women playing and hearing it. MichFest became their yearly highlight, a celebration of being queer women together and a moment of respite from the punishing climate of patriarchy for women and lesbians across the world.

Although MichFest preferred folk-leaning female artists, by 1981 we heard they were open to women rock bands, so we sent them a group photo and the demo songs we'd recorded for Bleeker Bob. The lesbian-feminist organizers deemed us 'too male-identified', and we were rejected.[1] Experiencing yet another dollop of homophobia from our supposed sisters seemed ridiculous. We laughed it off.

Word came back that Minou was thrilled with our demo tape when it arrived in Amsterdam. She immediately booked us on a tour of the Netherlands, and we were added to the line-up of bands to play the first ever all-women rock concert in Berlin, the Venus Weltklang Festival, alongside bands like the Slits, the Au Pairs, Malaria!, LiLiPUT, Unknown Gender, and the Delta Five. Good news kept on coming: the Clash's manager, Bernie Rhodes, asked us to open for the Clash at their notorious run of shows at Bond's in Times Square.

On 4 June 1981, the Bloods and the Bush Tetras opened for the Clash during that residency. Joe Strummer was a lovely guy

---

[1] Two and a half decades later, queer-core band Tribe 8 performed at MichFest with singer Lynn Breedlove brandishing a strap-on. I attended MichFest as a backing singer for Gail Ann Dorsey in the 1990s and felt euphoric about being on a planet of thousands of women, many topless, listening to the soul-stirring music of acts like Jane Siberry and Toshi Reagon. The wonders and politics of MichFest in all its complexity is a topic worthy of its own book.

and very supportive of women's bands. In anticipation of our gig, Kathy and I went to see the Clash the night that Grandmaster Flash and the Furious Five opened. The show is legendary for exposing the initial tensions that existed between white punks and hip-hop. Joe and the Clash were a political band committed to breaking through boundaries of genre as well as calling out the hypocrisy of racism, corruption, and the war machine. Grandmaster Flash and the Furious Five were one of the top rap groups of the moment, and their style was trailblazing. Idiot punks in the crowd started booing and throwing things at the band; racism disguised as punk anarchy. They were not having this new sound called hip-hop, ignorant of the fact that both bands on stage were fighting the powers that be.

The outdoor concert we played at Tompkins Square Park was memorable for several reasons. The entire affair was very out, very queer. Fabulous Lady Bunny was the emcee and David Wojnarowicz's band 3 Teens Kill 4 played, with Julie Hair and Brian Butterick aka Hattie Hathaway. It was a gorgeous day, and the audience was filled with dykes, punks, and queens. A Bloods fan slid a box filled with copies of Valerie Solanas's *S.C.U.M. Manifesto* onto the stage. We were on fire, performing the song 'Undercover Nation' that we'd recorded for the film *Born in Flames*, while I tossed copies of the book out to eager fans. Lizzie Borden was filming, and the footage would later be included as part of a montage in *Born in Flames*. We were riding high, quite literally. It may have been mescaline, but we had also started snorting speedballs, a mixture of cocaine and heroin that bestowed a euphoric buzz with enough speed to keep you excited and enough smack to keep you relaxed. The best of both worlds. This habit would soon become too serious for comfort. If they knew about the drugs, Brenda and Kathleen were not commenting, and certainly not imbibing.

One of the Blood's main groupies, Chris H., idolized Kathy, who wouldn't bed her, but that didn't stop Chris from being Kathy's willing servant. She followed Kathy like a shadow, carried her guitar, scored drugs for her, trimmed her nails, and shined her shoes if required. Another girl we called Big D was around too, and I'd heard Chris and Big D were junkies. One day, I walked into one of the Blood's apartments and a group were hovering surreptitiously in the kitchen around the stove where an acrid, burning smell hung in the air. I wandered toward their huddle and saw the belt being pulled tight around an upper arm. The works. The spoon being cooked over the stove. A woman was tied off and about to shoot up. The seriousness of it nearly knocked me over. I had seen a taste of this with James Chance and Anya and was adamant that heroin was poison; as so baldly stated by Brion Gysin at the Nova Convention: *junk is no good, baby*. Naively, I didn't think speedballs counted because the smack was cut with coke and snorted. Kid stuff.

For several weeks I would snort a little bit of smack while girls were shooting up all around me. I was judgemental about fixing, which didn't go over well – the junkie gang didn't want me near if I didn't imbibe, in their eyes meaning I imagined myself morally superior. Brenda and Kathleen stayed well away, and if they suspected, I don't think they understood the seriousness of how it might affect the band until much later. I didn't understand either, at first. Eventually, I used a needle. I couldn't bear to be on the outside of that inner circle. But (fortunately) I hated smack, hated the feeling of being utterly lost in a comfort I knew could be deadly.

BLOODS 2.0

I would vomit my guts out while internally hallucinating sinister beings out to get me.

Smack was cheap and strong. Where did it all come from? Friends you'd never imagine getting involved were crawling through holes in abandoned Alphabet City buildings to score, while others waited in lines in the cold for a bucket to descend from a tenement window with cellophane packets bearing skull-and-crossbones stamps. China White, Mexican Brown, Black Tar, DOA. At one point, it seemed like too many women I knew had these obligatory bedside props; a copy of Burroughs' *Junkie* and a fire-scarred teaspoon. These were the wild girls turned perforated girls, wanting to kill the fear of being free of gendered restrictions, wanting to fill the holes in their hearts with something warm, golden brown. Many of the girls and boys I hung out with were junkies for a time. Some recovered, others would die young because of it, or die a bit older from undetected Hep C, a liver disease contracted via needle that would only worsen over time, sometimes complicated by an extremely toxic treatment called interferon.

The trouble with heroin is that first taste. The devil always snares you with a kiss.

Lock Up Your Daughters

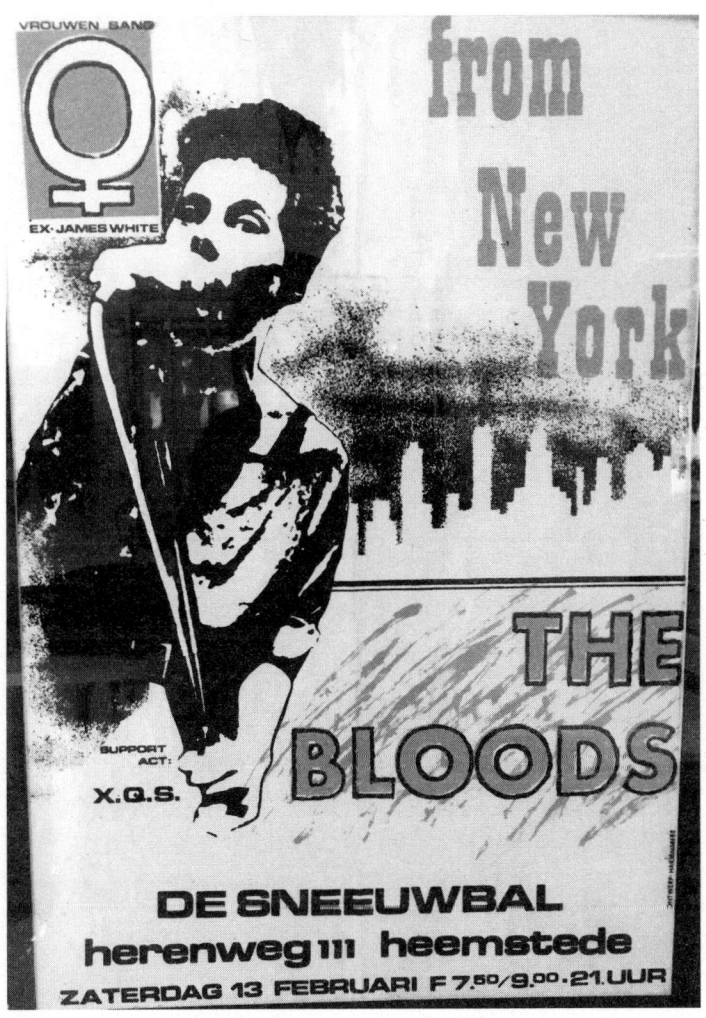

The Bloods arrived in Berlin in the June of 1981 to play the Venus Weltklang Festival, billed as the First International Women's Rock Festival. The venue was the Tempodrome, a large circus tent next to the Berlin Wall by Potsdamer Platz. Most of us stayed in a lesbian squat organized by Martina, the German woman Kathy had hooked up with during WOW. Thanks to Claudia Skoda's hospitality, I stayed at her loft again and, before the show, went out with her to the Dschungel on Nürnberger Strasse – Berlin's version of Studio 54 and hangout of Bowie and Iggy – to meet Tabea Blumenschein. She didn't speak English and because I was preoccupied with the band, it was the last time I'd see her. We Bloods were already tearing up the town, spray-painting THE BLOODS RULE next to the Turkish slang YASSASSIN (long live) on the Berlin Wall, and scoring drugs in Kreuzberg.

At the Tempodrome, the backstage area was a separate tent where the bands hung out and waited to soundcheck. Annie and I had snorted speed; we climbed up the tentpoles, goofing off like mischievous capuchins while Lesley Woods, the lead singer of the Au Pairs, watched. Lesley and I were enamored of each other on the spot. Venus Weltklang marked the start of a tempestuous relationship that would span several years.

The show at the Tempodrome would be the very best we ever played together and stands as a testament to our potential as a band – an indication of how far we could have gone had we committed ourselves to creating music and staying together. Fortunately, the performance was captured and can be viewed on YouTube. Berlin also signalled how the drugs and egos weren't about to disappear from the story of the Bloods.

A few days later, we played Kippenberger's S.O. 36 with the Au Pairs, and by this time Lesley and I were obsessed with one another. She was staying with me at Claudia's loft. Drugs were cheap and strong in Berlin then, and one night we got so high on methedrine and drink that I ran through a plate-glass divider door separating rooms in the loft, smashing it (and myself) to pieces. I was a bloody mess; Lesley played night nurse. Claudia's husband was livid and threw us out the next day. Lesley left for London; the Au Pairs had a gig, but the Bloods stayed — we had another show booked at the Music Hall in Berlin.

Claudia introduced me to Iggy Pop's drummer Klaus Krüger. I met him at his flat on the Hauptstrasse in Schöneberg and he kindly gave me the keys to stay there for the few days I remained in Berlin while he was going out on tour. I was surprised to discover it was Iggy's flat and that Bowie had a flat in the same building. There was a painting by Bowie sitting on an easel; it was Iggy, his back facing the painter. Shirtless and standing on a cliff, a ball and chain around his ankle, he is poised to take flight.

While staying at Iggy's, I listened to the Au Pairs' debut LP *Playing With a Different Sex*, a bomb of a gender-queer LP title. My obsession with Lesley was buoyed by intense admiration for her work on this LP. Her and the band's immense bravery and talent for melding politics with post-punk and making it danceable remains astonishing. The songs are hypnotically rhythmic, sexy, and lyrically scathing. Lesley sang about polyamory and the frustrations of hetero sex and misogyny, de-masking territory where no other woman in rock 'n' roll had dared venture.

Lesley was deeply concerned with the UK's treatment of political prisoners. As her band worked on the songs for the LP, protests were happening at the women's jail, HM Prison Armagh, in Northern Ireland. Thirty Irish Republican women were being treated violently by guards, and the conditions at the prison were horrendous. The women engaged in a 'no wash' protest, with several going on hunger strike, yet the women received far less attention than Bobby Sands and the IRA men on hunger strike at HM Prison Maze. Lesley would make sure all those listening to the LP would know about the women of Armagh.

Released in early 1981, *Playing With a Different Sex* is somewhat forgotten but merits new ears. Its relevance has not faded an inch as a revolutionary suite of songs about sex and gender, politics and oppression, and the power of music to address the unspoken anguish and rage lurking beneath society's masks.

★ ★ ★

Next stop for the Bloods was Nijmegen in the Netherlands, a warm-up gig before we played the Melkweg in Amsterdam. Brenda was not happy. Kathy, Annie, and I were partying like crazy. We played the show in Nijmegen and it went well, but by the time we landed at the lesbian commune squat we'd be staying at in Amsterdam, Brenda was spooked by the accommodation. She disappeared shortly after we arrived.

Why did she take off without telling us? She knew no one in Amsterdam and didn't speak the language. We panicked; not only were we worried about her, but the gig was that night. Annie got on the phone and with help from our Dutch friends, called every hotel in the city starting with the Holiday Inns, and found her. Brenda's explanation for the disappearance was that she couldn't stay in a squat; she needed her own bathroom, clean sheets, and blankets. And we Bloods were roughing it. She had hailed a kind English-speaking taxi driver who drove her to a proper hotel. Thankfully she remained with us long enough to play our European shows – with her own hotel room for the duration.

We set up in Amsterdam as our base for the month of July until we planned to leave for Birmingham to join the Au Pairs and record a single, and then a show in London. We raised holy hell in the Netherlands. Our motto was *Lock up your daughters and one of your sons – the Bloods are in town!* We also met and hung out with the coolest Dutch lesbians who gave us all places to stay, some becoming lifelong friends. Café Saarein ('Vrouwen only!'), Amsterdam's only lesbian bar, was in the Jordaan neighbourhood and became our clubhouse. The area was exquisite, its narrow streets and canals named after trees and flowers. Two women important to the

Bloods were Annetje (now Dia) Huizinga the poet, and Lidi, a bartender at the Saarein. Both women lived in a three-storey narrow Dutch house broken up into a few apartments on Egelantiersstraat (Egelantier meaning sweet briar, or Eglantine rose). The narrow house was probably built in the seventeenth century. The flats were tiny but cosy, and our friends super-hospitable. They'd never seen anything like the Bloods.

Kathy and I immediately started dating two gorgeous sisters: Ietje and Henneke, referred to as Eat and Drink. Lesley and I didn't have an exclusive relationship then. She'd show up in A'dam soon enough. Annie was seeing a gorgeous Israeli named Chanita who was close with Annetje. I cringe at how macho we were, so determined to out-perform the rock 'n' roll hooligan boys in outrageous behaviour. We'd strut into the Saarein and take over a wooden table playing poker, smoking rolled cigarettes laced with hash, drinking Pils with our girlfriends on our laps and our switchblades on the table. Not just a band, we were a gang and quickly became notorious for our outrageous antics. Some of the women customers at the Saarein did not approve of our absurd macho posturing but others were enthralled by the punk American girls with their take-all-prisoners attitude. Our shows were off the hook. Women flung their panties onto the stage and threw themselves at us backstage. We were out-bad-assing the boys, living an alternative reality and a freedom that most normals were incapable of imagining.

Our friend Liz had travelled over to meet us in A'dam, and she rented a van to drive us around the country to our assorted gigs. When it was time to return the van, she opened the engine, found the odometer, and flipped the number of miles backwards. One day we decided we were going to rob the grocery store across from

Chanita's flat. We cased the joint for a few days, chopped up some nylon stockings, pulled them over our heads, and were about to embark on the folly. Until we collapsed laughing.

Some nights we roamed around the Zeedijk and the red-light district, where the sex workers posed in windows garishly lit against flocked wallpaper. Drug runners from Turkey and the Middle East were bringing heroin into Amsterdam, the city being perfectly positioned on a drug trafficking route that played a major role in distributing heroin across the rest of Europe. The Zeedijk was crawling with dealers. Someone in the band had scored heroin. I had stopped doing heroin – I knew I didn't love it – but decided to snort some that night. Within a half hour I was overdosing. The strength of the heroin was formidable compared to what we had been doing in New York. Suddenly I couldn't breathe, my eyes began to roll. I needed to tear off my clothes to relieve the internal heat, my body temperature going crazy. Annetje rushed me to her flat and placed cold rags all over my face and head, held my body and kept walking me around the room. She wouldn't let me pass out – if she had, I'd not be alive to tell these tales. I swore to never touch heroin again.

Soon after, Annetje and I boarded a train to Italy, to Pisa. It was the first of many trips to the country of my paternal ancestors and I could not have experienced its discovery with a better companion. I wrote a poem, one of few I'd hang on to, about our time there, inspired by the woman who saved my life.

> in Pisa
> we were girls together
> flinging words at the immaculate sky
> speaking in rhyme

LOCK UP YOUR DAUGHTERS

to an audience of clouds that danced above
in a vast eye of silver
and you asked nothing of me
but to name the places where the light touched down.

in Pisa
we climbed the stairs of the tower
no other soul breathing
to break us
apart from our freedom
our youth
ascending to the cant
the campanile
ring of prayers waiting to be sung
a baby gazelle
arcade beam
tongue of a bell
and you wanted nothing of me
but seven notes
a vowel
and the fingers of sunlight streaking our hair

in Pisa
we were poets together
our words not remembered yet little it mattered
for past and future
we did not harbor

servitrici delle donne
for a day a year a century

surfing the pitch of the marble
tilt of the sky
and you needing nothing of me
but an easy arm around your shoulder
and a smile to match your shine

in Pisa
night came on yet bode no ending
drunk on red wine, with money
leaking through the holes in our pockets
we watched
as the moon lit up the Piazza dei Miracoli
and made of it a phosphorescent stage
where we danced
a waltz with fireflies.
lucciole

and you asked nothing of me
my friend
you asked for nothing
while we laughed and took hold of it all

Annetje's friend Betye had a houseboat on the Prinsengracht, which she graciously offered for a few weeks' stay – a restored antique boat with charming stained-glass windows, a galley kitchen, and a cosy double bed. The boat was surrounded by seventeenth-century architecture and was a quick walk from the Westerkerk church where Rembrandt was buried. The houseboat was moored directly across the canal from the house where Anne Frank wrote her diary while in hiding from the Nazis. Weeks spent on that boat brought on an overwhelming melancholy, a sadness I did not want to run from as I gazed over at the annexe where Anne had hidden. The stark contrast between Nazi evil and the courage of the family who kept Anne and her loved ones in hiding haunted me. Humanity's potential for cruelty and for goodness – especially of that family who endangered their own lives for the Franks – remains a stark testament to true courage.

★ ★ ★

Lesley had introduced me to the works of Hannah Arendt and Arendt's friend Walter Benjamin. Arrested by the Gestapo early into Hitler's regime, Arendt wrote extensively about the nature of evil and totalitarianism. I was reading *On Revolution* during my stay on the boat, alongside Benjamin's *On the Concept of History*. These books felt theoretically dense for me at the time, but I was intent on deciphering the language to consider the ideas. What I loved about Benjamin was his embrace of Jewish mysticism and the way he braided esoteric ideas with a Marxist analysis. Arendt and Benjamin: one was to survive the war, the other committed suicide.

My stay on the boat – the solitude, the reading, the haunted feel of the Prinsengracht – sent me into deep reflection. Was I being courageous in my choices? How was I confusing bravery with recklessness? Drugs and drink created the condition of sleepwalking, of living unconsciously. I wanted so much more. I came to understand heroin as an existential death, a death that would become literally too close for comfort as I'd soon discover on my return to the States.

To live free, in defiance of all societal expectations, was not enough. I was beginning to realize the band, with its self-sabotage, the drugs, the conflicting egos (including my own), would not be a conduit for the work I dared to imagine. Work that would take decades, discipline, and a huge heart in need of healing.

Lesley came to visit, and we'd lie in the boat listening to the carillonneur of Westerkerk playing Bach melodies on the bells. The bells all seemed a bit out of tune, enhancing the romantic sorrow of the music. Less than forty years earlier, young Anne Frank listened to the same church bells, dreaming of freedom while hiding in a secret annex a mere hundred feet away.

★ ★ ★

The Au Pairs and their manager Martin Culverwell wanted to record a single with us. Annie and I sat at the piano in the Melkweg – or was it a squat? – with the intention of writing a transgressive hit. I picked out three bass notes and we cycled the notes back and forth. It felt like I was coming up with most of the melody, based more on my background in soul than how the Bloods had been playing up to that point, and Brenda had everything to do with feeling the funk. Annie played some chords to accompany the melody, and I recall writing lyrics that were basically about bondage and discipline under the guise of 'buttoning up', as in being secretive. It was a simple progression, a song that would have been nothing if not for Brenda's scorching funk bass. The rhythm section made the song. We decided the songs we'd write together would mostly be full band collaborations, or written by myself, Annie and Kathy, which in retrospect should have been full band collaborations even if one person did most of the writing. Songwriting splits would become contentious much later.

LOCK UP YOUR DAUGHTERS

Suzanne, the booker at the Melkweg venue, was our champion in Amsterdam. She and Minou booked our last show in the Netherlands – an outdoor concert in a town called Venlo opening for Van Morrison. *Astral Weeks* was among my favourite LPs and opening for Morrison was a major thrill. But I was nervous – I could tell someone in the band was high and particularly out of it that night. We got on stage and my heart sank into my stomach; the first song was not only out of tune but was being played by that someone in a different key to the rest of the band. I looked around at the others on stage, their horrified faces. An awkward stab at recovery was made while we shifted around in front of a perturbed and fidgety audience that didn't know what to make of us. This insanity of wrong keys and bad tunings continued throughout the set. I was struggling to figure where to place notes as we all scrambled trying to match keys but at a certain point, keys no longer mattered. I started talking the lyrics like John Cooper Clarke, turning the set into a poetry reading with backing noise. When we left the stage, the entire band appeared shell-shocked. Leen and Brenda took me aside to ask what was going on with the drugs, but I was catatonic and needed to drink myself into oblivion.

We arrived in Birmingham and couldn't understand a word of Brummie-accented English. While staying at the Au Pairs' communal house, all the Brits drank milky cups of tea and ate 'chip butties': thick slabs of white bread slathered in mayo with fat, greasy French fries as sandwich filling. We were thrilled to be recording in England, but things were going from bad to worse in the band. One of the band members was getting high with Martin, the Au Pairs manager and our producer, and another's backing vocals were becoming so loud and aggressive that I practically had to scream to be heard. One night

I was so mad at Kathy for not coming up with a decent guitar part for 'Button Up' that I threw an ashtray across the room at her (thankfully, it hit the wall and not her head). I'm sure the acrid feelings were mutual. I had turned into a control freak devoid of all control.

I had been begging Kathy and Annie to rehearse more and this backfired, increasing their resentment. Who did I think I was, the leader of the band? It didn't help that Richard Grabel, a friend of Kathy's, reviewed one of our shows in the *NME* and focused on singing my praises. Envy had raised its ugly head to the extent where we were not getting along at all. I admit to wanting to control what I couldn't – wanting the band to focus, to push certain members to rehearse more and to concentrate on the music instead of the drugs, and to feel comfortable with me being the lead singer without throwing shade. But I was just as bad, drinking heavily, acting like a boss. In a sense it is easier for singers; we don't need to rehearse an instrument and lug gear around (although all of us chipped in on the gear-lugging). But a singer is only as good as the musicians around them. We were recording our first single. We needed to be on point but were pretending all was tight between us when we were being ripped apart by egos, a needle, and a spoon.

★ ★ ★

Before we returned to the US, we played a show in Birmingham with the Au Pairs, then at the Lyceum in London, again with the Au Pairs and Pigbag. Thanks to Brenda's bass playing and Leen's drumming, 'Button Up' was a success. The rhythm section and the vocal carried the song. John Peel loved 'Button Up' and was playing the single on his popular radio show in the UK. Shortly after our return to the States, Andy Schwartz, the publisher of the *New York Rocker* who gave me my first writing gig, interviewed us for a feature in the magazine and decided to out us as lesbians. Kathy was not out to her family and the article upset her tremendously. Homophobia was the norm for families and in business, never the exception back then. Especially in the music business.

★ ★ ★

We played a few gigs; one at the New Pilgrim Theater with R.E.M. opening, and at the Peppermint Lounge with the Au Pairs, who were dealing with their own set of band challenges. We played a show at the bar Tin Pan Alley in Times Square. Kiki Smith, Cookie Mueller, and Nan Goldin all worked there, and the owner Maggie Smith only hired women, many of them ex- or current sex workers. Tin Pan Alley had a fascinating array of customers, and conversations were heady, with downtown artists, the occasional pimp and his stable, No Wave filmmakers, bands, and punk musicians mixing it up and exchanging stories.

After the Van Morrison show disaster and the ongoing battles, Brenda officially quit the band. She'd had enough of the drugs and the egos. I was devastated. When she left, my Bloods enthusiasm dwindled away to zero. We hired a young bassist, Marina Saly, and returned to Amsterdam by popular demand. That second tour is a blur; I was drinking too heavily. I do recall us covering 'Communication Breakdown' by Led Zeppelin, which summed up the state of the Bloods then. Back in New York, we played a show at WOW, coming full circle from where we began. It's the last show I remember playing with them.

The news that ended the Bloods with tragic finality came shortly after my phone rang at 3 a.m. A band member was calling, asking that I come quick; something terrible had happened. When I arrived at the building, paramedics were wheeling out a gurney, loading a covered body into an ambulance. It was our young roadie, Bobby Battery. Chris Harkin had woken to find his lifeless body lying next to her. He had died from a heroin overdose.

Bobby was an extremely shy, faithful roadie to many of the bands downtown, a true sweetheart, and a mere twenty years old. Sometime after he died, my friend Patti Hudson went to visit his mother in Queens. Bobby's mother was a Holocaust survivor, and Bobby was her only child. In broken English she told Patti that *Bobby was a bad boy. He was a very bad boy. It's why he died.* Patti reassured her it wasn't true: *Everybody loved Bobby. He made a mistake. He wasn't a bad boy. Your son Bobby was beloved.*

The Bloods self-imploded due to heroin, rivalries, and the fact that no label would ever sign and financially support a band of 'out' lesbians, especially in the early 1980s.

I wrapped a tourniquet around my heart and tried to move on, with shaky steps.

Liquid Sky & the Crack-Up

Liquid Sky was filmed in New York during the Cold War years, created by a group of Russian emigrés in collaboration with the actress and writer Anne Carlisle and released in the summer of 1982. Despite its hollow female characters, including a truly repellent lesbian, the film was deludedly deemed 'feminist' and quickly became a cult classic due to its outrageous themes, music, and blood-lurid cinematic style. It is obvious the film does not fit into the No Wave or New Cinema group of films; it has none of the lo-fi charm, humour, or vitality.

I met the director Slava Tsukerman and his wife Nina Kerova in 1981 at a very shaky moment in my life. The band had broken up and I was spending nearly every night dancing, drinking, and drugging at the Mudd Club, Danceteria, Club 57, or Tier 3, and I was flirting dangerously with different addictions: amphetamines, cocaine, heroin, and Anne Carlisle. I'd met Anne, a beautiful blonde, Connecticut WASP while studying acting with Bob Brady. She was a classmate and Bob's lover at the time. We'd often hang out at the Mudd Club and I lived at her studio apartment off and on, crashing there with my friend Hal Ludacer. Hal was strikingly handsome and equally hilarious. Anne would portray him as her male twin in *Liquid Sky*.

I can't recall how I met Slava and Nina – it may have been through Anne, or they may have seen me perform at some point. I started spending time with them, perhaps taken under their wing because they were initially captivated by my love for Russian literature, especially Mikhail Bulgakov and the agit-prop poet Vladimir Mayakovsky. They were conceptualizing a film and wanted me to tell them about the downtown scene and act in the film they were developing, offering a weekly salary. After the Allan Moyle debacle, I was suspicious, but needed the money.

NO NEW YORK

We started spending evenings together talking over dinner. I was eager for what they had to teach. Slava was Jewish and spoke about Russia's pogroms, a history of antisemitism I was unaware of. They turned me on to Shostakovich, Anna Akhmatova, the Russian Constructivist movement, Rodchenko, Diaghilev, Nijinsky and the Ballets Russes. I had terrible acne at the time and Nina, with her immaculate porcelain skin, taught me which soap to use and the secrets of apple cider vinegar. Slava and Nina quickly became proxy for the intelligent, nurturing parents I'd never experienced.

But my shadow side took over. I had slipped further into alcoholism and often self-sabotaged when situations seemed too good. When I started showing up late for our meetings, or not at all, they discovered I was doing drugs. I also befriended a young woman from Russia they were sponsoring; it was not romantic, but I did share my amphetamines with her once. The news of this and of my drug use killed our relationship.

Years later, after watching the film, I imagined the Russian filmmakers in the States on a mission to document the strange perversions of American youth. Slava had told a writer at *The Daily Beast* that 'during the August Putsch of 1991, when Gorbachev was held prisoner by KGB guards in the resort of Foros, in the Crimea, he was allowed to make an "entertainment" order for himself and his wife Raisa. So, while the Old Guard was attempting to restore rigid Communism in Moscow, the KGB agents provided Mikhail and Raisa Gorbachev with something to take their mind off things; a few bottles of white and the film *Liquid Sky*.'[1]

---

1 Daniel Genis, 'Punks, UFOs, and Heroin: How *Liquid Sky* Became a Cult Movie', *The Daily Beast*, 2 June 2014.

LIQUID SKY & THE CRACK-UP

The same writer reiterates a story Slava told him about his experience during the Moscow Film Festival. During the screening, he was approached to show *Liquid Sky* to an 'organization'; it turned out to be the Russian police and KGB. Apparently, they loved the film. If Russian intelligence wanted a more damning indictment of how the youth of America's supposed avant-garde thought and played, they'd be hard-pressed to find it.

And, yet, this film was the antithesis of what downtown art culture was all about. Yes, there was heroin in the scene. Yes, there was gender fluidity and lots of sex. But the people experiencing it were all on fire with ideas, collaborations, curiosity, intelligence, and genuine comradery.

Released in 1982, an exaltation of gender-bending sexual fluidity in *Liquid Sky* is ultimately punished via people dying from sex, a foreshadowing of the AIDS epidemic (the first cases would be reported in June 1981 when the film was in early production). Characters look otherworldly stylish in a 1980s-gone-berserk mise en scene, with makeup and outfits screaming in saturated colours – perhaps in an attempt to offset the dead-eyed, zombie personalities of the characters, none with any redeeming qualities whatsoever. The sex is ugly, everybody's on dope, the supposedly feminist lead character's iconic line is, 'I kill with my cunt.' That would be funny if it were about rape revenge, but she 'kills with her cunt' before she gets raped. Aliens suck the endorphins from her victims as they climax.

The film is a cruel pastiche of a fake, garish scene representing hipster youth in 1980s New York, taken over by sex-crazed aliens. There's a deceptive and deliberate cruelty in films like *Times Square* and *Liquid Sky*. In a sense, I feel the filmmaker's resentment of a freedom they will never experience – they must demonize the 'other', especially lesbians, who they portray as mentally troubled, sick, and depraved, spiritually dead, lesser-than-human things who will never ever be granted a happy ending.

I remember Anne letting me read the finished script for *Liquid Sky*. The lesbian character Slava initially wanted me to play turned my stomach; she was a disgustingly reprehensible goblin who mounts dead men's faces. I understood that they were upset about my irresponsibility and drug use. I was young, and because of a childhood that included rape, abandonment, and torture, I was a mess. But to create a character supposedly based on me – a 'thing' devoid of curiosity, wonder, a longing to learn, dull to the poetics of Shostakovich and Akhmatova, without the need to give or receive love – was heartbreaking. After exposing so many personal details to them and to Allan Moyle, including aspirations and excitement for the future, I felt these characterizations as soul-crushing cruelties; a slap in the face to not only mine but to any young woman's resilience and longing for freedom, sovereignty, and knowledge.

★ ★ ★

The personal unravelling that had begun earlier in the year came on full force. I shattered into pieces and feared I would never reassemble. I had given so much of my yearnings, my poetry and the loneliness of what it was like to survive as a young woman in the world alone, eager for knowledge and love . . . to have all of it ignored and made over into a monstrous caricature, not once but twice, felt worse than defeat. My recent past of drinking and drugs escalated, pushing me toward a cliff, and crystal meth, a horrible drug, nearly buried me. I remembered my mother being addicted to speed in the form of Black Beauties. She had sent me a long nylon purple robe, and one day, I found myself walking the streets barefoot in the robe, all the money I had in the world in a brown paper lunch bag. I pulled myself together enough to make a call, to Lizzie Borden's loft.

Honey answered. I had met her while working on Lizzie's *Born in Flames*, and I liked her immediately. She and Lizzie would fall in love and live together during the filming and beyond. Honey reminded me of the girls I'd been in reform school with – a sister veteran, having made it through the kinds of wars I knew well. Tough, yet with a tremendous sweetness just beneath, she had a voice any gospel choir would push up front to the solo seat. Although she remained a gentle spirit, she could never give up drinking, and when she drank she imagined she gained control enough to become one with the demons who haunted her. She scared me when she drank, and she drank a lot (as did I).

When she asked me that day of the phone call 'Where are you?', I told her where to meet and sat down on a stoop to cry. Honey came to collect me, took me to Lizzie's loft, stroked my head, and drew me a hot bath. This was medicine. She took out a book and read to me by candlelight and I heard the call, soft and beckoning, like velvet in the room come to cloak me. Like a mother.

The book was *Science and Health* by Mary Baker Eddy. Eddy believed thought created good or evil conditions, including disease, and that through faith and right belief, one could be healed. Honey believed Eddy, and in a God who I knew had forsaken me long ago for no reason I could fathom. And if I were to judge the circumstances of her life, that same God had forsaken Honey too. Yet she did not feel the same as me. As she read to me, my not believing in anything or anyone outside myself, and with only her voice to hang on to, I felt a growing buoyancy, a life raft building there through the sound of her voice. I came to trust that I could be healed by faith, in something I'd felt had abandoned me. I replaced the name of God with Love. It was just that simple. Because Honey chose to love me in that moment, I chose to try to love life. And I began to heal.

Lizzie had an old upright piano in her loft, worse for wear, but it still held a tune. I grew stronger, day by day, as Honey and I sat at that piano singing harmony to a song she wrote called 'Tropical Storm', about the sky falling on a world of fantasy. We must have sung that song a thousand times. One afternoon we were singing at the top of our lungs when the loft door flew open, and a tiny nun – a *nun*! – in full regalia was standing there grinning at us like the Cheshire Cat. We howled with laughter and so did the sister, as if it were a staged walk-on blessing, and she disappeared just as quickly as we'd conjured her.

I'll always be grateful for Honey, the woman who gave me the time and the choice to see through a different prism. The goosebump resonance of our voices together in song lifted me. I imagine that when she sang, Honey felt healed too. Music can do that.

Honey died in June 2010 when she was sixty years old. She suffered from congestive heart problems. Although she lived alone in a YWCA in Springfield, Massachusetts, the last year of her life wasn't lonely, for she had fallen in love and her love was returned. I wonder if the loss of control that walks arm in arm with falling in love led her to drink more than she usually did. The night she passed, she drank. A sailor floating in her own warm boat of sweet oblivion, her heart gave out while she slept, and she passed away from this world without knowing the seam had been gently torn asunder.

Cabaret to Compromise

Lesley and I continued to correspond and talk on the phone, trying to keep our relationship alive. I began doing solo shows at the Mudd Club and Max's featuring my poetry and lyrics set to backing tapes.

Binaural headphones first appeared in the late 1970s and were akin to the first virtual reality audio. On the outside of each padded earpiece was a high-quality microphone so that while wearing the headphones attached to an audio recorder, like a portable Nagra or a Sony cassette deck, you could record what you were hearing around you in vivid aural detail. (Lou Reed recorded his masterpiece *Street Hassle* using a mannequin head and binaural headphones, placing the musicians around the head and recording the musicians live.) Scott B had a pair, and I borrowed them for a stroll up and down 42nd Street, recording the voices of hustlers and dope peddlers hawking their wares around me as I walked. Because of the discreet design, no one was aware they were being recorded. The results were an ambient street hassle of another kind.

I had a guitarist and a drummer lay a track over the live ambience recordings and would use the tapes in my performances, singing and reciting poetry live over the tracks issuing from a boombox on stage. I always did a cover version of 'Pirate Jenny' whenever I performed, loving this song's first-person story about a scullery maid rendered invisible, and her revenge. One day I would record my own version of this song and call it 'Can't Stop the Dance'. It would become the most accomplished and powerful track on my solo LP for Chrysalis Records, the one I'm most proud of – a song that must have scared the pants off the company and hence would end up permanently buried.

Lesley came to New York, and we lived in various places; apartments of friends who were out of town, and at the B's loft, where

NO NEW YORK

I was living while working on the soundtrack for their film *Vortex*. We did a show together at the Mudd Club, dressed in matching tuxedos singing cabaret songs like 'Lili Marlene'. When drunk and high, I could be physically and ashamedly brutal. We had a passionate, highly volatile relationship heavily infused by drugs and booze. My past haunted our relationship; experiences, traumas, and insecurities in desperate need of healing, hurts I could not untangle that I brought to the relationship, that would take decades to come to terms with.

I stayed in touch with Brenda Alderman and brought her in to play bass on the B's LP. Along with the B's, Richard Edson, John Lurie, and Angel Quinones of the band Konk, we had a great time collaborating and recording the music.

★ ★ ★

Danny Heaps was one of the founders of the New Music Seminar along with Marc Josephson. Danny had been paying close attention to me. He'd seen the Bloods and scoffed at the band, but said he was a fan of mine. Maybe he was in the audience at the Mudd Club when I performed solo, but he was definitely at a Max's show when I babbled from the stage about how Hitler accused the Jews of breaking the economic circle in Germany as intro to 'Pirate Jenny'. I heard Danny call out 'Careful, Adele!' from the audience. Far from being antisemitic, it was my clumsy attempt at explaining the Nazis and why the Holocaust had happened, the crimes of the 'gentle men' Jenny calls out in the song. But perhaps Danny's warning was a foreshadowing of our future relationship.

In 1982, David Geffen had started his own company, Geffen Records, and he hired Danny as an A&R man. Danny was affable, always smiling and good-natured. He was short and wore cosy clothes in muted tones; lots of corduroy pants, chinos, rolled-neck button-down sweaters, all a little too large. His style made him look cuddly, with his curly reddish hair and constant grin. He began approaching me after a couple of these solo shows and was always warm and complimentary but not overzealous in the way that would have felt creepy. I liked him immediately.

When Danny was hired by Geffen, the only two acts the label had signed were Donna Summer and John Lennon. Was (Not Was) and I were Danny's first signings. It began with Danny asking if I'd be interested in demoing a few songs for Geffen. I was astonished. A major label interested in *me*? He laughed, saying he'd take care of the money, and I should start writing songs in haste.

David Geffen had discovered Laura Nyro and signed Joni Mitchell to Asylum. Allegedly, he was gay. This shouldn't matter, but it did for all of us in the closet. I figured I'd have a longer leash to be myself if another gay person behind the scenes was supporting my career. If I was going to sign to a commercial record label, Geffen looked like the perfect home. Later I'd find out this was far from true; you should never assume you're compatible with anyone if you're basing your friendships and collaborations on which gender people choose to bed.

John Clifford's sofa bed was the place I called home on West 16th Street when Danny's invitation turned my world into a new spin. Susan Seidelman and I were hanging out a bit after she'd made her debut film *Smithereens* and John was Susan's boy-pal at the time, a photographer and a great guy. I needed a place to lay my head without having to worry about the stresses of paying rent – wanting to concentrate on writing music and performing, and John was kind enough to let me use his living room as a bedroom, if I chipped in on cleaning and groceries. Lucky for me, I also acquired an education in the music of Brazil. An amazing parade of artists revolved on his turntable. Caetano Veloso and his sister Maria Bethania, Milton Nascimento, Elis Regina, Gilberto Gil, Antônio Carlos Jobim . . . I heard them all at John's place and he was thrilled to turn me on to all these great musicians and singers.

Danny Heaps heard a track Brenda and I had recorded for the *Vortex* soundtrack called 'Once in a Lifetime', which helped convince him to give me a shot at some demos, but he wasn't aware I was still working with Brenda. My first call for a musical collaborator on the Geffen demos was her. She was responsible for the funk of 'Button Up'. Spanking the bass was the popular funk style of the time, and no one could spank the bottom out of a bass guitar like Brenda. I'd never had any friction with her in the Bloods, except for when she ran away from us in Amsterdam. Looking back on what was happening then, I don't blame her. I knew I could count on her for a fun and stress-free collaboration.

Throughout my upbringing, and despite my father's extremely vocal prejudices (this, in the face of the fact that he didn't have the moral fibre to support and take care of his own children), I always knew racism was evil. I remember watching newscasts about race riots in Detroit and Watts on TV in the mid-1960s, spellbound and horrified by the injustice of it. Ironically, and my father never knew nor cared about this, it was Black women who looked after me, cooked my meals and nursed me back to health when I was sick. That they were being paid for their duties didn't matter. What counted was their kindness, their acknowledgement that a young white girl could suffer the misfortune of being thrown away just as easily as a young Black girl. I grew up with Black girls and women, felt safe with my 'lost girls' as we found each other. The complications and the beauty of race are fundamental to the fabric of my life and story – the strongest threads binding our authenticities together as human beings and artists are the lessons learned from the people in our lives and the paths we've travelled. Soul was as important as rock and punk in my musical hegemony. My heart sang of soul; it would always leak through the cracks of my voice.

The sound I wanted to create was a soulful pop shimmer with lyrics you wouldn't ordinarily hear from a woman, or an androgyne. And aside from Patti Smith, I couldn't think of another androgynous woman doing music at the time. Even though I was still influenced by Bowie and his work in the mid-1970s (especially 'Station to Station' and 'Young Americans', his funkier tracks), he had left Ziggy and his bisexual glam persona in the dust. He was nearly finished with the Berlin trilogy and *Scary Monsters* at this point. The possible backing of a powerhouse like Geffen Records had me fantasizing about growing into a major artist to contend with, stepping into the gap as a punk-funk androgyne breaking new ground, bringing new ideas of theatre to rock 'n' roll stages. My hubris and naiveté about the music business stage-whispered to me of a void in the pop star hierarchy that only I could fill.

Pop stardom certainly wouldn't materialize unless I stopped all drugs and cut way down on the drinking, which I did, and to good effect. I was safe and secure at John's place, had musical gear to write on, and was diligent about creating music. I felt healthy and positive, looking forward to what was coming with a bright attitude for the first time since the Bloods had dissolved. Brenda and I set to work on two new songs, both funky in the style of Shalamar and Cameo, with the intention that once I had a recording contract we'd glam the songs up with Bowie-esque rock touches. The songs were 'You Can Bet' and 'Queen's Strut' and we had a fantastic time recording at Sorcerer Sound in SoHo. Bloods drummer Leen came in to play drums, and a funky guitarist the engineer had suggested laid down stellar rhythm tracks. Brenda played bass, keyboards, and pitched in on backing vocals. I always thought she would make an amazing record producer, an impossibility at the time since there weren't any women producing. (In the 1980s, the only woman producer I could name was Roma Baran, Laurie Anderson's producer, and she was doing more experimental work, or I would have lobbied to record with her. I had worked with Roma when Lizzie Borden asked me to record a song for the soundtrack of *Working Girls*.)

Danny applauded the songs and the demo tracks, and I was elated that he truly supported my work. I'd soon find out his support was conditional. He brought the demos to the company heads, Carol Childs and Geffen himself, and called within the week. Geffen Records were offering me a contract for a single with an option for an album and I should start thinking about a lawyer. I couldn't believe it. Danny tossed out a few names of music business attorneys, but I knew better than to go with a lawyer suggested by my potential record company.

Alan Bomser had represented another of my heroes, Laura Nyro. Alan was flattered I'd contacted him, loved the music, and after hearing about the Geffen deal was eager to take me on. He explained the way he worked and asked that I sign a contract giving him 5 per cent of any monies earned through my career as an entertainer and songwriter. I discovered this was standard in the music industry. In turn he'd provide all legal work and protect my interests. He seemed

CABARET TO COMPROMISE

like a good enough guy, and I trusted him based on the career of Laura Nyro. I signed the contract, completely missing how his last name sounded out two distinct words: 'bombs-her'. I called Brenda to tell her the good news that we had a deal! Even though it was my name on the contract, she'd be coming with me.

As soon as the ink was dry on the contract, Danny demanded I drop Brenda, implying, *You can't work with . . . well, you know! The Bloods are over! I mean, come on Adele!* Without saying it out loud, Danny had his own transparent way of towing the line of all record labels in the 1980s – gayness, and the appearance of gayness, was verboten. We never discussed being gay, or the closet, or homophobia back in those days. People knew but didn't bring it up, certainly not in professional circles. I felt like I'd been sucker-punched. Brenda wasn't only a great musical collaborator, she was my friend. She trusted me and I her. I protested, asking why he'd want me to drop the person I wrote the demo songs with, the same tracks that had convinced him and the company to sign me. But Danny was in control and his confident grin said it all. He assured me I was moving up and into the business in a big way. I shouldn't hold on to the past; it was time I started reaching higher.

Finding the nerve to call Brenda and tell her the news was excruciating. She was disappointed but gracious about it, wishing me luck on the deal while I squirmed and told her I'd try to record the songs we'd written and demoed. I felt horrible. A part of me knew I wouldn't be hanging out with Brenda for a long, long time and I felt ashamed. Danny must have known how distressed I was about losing my collaborator. His fix was to make good on his promise. He pulled out the best card he could at the time, and it was a King of Diamonds – Chic's keyboard player, Raymond Jones.

Raymond was Nile Rodgers and Bernard Edwards' secret weapon, the guy responsible for the sound of all those lush percussive chord progressions on hits like Chic's 'Good Times', Sister Sledge's 'We Are Family', Diana Ross's 'Upside Down', songs that Studio 54's glammerati would dance to endlessly. Raymond's piano sound was just as important to Chic's style as Bernard's bass and Nile's guitar licks. Raymond played on dozens of hits and would produce soundtracks for Spike Lee's films, notably *Do the Right Thing*.

Danny arranged for us to meet and write together. I was thrilled and completely intimidated, expecting Raymond to be arrogant and somewhat removed because of his place in the pop music stratosphere, but he was the loveliest and most talented musician I'd ever met. The moment I sat down with him at his piano and he started seat-dancing on the bench next to me, playing his signature percussive progressions, I instantly came up with a melody line. We clicked immediately, laughing at the magic of it and constructing the music for the entire song in one sitting.

Lesley was in town, and we were staying together at the time. At Raymond's, we came up with the lyrics for the song 'Build Me a Bridge', thinking of the missed connections; of us being oceans apart and universally as a need for uniting across chasms of misunderstanding. Lesley was a great lyricist and songwriter and together we dared to have high hopes of a major deal. Raymond finished arranging the song with his gorgeous piano chords.

Danny and everyone at Geffen loved the song. It was time to find a producer. Excitement was mounting and I wanted to ride the wave of it, that possibility of a career in the music business and the implications of what I might be able to create. Working with Raymond had bolstered my confidence.

CABARET TO COMPROMISE

Danny asked if I had any ideas on producers, and suggested I work with Thomas Dolby. I'd thought of Brian Eno as a potential producer but I recall Danny nixing it, thinking 'Build Me a Bridge' a bit too pop for his taste. His innovations combined with my funk-pop sensibilities were exactly what I needed at the time, but Danny thought Eno was too avant-garde. I guessed he must have missed the Talking Heads hit 'Once in a Lifetime' from the Eno-produced *Remain in Light*.

I suggested Tony Visconti, based on his work with Bowie, but he was living in London, busy working on records by groups like Haysi Fantayzee and Modern Romance after Bowie traded him in for Nile Rodgers on *Let's Dance*. I remember asking for David Byrne to produce – twice, when I was signed to major labels – but he always turned me down. He must have seen me slug someone at the Mudd Club or heard the stories and was petrified.

Although I wasn't crazy about 'She Blinded Me with Science', I really liked Thomas Dolby's *The Golden Age of Wireless* LP – his chunky synth sounds, his musicality, and the stories he told in songs like 'Airwaves'. I met with Thom and found him charming in a nerdish sort of way. He talked about how he'd like to add a new synth sound to the signature musical line of the song and add backing vocals to fatten the choruses. I liked his ideas, and we settled it – he would produce 'Build Me a Bridge' in London at the Townhouse Studios. Danny sanctioned the deal, and I was off to the UK. Another perk: I'd be with Lesley in London while we recorded.

Working with Thom at the Townhouse was a fantastic experience. We got on well, and his synth sounds were unique; fat, analogue and resonant. He was using Roland Jupiters 4 and 8, an Oberheim, a PPG Wave, and a Linn Drum, all perfect tones and timbres for the song. Thom played all the keyboard parts and was not funnelling the parts working with a sequencer; he played everything live to tape. Thom was good about asking me what I liked and didn't like, and we spoke about writing songs together and possible collaboration on an LP.

I returned to a thrilled Danny in New York; he was champing at the bit to have the single remixed for the dancefloor. He gave the master tapes to Mark Kamins, a popular DJ, remixer, and up-and-coming producer. Mark was also working with a new singer who called herself Madonna.

When I heard the remix, I baulked. Remixing requires taking all the separate instrument tracks and extending three and a half minutes of song to as much as ten minutes by adding extra beats and playing around with the tracks for a wildly different assemblage geared toward club play. Thom did not sequence his keyboard parts – he played and recorded live. On the remix, there was a very bare section where the music drops out and Thom's keyboard parts are played solo over the drum track. He had made what musicians call a 'clam' – bungled a trill of notes which could not be heard on the single, and Kamins, who was working on Madonna's first 12-inch at the same time, exposed the mistake on the remix.

He(art) Lost and Found

Whether Mark Kamins highlighted Thom's mistake unintentionally or deliberately is uncertain. He was sleeping with Madonna at the time; he had just produced her first record 'Everybody', and the business had placed her and me in direct competition: two white girls doing dance music. Neither Madonna's label Sire nor Geffen wanted either of us to put our photographs on the record covers; they actually wanted to hide the fact that we were white! The 12-inch and 7-inch versions of 'Build Me a Bridge' and 'Everybody' were released at the same time, in October 1982. (As was the reality for a women climbing up any ladder, be it corporate or artistic, the competition was fierce because of the dearth of women in positions dominated and controlled by men. The idea that *There's only room for one* was often true and internalized by women, creating an ugly lack of alliances.)

Madonna and I started out as casual friends, both living in the East Village on East 4th Street, hanging out at the Pyramid Club. I adored her friend, the bartender Martin Burgoyne, who was also one of Madonna's early dancers. When she was recording her first LP in 1982, she asked me to sing backing vocals on the song 'Physical Attraction'. I went over to her apartment to rehearse. It was extremely bare: a bed on the floor, a ghetto blaster, assorted cassette tapes, and not much else. When I met her in the studio, she was being produced by Reggie Lucas and he'd brought in the singers from Chic – Alfa Anderson and Luci Martin – to do backing vocals. I don't think Madonna had told Reggie about me. It did not go well. The Chic singers were dripping with attitude and looked at me as if I'd rolled out of a garbage bin. We stood around the microphone, and I tried to blend with them but they were being snobbish, throwing shade. Not wanting to feel utterly useless, I hummed a melodic backing part consisting of *bum-bum-bum-bums* for the second half of the chorus. Madonna liked the part. I hung around and listened to the Chic girls sing it. Badly, I thought.

Madonna later brought in Gwen Guthrie and another singer to replace the Chic women. I was surprised when I heard the same backing vocal melody I'd created repurposed for Madonna's hit single 'Crazy for You'. The song became a number 1 hit, but I was never compensated for my arrangement contribution – a story not unusual in the music business.

★ ★ ★

While Madonna was recording her first LP, the 12-inch of 'Build Me a Bridge' debuted on Billboard's dance club charts at number 20, hitting number 5 within weeks, while Madonna's 'Everybody' debuted at 40 and languished. Madonna became catty. There were snide remarks at the Pyramid, swipes at my motorcycle boots and outfits, haughty looks, and bitchy stares.

A young Black graffiti artist, Michael Stewart, who we all knew in the scene, had been brutally beaten to death by the police while caught writing graffiti in the First Avenue subway station. The medical examiner initially blamed Michael's death on his drinking, but his body was beaten to a pulp and there was a spinal cord injury to his neck. Pressure from family and friends resulted in an independent autopsy; he died of strangulation. Murder was out as a verdict due to Michael's eyeballs having gone missing, which would have proven strangulation. We all got together to help with financial support and raise awareness of Stewart's death with a benefit gig at Danceteria – the Lounge Lizards, John Sex, 3 Teens Kill 4,

HE(ART) LOST AND FOUND

and others. Madonna performed tracks with her dancers that night. I sang the Dylan song 'It's All Over Now Baby Blue' as a warning to the cop murderers, accompanied by Patti Smith's little sister Kimberly on guitar.

Freddy DeMann, famous for having managed Michael Jackson during the time of his *Off the Wall* and *Thriller* LPs, was now managing Madonna. Career-wise, she was about to launch into extraterrestrial orbit and everyone knew it. Especially her.

Kim and I were in the smaller of two basement dressing rooms at Danceteria warming up in a corner, Kim tuning her guitar to my harmonica in the crowded dressing room. Madonna and Freddy appeared in the doorway whispering and giggling, pointing at me and Kim. Suddenly he marched toward us (he was short and hardly intimidating), yelling at us to get out the way. He wanted to take Madonna's photo precisely where we were standing. At first, I was stunned and looked around to see if maybe there was a Basquiat mural or special graffiti behind us, but it was a blank corner. Madonna stood in the doorway cracking up. I glared at Freddy.

'What the? Can't you see we're tuning here?!'

His eyes bugged. I moved toward him.

'There's a huge dressing room next door! Get out! Go on, get!'

If only I could have frozen his terrified face in amber. Madonna scurried off with her humiliated manager in tow.

★ ★ ★

Meanwhile, 'Build Me a Bridge' had become a major dance 12-inch, so I guess club DJs were not bothered by Thom Dolby's keyboard mistake, which was only noticeable if you listened very carefully.

But Thom was listening. Furious that Danny had not consulted with him at all about a dance mix, and hearing the exposed mistake on Kamins' mix, Thom refused to work with Danny Heaps and Geffen and would not be producing my LP. Thom was a perfect creative match for what I'd envisioned as my first collection of songs, and Danny had ruined the relationship. Almost. In 1983, Thom brought me to London to work with him on his follow-up LP, *The Flat Earth*. (We duetted on his song 'Hyperactive!', which would become Thom's second-biggest hit, charting at number 17 in the UK pop chart.)

I was treading in deep waters with Danny, Bomser, and Geffen Records and could not find my sea legs. 'Build Me a Bridge' was now climbing the singles chart, but the team at Geffen stopped promoting due to me not having an LP in the wings. Geffen wanted to pick up the option for an album, and I was in desperate need of a manager. Because I followed any Patti Smith-adjacent leads, I reached out to Jane Friedman.

Jane had been managing Patti Smith through her company the Wartoke Concern, and Patti was the reason I felt brave enough to become a performer. Jane had started out with Patti early on when she was business and romantic partners with John Cale, helping Patti record and release her first single 'Hey Joe' / 'Piss Factory' with Cale producing, and negotiating her contract with Clive Davis and Arista Records.

Jane loved the demos I did with Brenda, and I adored her instantly. She was little, like me, and whip-smart and confident about her music business knowledge, with a mischievous grin that felt conspiratorial and made me feel like I'd be in safe hands. We'd be a team. I started spending a lot of my time with her. I'd never tell her this back then, but she was a maternal figure for me. I instinctively felt she would protect me. Jane hit every mark.

On my second meeting with Bomser concerning the Geffen contract, I brought in the management contract Jane Friedman had given me. He read it, flushed red, and hit the roof. Jane had asked for 5 per cent more than a manager's usual 20 per cent share of my publishing and songwriting. I didn't have a clue as to what was standard for managers, aside from reading about how egregious Colonel Tom Parker's deal had been with Elvis. I went back to Jane and we talked about this split, with her explaining how song royalties and mechanical royalties worked. Honestly, I can't remember what she asked for but didn't think it was anywhere near Bleeker Bob shenanigans. I was more than willing to give her the extra 5 per cent.

I recall raving to Danny about wanting Jane to manage me but him joining ranks with Bomser, telling me I should drop her, that she wasn't powerful enough and would be ineffectual. They continued lobbying to convince me that I should choose a powerful manager who could work in harmony with the company and catapult my career. I argued that Jane worked well enough with Arista Records, but they weren't having it. Danny thought I should be managed by Marc Josephson, his ex-partner in the New Music Seminar. Marc and I got along well, but we mutually decided he'd be too busy and I needed someone with more experience.

I asked Jane if we could put the contract on hold and she seemed fine about it, in part because I didn't tell her about the pushback I was getting from Bomser and Danny. My head was already spinning. I decided to make sure the legal side of the Geffen deal went through smoothly while I concentrated on writing new songs. But the pressure from Bomser and Danny was mounting; they were tag-teaming me to drop Jane and hire a manager. I sat down with Jane and told her what was happening, that we wouldn't be able to work together. Sacrificing Jane to make sure I sealed the contract with Geffen would become one of my biggest regrets.

Breaking up with yet another person crucial to my safety in a treacherous business was taking its toll. And life was off to a frenetic pace. I had followed directions and separated from Brenda and Jane with the understanding that, with a major deal like Geffen, I would not have a chance at a successful singing career if I didn't follow orders. Brenda and I had worked so well together, and I wanted to take her with me on the ride. I needed and enjoyed her companionship, both musically and as a friend. Jane was like my surrogate mother; she made me feel safe. I felt secure with them, both as an artist and as a woman in an industry in which men held the power.

The ground was being stripped from beneath my feet by these music men – the Machiavellian 'star-making machinery' demanded absolute control. I was experiencing the antithesis of the creative and personal freedoms of No Wave and the downtown scene. My drinking escalated again. I sincerely tried tightrope-walking the corporate line, until the tension snapped the line completely.

*   *   *

By the end of the 1980s, many of the women and men I'd gotten high with in New York were completely sober and had joined the fellowship of Alcoholics Anonymous meetings. I'd been attending ACT UP meetings and actions with a sober friend, Ivonne Casas, and she could tell I was in distress. Ivonne was a Cuban emigrée, another who had lost her mother when she was a young girl. She introduced me to AA meetings. I recall walking into my first one and feeling so much shame, having had problematic relationships with many of the people in the room. All opened their arms to me with compassion and forgiveness, saying they'd been saving a seat for me. It was an excruciating moment and a chance at a new way of life, of redemption. I didn't have a problem with the God language and was used to ignoring pronouns in my search for heroes, for my survival as a woman, throughout my life. A patriarchal concept of God was easy to ignore.

I stopped drinking a day at a time, got a sponsor, and would physically shake in soul-deep acknowledgement every time I held hands in a group and recited the wisdom of the serenity prayer: *God, grant me the serenity to accept the things I cannot change, the courage to change the things I can, and the wisdom to know the difference.* I began to recognize God as the kindness I saw in others.

★ ★ ★

Sometimes, when all is still in my garden, a few finches with distinctive markings come to visit. These are my ghosts, the lost girls and boys who sing to me. I think of them often: Peter Laughner, Lester Bangs, George Scott III, Laura Kennedy, Lizzy Mercier Descloux, Peter Graute, Edwige Belmore, Bobby Battery, Sally Ven Yu Berg, James Chance, Anya Phillips, Honey, Ivonne Casas, Kathy Acker, Nancy Brooks Brody. And now, Sinéad O'Connor.

A return to poetry, to new understandings, has taken decades. Getting down the words is a demand the ghosts now make of me. I'll close out this book with a eulogy for an artist from No New

York, Nancy Brooks Brody. They left this earth while I was writing the book. And I'll end with an epilogue in the form of a lyric unsung.

★   ★   ★

Brody. Do you remember the exquisite painting you gave me when we were together? I recall the image – a feminine yet androgynous figure playing a violin, and you had painted an abrupt thin black line through the playing wrist. I loved that painting. To me it represented all the musics and magics women have made through the ages, cut off, made invisible to girls like us who grew up without mirrors or models of who to be. Whoever has it now – may they follow that line to the ghost girls past who never had the chance to shine, like you did, Brody.

We were free and young and on fire to be. To be ourselves without the punishing strictures of a world filled with gendered expectations. We were boy-girl creatures together and you were so pure, so sweet and playful. You were a miracle of light to me, an antidote to a downtown scene that could be very dark at times. I adored your smile, adored you, Brody. When I think of you, I always see your joy and hold it carefully in my memory, a glittering treasure. I am sorry you suffered in your body. I am happy you were loved by so many and moved that you are now free, navigating through stardust with your wise, childlike enthusiasm, painting lines and connecting dots in the ethers while you dance. Shine on, little warrior. I'll see you again one day, where time is a circle and within it, your smile and beautiful heart will be there, forever immortal.

Epilogue

Town of Empty
by Adele Bertei
(a song lyric, title inspired by Mark Boone Jr)

you were our holy poet
your words like a gun
black hair of a rock-n-roll magdalene
mythologizing the lice in your crown
and pumping your fist
to the new sins you found
o they fell at your feet
a salvation bazaar
pasolini's daughters and sons
accattone on the run
in the empty
town of gone gone away

the children all followed in buses and trains
with mottos tattooed on their eyes
dying is easy it's living that's tough
and art without comfort is comfort enough
o we claimed our lost and found
forsaken rooms
broken english scrawled on the walls
internationale
town of empty
town of gone gone away

we played through the ruins, a palace we made
the wild girls the junkies the renegades

NO NEW YORK

waltzing the breakdown
our own port of call
with hooligan hearts the most tender of all
what we need we didn't need
all we wanted
was our ugly beautiful time
in the blink of an eye
town of empty
town that's gone gone away

they're closing the doors on the chelsea hotel
they're signing the papers today
the old dame is dead
long live the dame
who cradled our gutter of singers and saints
among stars
endless stars
broken hearts
beating through that glittering dark
dancing night
town of empty
town of gone gone away

a french girl is singing alone in her room
a song of utopian helium
damn this nostalgia
this heavenly hell
and damn all the money
that strangled the call-out to arms
beautiful arms

EPILOGUE

in the dawn
Icarus falling out of our sight
ashes in flight
town of empty
town of gone
gone away

FIN

Acknowledgements

I am deeply grateful to the fellowship that has helped me remain sober through the decades. If you were to ask what I am most proud of having achieved to date, it is my sobriety. Alcohol and drugs had taken away my awareness of the sacredness of life and of others. AA offered spiritual tools to heal, to forgive, and be forgiven, and to connect with people in ways I'd never dreamed possible. Without your fellowship and ongoing support, I would not be alive today. You all know who you are.

Thank you for being the loving ground beneath my feet: Natalie Hill, Jeffrey Hill, Glen Nafziger, Liz Graves, dama and Maya. I'm humbled by your generosity and love. Thanks to the following people who have provided friendship, inspiration, and support on my writing journey: Jack Ryan, Lizzie Borden, Hugh W. Harris, Nan Goldin, Michael Zilkha, Marina Saly, Suzanne Fletcher, Sandra Bernhard, Lydia Lunch, Cathay Che, Mary Ann Livchak, Susan Seidelman, Eszter Balint, Kiki Smith, Jim Sclavunos, Scott Billingsley, Brenda Alderman, Nona Hendryx, Vicki Wickham, Evelyn McDonnell, Andy Schwartz, Matias Viegener, Róisín Davis, Barney Hoskyns, Jill Kroesen, Mary Harron, Wayne Kramer, Nina Zilkha, Tanya Pearson, Patti Hudson, Willij Vanderlinden, Thurston Moore, Susan Berman, Maripol, Ann Magnuson, Maria Elena Buszek, Peter Gordon, Debbie Harry, Quito Cooksey, Michelle Tea, David Siegfried, Sylvia Morales Reed, Pat Place, Jamie Nares, Weasel Walter, Matthew Hamilton, and Evelyn McDonnell. Thank you to the original Kickstarter supporters who made it possible for me to complete my first book, *Peter and the Wolves*. Segments from that work are reprinted

ACKNOWLEDGEMENTS

here in the chapters 'Nan, 1975' and 'Peter and Lester, 1977' .

Thanks Natalie Hill, for laying out the 'women in bands' graphic. I am grateful and humbled by the generosity of the following photographers, some of whom are cherished friends (and thanks to those contributing courtesy photos). The photographers didn't just capture the scene – their eye for the moment amplified our revolution.

Nan Goldin, Vivienne Dick, Julia Gorton, Richard Prince, Jamie Nares, Kiki Smith, Marcia Resnick, Michael Granros, Beate Nilsen, Laura Levine, Robert Carrithers, Leslie Ann Duffy and Linda Duffy, John Clifford (photos courtesy Susan Seidelman), Lizzie Borden, Bobby Grossman, Jane Cantillon, Jill Kroesen, James Muscarella, Amsterdam Sasha, Tom Bessoir, and Mick Rock.

Thank you, Faber & Faber and Dan Papps, for the opportunity to tell these stories, and for being so wise and wonderful. To my editor Emmie Francis – gratitude abounds. And thanks Nige Tassell and Anne Owen for your keen attention. Thank you Amy Caldwell for the honour of releasing the book with Beacon Press. Last but not least, Elias Altman, my agent – the sincerest of gratitude for your wise stewardship. ♥

★ ★ ★

The chapter 'Anti-Fashion' is taken from an essay published in the book *It's So You: 35 Women Write About Personal Expression Through Fashion and Style*, Seal Press, 2007. (Thank you, Michelle Tea.)

Chapters 'Nan, 1975' and 'Peter and Lester, 1977' are reprinted from *Peter and the Wolves*, Smog Veil, 2021 © Adele Bertei, all rights reserved by Adele Bertei. Complete poems and song lyrics © Adele Bertei. All rights reserved.

Photo Credits

page

7 Adele passport photo, 1977, courtesy of the author.
13 Nan by Nan Goldin.
23 Peter Laughner, courtesy of Jane Cantillon.
35 (*top*) Anya Phillips smoking, photo by Julia Gorton; (*bottom*) Lydia Lunch and Diego Cortez, photo by Bobby Grossman.
47 (*left*) Pat Place, photo by Kiki Smith; (*right*) James Chance, photo by Marcia Resnick.
53 James Chance (Robert Fripp watching), photo by Julia Gorton.
61 Anya and Sylvia Morales Reed, photo by Bobby Grossman.
66 Anya, photo by Julia Gorton.
71 Adele, photo by Beate Nilsen.
77 (*left*) James Nares and Diego Cortez, photo by Bobby Grossman; (*right*) Jamie Nares, photo by James Nares.
83 Adele at CBs, photo by Julia Gorton.
91 Pat Place, Kiki Smith, Adele, courtesy Kiki Smith (photographer unknown).
94 (*left*) Kiki Smith, photo by Adele; (*right*) Adele, photo by Kiki Smith.
99 The Contortions, photo by Anya Phillips.
103 The Contortions, Bob Quine, photo by Julia Gorton.
107 Brian Eno, James Chance, photo by Julia Gorton.
111 James Chance, Robert Christgau, Artist's Space, photo by Julia Gorton.
115 *No New York* album cover (front), courtesy of Universal Music, Brian Eno, and Steve Keister.
117 The Contortions, photo by Beate Nilsen.
122 James White, photo by Marcia Resnick.
123 Michael Zilkha, courtesy of Nina Zilkha.
133 Adele portrait, by Julia Gorton.

PHOTO CREDITS

136 Kathy Acker, courtesy of Jill Kroesen.
138 First cover of *The Childlike Life of the Black Tarantula* by Kathy Acker, courtesy of Jill Kroesen.
141 Jerry Nolan, Adele, Walter Lure, photo by Leslie Ann Duffy, courtesy of Linda Duffy.
147 Williams Burroughs and Patti Smith, Nova, photo by Marcia Resnick.
152 Adele and Brion Gysin, Nova, photo by Marcia Resnick.
156 Kathy Acker reading at Nova, photo by Marcia Resnick.
163 Adele, Bowery, photo by Michael Granros.
175 Adele, photo by Richard Prince.
183 Adele and Lizzie Mercier, photo by Marcia Resnick.
188 Lizzy Mercier Descloux, April 1973.
189 NYC, 1983: (*left to right*) Susan Seidelman, Scott B., Amanda Plummer, James Russo, Adele, courtesy of Susan Seidelman.
196 Lizzie Borden, *Born in Flames*, courtesy of Lizzie Borden.
212 Patti Astor mural created by Charlie Doves, Al Ruiz, Shiro One and Al Diaz. Organizers of the memorial: Kate Storch and George Ibanez, and the Patti Astor Family Trust. Photo by James Muscarella.
223 Adele, *Les guérillères*, Vivienne Dick, photo by Vivienne Dick.
226 Adele and Jamie Nares, photo by Nan Goldin.
229 Adele, photo by Robert Carrithers.
235 Adele and Peter Graute, Rotterdam.
237 Adele and Janet Hamill, photo by Nan Goldin.
245 The Bloods backstage.
251 The Bloods, photo by Tom Bessoir.
265 The Bloods, photo by Mick Rock.
273 The Bloods poster Holland, courtesy of the author.
278 The Bloods in Amsterdam, photo by Sasha.
288 The Bloods, photo by Tom Bessoir.
289 Honey in Paris, courtesy of Lizzie Borden.
297 Adele and Lesley Woods, NYC, 1981, photo by Laura Levine.
309 Adele and Thomas Dolby, courtesy of Susan Seidelman.